Macs TRANSLATED for PC Users

Dwight Spivey

ALPHA
A member of Penguin Group (USA) Inc.

ALPHA BOOKS

Published by the Penguin Group

Penguin Group (USA) Inc., 375 Hudson Street, New York, New York 10014, USA • Penguin Group (Canada), 90 Eglinton Avenue East, Suite 700, Toronto, Ontario M4P 2Y3, Canada (a division of Pearson Penguin Canada Inc.) • Penguin Books Ltd., 80 Strand, London WC2R 0RL, England • Penguin Ireland, 25 St. Stephen's Green, Dublin 2, Ireland (a division of Penguin Books Ltd.) • Penguin Group (Australia), 250 Camberwell Road, Camberwell, Victoria 3124, Australia (a division of Pearson Australia Group Pty. Ltd.) • Penguin Books India Pvt. Ltd., 11 Community Centre, Panchsheel Park, New Delhi—110 017, India • Penguin Group (NZ), 67 Apollo Drive, Rosedale, North Shore, Auckland 1311, New Zealand (a division of Pearson New Zealand Ltd.) • Penguin Books (South Africa) (Pty.) Ltd., 24 Sturdee Avenue, Rosebank, Johannesburg 2196, South Africa

Penguin Books Ltd., Registered Offices: 80 Strand, London WC2R 0RL, England

International Standard Book Number: 978-1-61564-197-0
Library of Congress Catalog Card Number: 2011941055

14 13 12 8 7 6 5 4 3 2 1

Interpretation of the printing code: The rightmost number of the first series of numbers is the year of the book's printing; the rightmost number of the second series of numbers is the number of the book's printing. For example, a printing code of 12-1 shows that the first printing occurred in 2012.

Printed in the United States of America

Publisher: Marie Butler-Knight
Associate Publisher/Acquiring Editor: Mike Sanders
Executive Managing Editor: Billy Fields
Development Editor: Mark Reddin
Senior Production Editor: Kayla Dugger
Copy Editor: Amy Borrelli
Designer: William Thomas
Indexer: Julie Bess
Layout: Brian Massey
Proofreader: John Etchison

ALWAYS LEARNING PEARSON

To my children: Victoria, Devyn, Emi, and Reid
I thank God for blessing me with each and every one of you. Being your dad is an honor and a privilege, and nothing less.

Contents

Appendixes

Introduction

Change isn't something that most of us particularly enjoy. However, the fact that you're holding this book in your hands is testament to the fact that changes in your computing habits are exactly what you're experiencing. Whether this change in technology is voluntary or being foisted upon you, the process can be a tad painful, especially if you're left to face the change on your own. That's why *Macs Translated for PC Users* was written: to be a competent guide and knowledgeable companion during this transition from Microsoft Windows–based PCs to Apple's Mac line of computers running the Mac OS X operating system.

Let me quell a few fears before we begin. You're obviously not new to computers; you've most likely logged many hours of experience with PCs. So just remember these computer-related truisms: a mouse is still a mouse, a keyboard is still a keyboard, a window is still a window, a monitor is still a monitor, a web browser is still a web browser, email is still email. Do you see a pattern developing here? Sure, some things are going to be different when it comes to performing tasks on your Mac that you've become so adept at on your PC, but the basic tools are still the same. Getting to know the slight variations in tools and usage won't be that bad, certainly not when you incorporate the tool you are currently holding.

Macs are increasing their infiltration onto the desks and into the consciences of the world's computer users, and with good reason: there is simply no better computing experience on the planet. The aim of this book is to quickly acclimate you to your new computing environs, help you assimilate your knowledge from your old platform to the new, and to do so with a nice dash of levity to ease the transition.

Happy Mac-ing!

Acknowledgments

A very heartfelt "thank you!" to all those who were involved in bringing this book to the masses!

I would like to extend a special thanks to my agent Carole Jelen for her part in bringing this title to my attention, and to Mike Sanders for bringing me on board.

Mark Reddin, Kayla Dugger, Amy Borrelli, and Guy Hart-Davis: thank you for making my contributions to this book so much better than they originally were.

Special Thanks to the Technical Reviewer

Macs Translated for PC Users was reviewed by an expert who double-checked the accuracy of what you'll learn here, to help us ensure that this book gives you what you need to know to hit the ground running with your Mac. Special thanks are extended to Guy Hart-Davis.

Keyboards, Mice, and More

You're a Windows user since the first day you were introduced to a computer. And now you're sitting in front of a Mac. You look at the keyboard and mouse, and think, "This doesn't look so different," and you're right—they really aren't that different. The alphabet is still the same, whether you use a Windows-based PC or a Mac, and everyone knows what the Caps Lock, Tab, Spacebar, and other keys do. And the mouse looks pretty much like your PC's mouse, although the buttons seem to be missing. Sure, there are differences here, but nothing insurmountable, I assure you.

In this chapter, I will introduce you to some of those similarities and differences, and help familiarize you with what many consider to be the finest computer experience around.

Keyboard Layout Differences

"Okay … where did the Windows key go?"

"What the heck is that squiggly looking key next to the Spacebar?"

"Return? What happened to Enter?"

"What in the world? There's no Print Screen?"

"How do you backspace on this thing?"

These are common questions that most Windows users ask (although sometimes not quite so politely) when they first begin poking around on a Mac keyboard.

Figure 1.1 shows you examples of a wired Apple keyboard (top) and a wireless Apple keyboard (bottom). The biggest difference (besides the wire, of course) is the absence of the numeric keypad on the wireless model.

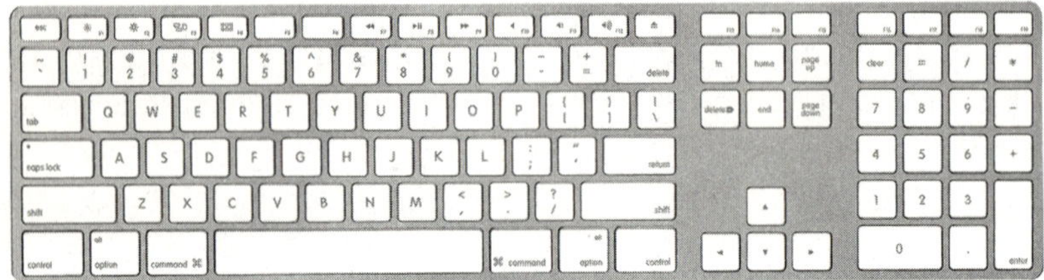

Figure 1.1: *Apple wired and wireless keyboards.*
(Both images courtesy of Apple)

There is one main key that stands out from all others for PC users, and that is the Command key. There are actually two Command keys, one on either side of the Spacebar, which are also represented by the iconic Command symbol: ⌘.

The Command key works much like a combination of the Ctrl (Control) and Windows keys on PC keyboards. It acts as a modifier, meaning that if you press it in conjunction with another key (or keys), it will alter the behavior of that key. For example, pressing Ctrl-P on a PC keyboard will typically open a Print dialog box within an application. In the same manner, ⌘-P on a Mac keyboard will open a Print dialog in an application.

The Return key acts just like the Enter key on a PC keyboard. The Apple wireless keyboard even has the word "Enter" in small type on the Return key to give a helping hand to PC users and those running Windows on their Mac (oh, yes, you can do that).

Many Windows aficionados use the Print Screen key to take screenshots. With the Mac you use the key combination of ⌘-Shift-3 to take full screen captures and ⌘-Shift-4 to take shots of a selected portion of your screen.

And finally, the absence of a Backspace key can throw some folks for a loop, but don't fear: the Delete key on the Mac keyboard operates the same way as the PC keyboard's Backspace key.

Common Keyboard Shortcuts

Keyboard shortcuts are great ways to perform a task with just a couple of keystrokes as opposed to moving the mouse from menu to menu. Table 1.1 gives you a nice list of Windows commands, their functions, and the Mac equivalent.

Table 1.1 Mac Equivalents to Common Windows Keyboard Shortcuts

Windows Shortcut	Function	Mac Shortcut
Backspace	Backward delete	Delete
Ctrl-W	Close active window	⌘-W
Ctrl-C	Copy	⌘-C
Ctrl-X	Cut	⌘-X
Ctrl-V	Paste	⌘-V
Ctrl-P	Print	⌘-P
Ctrl-F	Find/search	⌘-F
Ctrl-N	New folder (within Finder)	⌘-Shift-N
Ctrl-O	Open file	⌘-O
Ctrl-S	Save file	⌘-S

continues …

continued

Windows Shortcut	Function	Mac Shortcut
Ctrl-A	Select all	⌘-A
Ctrl-Z	Undo	⌘-Z
Windows-M	Minimize window	⌘-M
Delete	Send items to Recycle Bin/ Trash (within Finder)	⌘-Delete
Alt-Tab	Toggle among open applications	⌘-Tab
Right-click	Open contextual menus	Control-click
Ctrl-B	Make text bold	⌘-B
Ctrl-I	Italics	⌘-I
Ctrl-U	Underline	⌘-U
Ctrl-N	New document (within applications)	⌘-N
Ctrl-T	New tab in web browser	⌘-T
Ctrl-R	Refresh web page	⌘-R

Mouse Differences

The mouse has been working hand in hand with the keyboard for years as the primary means of input for computers. Children typically learn how to use a mouse long before they can even read.

Windows users are quite happy with the mice they currently use on their PCs, which usually have two buttons and perhaps a scroll wheel. Left-clicking selects items and takes action upon them, while right-clicks yield contextual menus for accessing options that can be taken with a particular item. For example, right-click a folder within Windows and a huge list of options pops up, including commands such as opening the folder or sharing it with other users.

When Windows users take a gander at the mouse that comes with a Mac, they are understandably confused. Apple's Magic Mouse (Figure 1.2), which ships with the iMac and Mac Pro, appears to have only one button (even though upon first glance you may be inclined to think it doesn't have any).

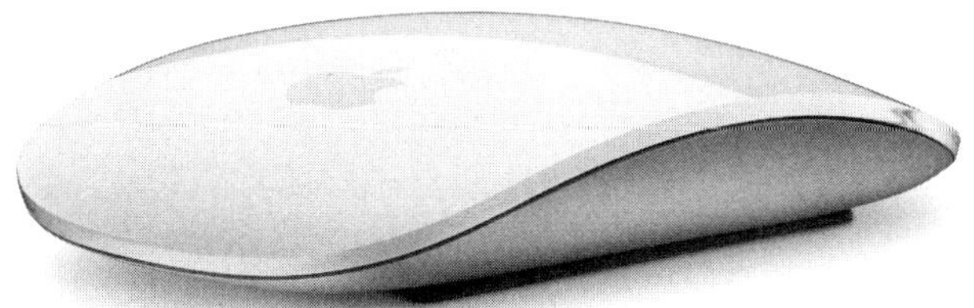

Figure 1.2: *Apple's Magic Mouse ships with iMac and Mac Pro desktops.* (Image courtesy of Apple)

In fact, the Magic Mouse does have two buttons, and even a few other hidden surprises. The top half of the Magic Mouse not only acts as a button; it is also a Multi-Touch surface that you can use to perform some pretty cool actions, such as:

- Brush a finger across the top to scroll in any direction.
- Hold down the Control key on your keyboard and scroll back and forth with one finger on the Multi-Touch surface to zoom in and out.
- Use two fingers to swipe left or right to "turn" pages in the Safari web browser or when viewing pictures in iPhoto.
- Double-tap (lightly) with two fingers to open and exit Mission Control.

You can also use the Mouse System Preferences to set options such as tracking speed and to enable the secondary click (which makes the Magic Mouse perform like a two-button mouse):

1. Click the **Apple** menu in the upper-left corner of your screen and then click **System Preferences**.
2. When the System Preferences window opens, click on the **Mouse** icon in the Hardware section of the window.
3. The Mouse preferences (Figure 1.3) allow you to configure how your Magic Mouse behaves.

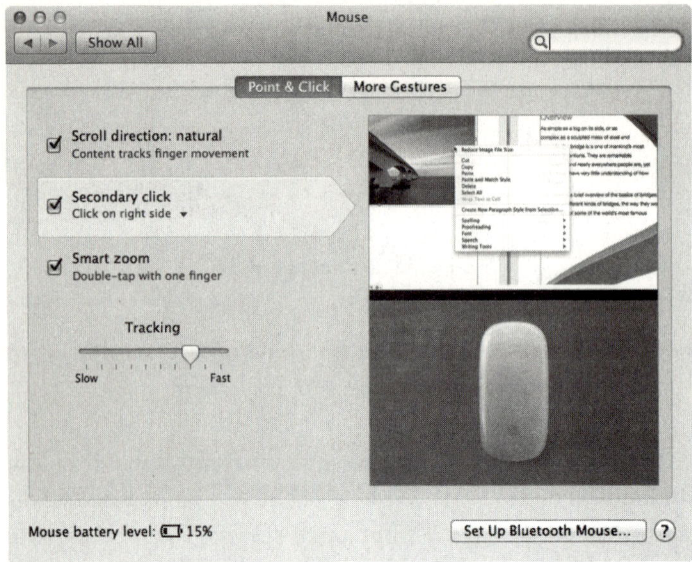

Figure 1.3: *Use Mouse preferences to adjust how your Magic Mouse works.*

But I Like My PC's Mouse!

Should you find that you simply can't get along without the mouse you used with your PC, don't fret. If the mouse is a USB device, you can still use it with your Mac. Just plug it into one of your Mac's USB ports and away you go.

Navigating with a Trackpad

If you've used a Windows-based laptop, the chances are darned good that it had a trackpad. Trackpads allow you to use your finger as a mouse, dragging it across the surface of the trackpad to move the mouse pointer onscreen.

Should you be lucky enough to be using one of Apple's current lineup of laptops (MacBook Air or MacBook Pro), you have the best trackpad on the planet built right in. Should you have one of Apple's desktop models, you're still in luck, though. Apple has another Magic device in its stable: the Magic Trackpad (Figure 1.4). The Magic Trackpad does exactly the same thing as the trackpads built into the Apple laptops, only as a stand-alone device.

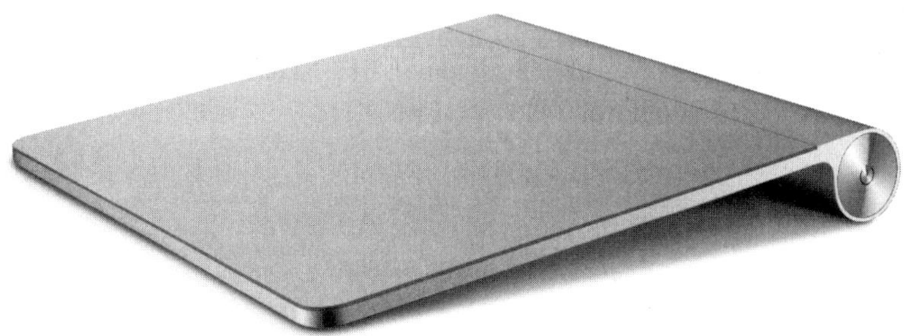

Figure 1.4: *Apple's Magic Trackpad performs the same functions as a laptop's trackpad, but as a stand-alone device.*
(Image courtesy of Apple)

As with any other trackpad, Apple's trackpads allow you to drag your finger around on their surface, moving the mouse pointer around the screen. However, Apple's trackpads are also Multi-Touch devices, allowing them to do tons more with just the swipe of your finger(s):

- You can click or double-click any item on the screen by pressing down anywhere on the surface of the trackpad.
- Scroll in any direction by brushing two fingers "any which way you can" (to borrow a line from Clint Eastwood).
- You can "turn" pages by brushing three fingers to the left or right.
- Rotate images by placing your thumb and index finger on the trackpad, and then twist them clockwise or counter-clockwise.

There are many other actions you can take with a trackpad, and you should use the Trackpad preferences pane in System Preferences to learn about and set them up:

1. Click the **Apple** menu in the upper-left corner of your screen, and then click **System Preferences**.
2. When the System Preferences window opens, click on the **Trackpad** icon in the Hardware section of the window.

3. The Trackpad preferences (shown in Figure 1.5) help you configure how your trackpad works. View the movies that are available, which show you how to use your trackpad efficiently.

Figure 1.5: *The Trackpad preferences pane allows you to customize how your trackpad works.*

First Glance at the Desktop

2

Lots of people have the mistaken notion that Macs and Windows-based PCs are just worlds apart. The fact is that they have much more in common than you might think. I promise that if you sit a long-time Windows user in front of a Mac and tell him to check it out, his head will not explode. He'll take a look around, grip the mouse (just as he would when at his PC), and begin to guide the pointer around the screen. He will certainly click on various elements, such as menus, because they look familiar. He may even click on the happy face on the left side of the Dock just to see what happens, and he'll be pleasantly surprised when a new window opens. The window will show him other things he's familiar with, such as files and folders. Suddenly things aren't so scary anymore. Once the initial jitterbugs are gone, the savvy Windows user will figure out what the icons in the Dock do and will be surfing the web in a matter of minutes.

Don't get me wrong; of course there are differences. My point is that those differences don't amount to all that much once you get your hands on a Mac. This chapter will help you recognize that much of what you know on a PC is still here on a Mac, but in a slightly different (and, dare I say, better) form.

What Is Mac OS X?

First of all, the "X" is the Roman numeral 10, not the letter. Mac OS X is the operating system that runs on Apple computers, just like Windows XP or Windows 7 are operating systems that run on PCs. The current version of Mac OS X is 10.7, also known as "Lion." Each of the previous iterations of Mac OS X also had a big-cat name, such as Snow Leopard (10.6) and Panther (10.3).

The Lay of the Land

When you take your first gander at the Mac desktop, some things may be a little confusing, but others will look oddly familiar. As a Windows user, when you first turn on your PC and the desktop appears, you know exactly where you are and what to do next. This is probably not the case the first time you turn on a Mac. Figure 2.1 will show you a snapshot of a typical Mac OS X desktop and point out major items of interest.

Apple menu

Finder window

Menu bar

Volume

Clock

Spotlight

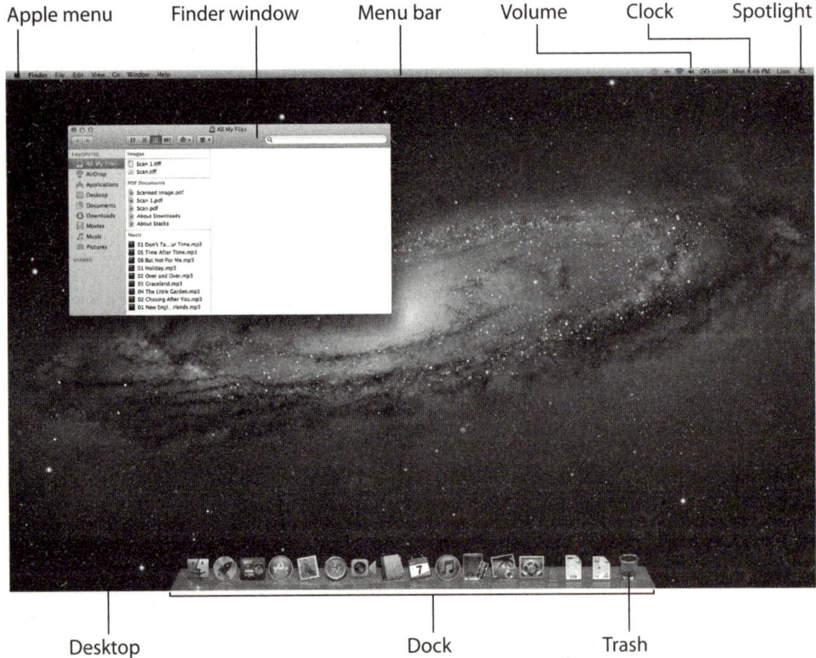

Desktop

Dock

Trash

Figure 2.1: *The Mac OS X desktop is nothing to be afraid of.*

Now that you've got the bare-bones basics, let's take a deeper look.

Explorer = Finder

For many computer users, the word "Explorer" as it pertains to PCs is taken to mean Internet Explorer, but that's not the case. Windows Explorer is an application that runs above all others and is your gateway into the Windows operating system. The windows, folders, taskbar, Start menu, icons—all of it comprises Windows Explorer. Windows Explorer is the graphical user interface of the Windows operating system, and is what makes it possible to work in Windows without a DOS prompt.

Finder is the Mac OS X equivalent of Windows Explorer. Finder is the application that gives you access to the file system and all the other apps on your Mac.

I'm sure you've noticed the really jovial-looking fellow on the left side of the Dock by this point. That smiley-face icon is the icon for the Mac OS X Finder. Clicking that smile will instantly open a new Finder window (if one isn't already open) or bring an already-open Finder window to the fore.

Figure 2.2 lays out the anatomy of a Finder window so that you can get a handle on getting around. Here's a brief description of each of the major elements:

- The toolbar provides access to tasks you frequently perform.
- The sidebar gives you instant access to frequently used items, such as folders and other computers on your network.
- Select one of the Finder window's four viewing options. It won't take you long to discover a favorite.
- Enter search words into the search field to find items on your Mac.
- Select a file or folder and then click the **Action** button to perform one of the actions found in the resulting pop-up menu.
- The Arrange button sorts items in the folder you're currently viewing.
- Select an item in the sidebar and its contents will show in the Viewing pane.

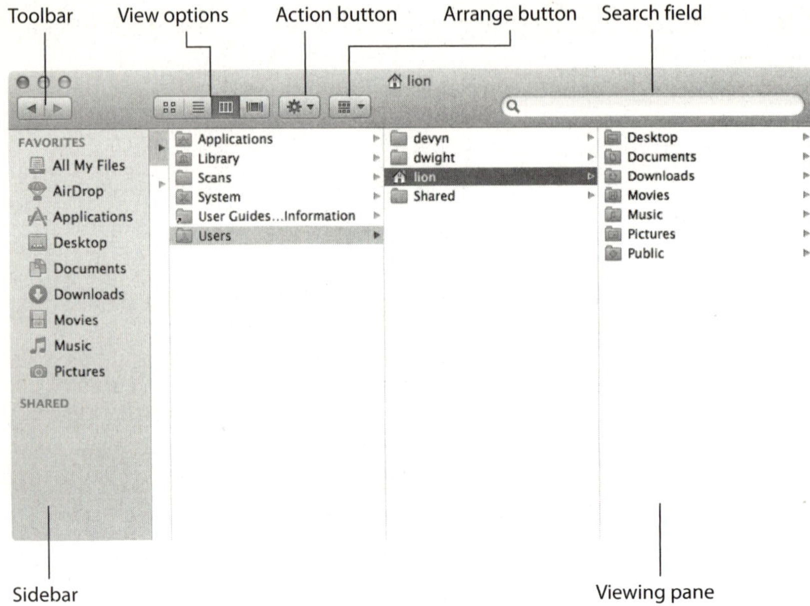

Figure 2.2: *A typical Finder window, which is your doorway into the Mac file system.*

Start Menu and Taskbar = Apple Menu, Menu Bar, and Dock

One of the biggest landmarks when it comes to navigating around in Windows has got to be the iconic Start menu. The Start menu gets its name because it's a good place to start when you're ready to open an application, find an item in your folders, and the like. The Apple menu in Mac OS X is not an exact equivalent to the Start menu, but it's pretty close. Throw in some of the tasks of the Mac OS X menu bar and you're in the ballpark.

Windows' Start menu gives you access to the programs installed on your computer, files and folders, Control Panels, Help, your network, and more, as well as allowing you to restart, shut down, or log in as another user.

Click the **Apple** menu in the upper-left corner of your Mac's screen and you will see much of the same. From the Apple menu (Figure 2.3), you can do the following:

- Get information about your Mac.
- Check for updates to software.
- Find new applications.
- Set preferences for the Dock, which I'll cover in a bit.
- View recently used applications and documents.
- Force unruly applications to quit, even if they don't want to.
- Put your Mac to sleep, restart it, or shut it down.
- Log out of the current user.

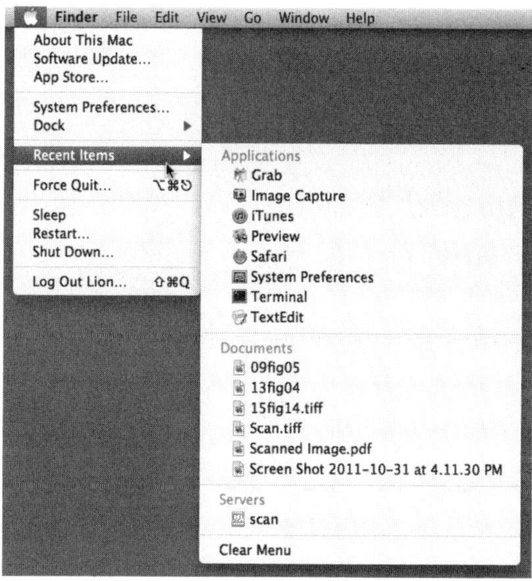

Figure 2.3: *The Apple menu is similar in many ways to Windows' Start menu.*

One of the features found in the Start menu that is lacking in the Apple menu is the ability to log in as another user. It's the menu bar that handles this task in Mac OS X. Notice the user name, Lion, on the right side of the screen in Figure 2.1 (you'll need to turn back a couple of pages). If there are multiple user accounts on your Mac, you can click the name of the user currently logged in to see a list of other users. Simply select the other user's name from the list and enter the correct password to access the account. You can have multiple accounts logged in at once. You must first go to the Users & Groups preferences pane in System Preferences, click **Login Options**, and check the box for **Show fast user switching** to enable this feature.

Another feature found in the Start menu that isn't quite in the Apple menu (it's close) is Help. Should you find yourself getting lost at any point, click on **Help** in the menu bar and select **Help Center** (Figure 2.4). From here you can get a ton of helpful information on just about everything in Mac OS X.

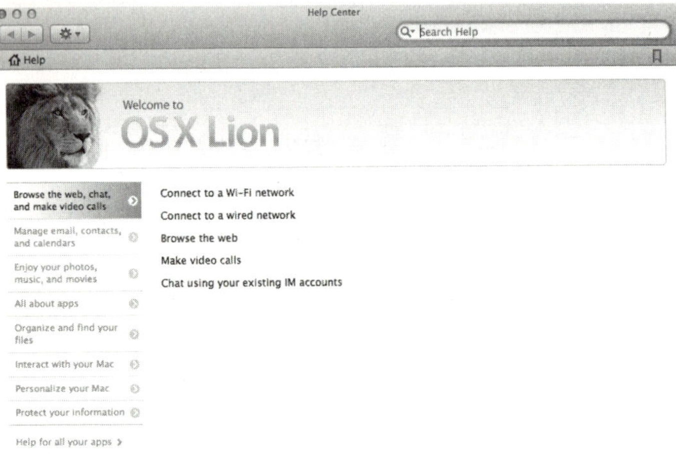

Figure 2.4: *Help Center will set you in the right direction should you get turned around a bit.*

A big feature of Windows' taskbar is quick access to applications you use the most. The left side of the taskbar is populated with icons for those applications you need to get to in a hurry.

The Dock, which is the row of icons you see at the bottom of your Mac's screen, acts in a very similar fashion. It comes preloaded with many of the most popular apps, such as the Safari web browser, the Mail email application, and others, as well as folders that you may frequently store files in. The icons you see in the Dock are shortcuts to the actual applications and folders themselves, so removing an icon from the Dock won't delete the folder or application.

As I'm sure you gathered by that last sentence, you can customize which icons are in the Dock, with the exceptions of the Finder and Trash icons. All the others can be dragged-and-dropped out of the Dock and onto the desktop to clear them from the Dock, or you can add an item to the Dock by dragging it from the Finder and placing it into the Dock. You can also rearrange items in the Dock by dragging-and-dropping them into your preferred order. You can't just place things all willy-nilly, though: icons for apps (or applications, whichever you prefer to call them) are stored on the left side of the Dock, while folder icons are on the right.

You may have noticed the little glowing dots underneath some of the icons in your Dock (Figure 2.5). These dots don't mean the app is radioactive, but merely indicates that it is open.

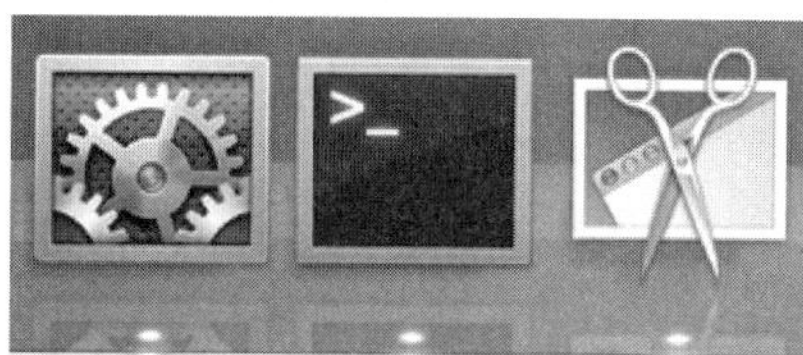

Figure 2.5: *Glowing dots under the Dock icons let you know an app is open.*

The Dock has many preferences you can tweak (Figure 2.6) to make it work the way you want. Click the **Apple** menu, move your mouse pointer over Dock, and select **Dock Preferences**. You can modify the Dock's size; use Magnification (if you make the Dock small enough you'll need this); position the Dock on the left, right, or bottom of the screen; minimize items into the Dock using some really cool effects; and other options. Of particular interest to Windows users will be the "Minimize windows into application icon" option.

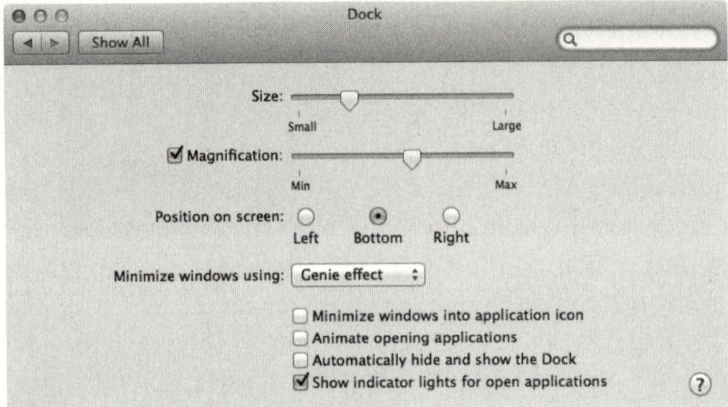

Figure 2.6: *Set the Dock's preferences to make it work the way you like.*

Notification Area Icons = Menu Extras

One of the best features of Windows' taskbar is that it offers quick access to important items such as the system volume, your network status, a clock, and system alerts in the notification area. Many Windows users aren't aware that the right side of the taskbar (where the clock is) is called the Notification area. That's what Microsoft calls it, I promise!

Mac OS X's menu bar extras (or simply, menu extras) serve some similar functions. The menu extras are found in the upper right of your Mac's screen. Simply click them to access their information and functions.

Some of Mac OS X's menu extras are for volume (shown in Figure 2.7), battery life (for laptops), wireless network status, date and time, Bluetooth status, and Time Machine status (some of these are covered in later chapters).

Sometimes applications may add their own menu extras to the menu bar; there are some Mac OS X preferences that do so as well (the wireless network status is a good example). You can usually remove these, if you wish, by enabling or disabling an option in the applications preferences or from within Mac OS X's System Preferences (more on them later in this chapter).

Figure 2.7: *Menu extras provide quick information and access to system functions, such as volume.*

Gadgets = Widgets

Windows Vista introduced a new item into the lexicon of Windows users: gadgets (or some may say, desktop gadgets). Gadgets are essentially miniapplications that perform very particular tasks in a very basic fashion within a very small floating window (typical gadgets would be for local weather or displaying information about your CPU). These gadgets are seen usually on the upper-right side of the screen, but you can move them around. Since they are floating windows, they stay on top of other windows you may have open, hence their information is always easily viewable.

The Mac OS X equivalent of a gadget is known as a widget, and they pretty much do identical types of things. Just so you know, Mac OS X had widgets well before Windows had gadgets.

Widgets can be accessed in a number of ways. First, and most convenient, is via the F4 key on your keyboard; simply press **F4** to launch into the Dashboard (Figure 2.8), which is the interface where widgets can be viewed. Pressing **F4** again will whip you back to the desktop. You can also access Dashboard by clicking its icon in the Dock (if it's not there this will be good practice for you with adding applications to the Dock) or through Mission Control (its icon is in the Dock by default).

Figure 2.8: *Dashboard is where Mac OS X's widgets are kept.*

When you open Dashboard, you will notice there are already some widgets that are open and ready to go. To give you a quick example of how to get around in widgets, let's look at the Weather widget.

Unless you live in Cupertino, California (the weather widget's default location—home to Apple, Inc., in case you're wondering), the default information in the widget won't be of much help to you. Click the small "**i**" you see in the lower-right corner of the widget window and the widget will "flip over" to reveal its settings. Change the settings to reflect your hometown and click **Done** to see relevant forecasts (Figure 2.9).

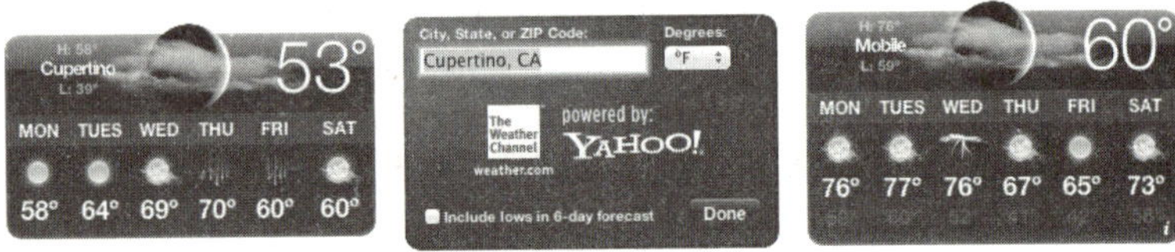

Figure 2.9: *Set a widget's preferences to make it more relevant to you.*

Many widgets (such as Movies and Stocks) offer ways to customize their settings to make them relevant to you, so just be on the lookout for small i's in your widgets' windows.

You can find more widgets by clicking the **+** button in the lower-left side of the Dashboard window. To remove widgets from Dashboard, click the **+** button in the lower left of Dashboard's window and then click the tiny **x** that appears in the upper-left corner of the widget's window (Figure 2.10).

Figure 2.10: *Delete widgets from Dashboard by clicking the small* **x**.

Control Panels = System Preferences

Every Windows user knows that Control Panels are what you use to configure the behavior of Windows features and manage certain types of devices, like printers.

System Preferences are the dead-on Mac OS X equivalent of Windows' Control Panels. Experienced Windows users will intuitively know what most of the available options in System Preferences are from the moment they see them.

To open System Preferences, click the **Apple** menu and select **System Preferences**, exactly like you would click the **Start** menu to access Control Panels (you could also click the **System Preferences** icon in the Dock). System Preferences (shown in Figure 2.11) is divided into four categories: Personal, Hardware, Internet & Wireless, and System. Figure 2.11 shows a fifth category, Other, but this category is only there after third-party applications requiring a preferences pane are installed.

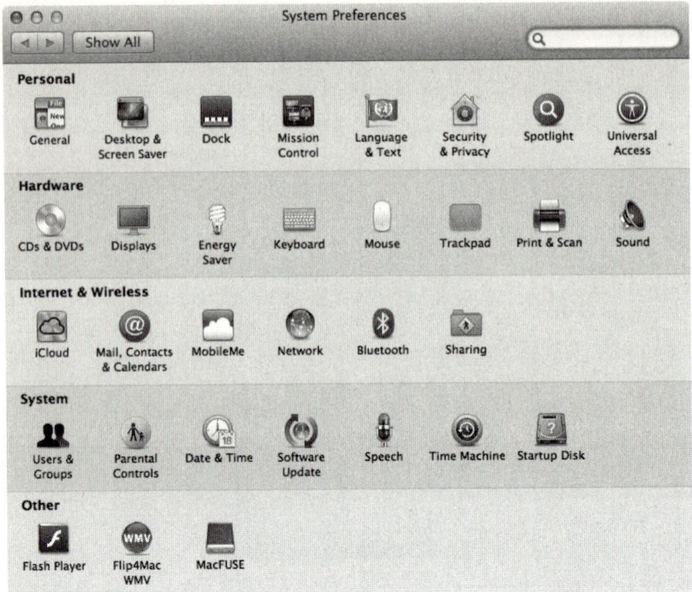

Figure 2.11: *Click the* ***System Preferences*** *icon in the Dock to access the System Preferences window.*

Each of the items under the categories gives you access to their preference panes. Tables 2.1, 2.2, 2.3, and 2.4 afford brief descriptions of each category's items, and many of them are discussed in detail in upcoming chapters.

Table 2.1 Personal Preferences

Pane	Description
General	These options affect the overall look and feel of Mac OS X.
Desktop & Screensaver	This is where you go to customize your desktop picture and screensaver.
Dock	Set options for the Dock here.
Mission Control	Mission Control (activated by pressing the **F3** key on your keyboard) gives you a bird's-eye view of all your open windows and other items. Configure its options here.

Language & Text	The Mac can speak more than 110 languages, and this is where you go to determine which of them it uses.
Security & Privacy	Allows for setting of passwords for system access, encryption of a user's entire account folder, and setting up Mac OS X's built-in firewall.
Spotlight	Determine in what order categories of search items are displayed and what keyboard shortcuts invoke a Spotlight search.
Universal Access	These settings allow those with physical difficulties (such as hearing loss) to more easily use their Mac.

Table 2.2 Hardware Preferences

Pane	Description
CDs and DVDs	Decide how Mac OS X behaves when CDs and DVDs are inserted into your Mac's optical disc drive.
Display	Adjust your Mac display's resolution and color settings.
Energy Saver	Set options for more efficient energy use—especially helpful if you have a laptop.
Keyboard	Modify how your keyboard inputs data and edit/create keyboard shortcuts.
Mouse	Customize the way your mouse works with Mac OS X.
Trackpad	Configure how your trackpad (if you have one) interacts with the operating system (OS).
Print & Scan	Install, configure, and manage printers and scanners.
Sound	Select sound effects as well as input and output devices.

Table 2.3 Internet & Wireless Preferences

Pane	Description
iCloud	Apple's cloud computing service, which allows you to use and save the same information across multiple devices. Learn more by visiting www.apple.com/icloud.
Mail, Contacts & Calendars	This is a one-stop shop for setting up accounts for Address Book, iCal, iChat, and Mail.
MobileMe	MobileMe is being replaced by iCloud, but this pane is still available for those who are members of MobileMe.
Network	Manage how your Mac accesses a wired or wireless network.
Bluetooth	Configure how your Mac works with other Bluetooth devices, such as wireless keyboards and mice.
Sharing	Your gateway to sharing anything, from folders to printers to internet connections, and everything in between.

Table 2.4 System Preferences

Pane	Description
Users & Groups	Add, remove, and manage user accounts.
Parental Controls	Determine what level of access and other privileges some users have.
Date & Time	Set up date and clock options for Mac OS X.
Software Update	Configure how to check for updates and view recently installed software.
Speech	These settings allow you to customize your Mac's speech abilities.

Pane	Description
Time Machine	Set up automated backups for your system.
Startup Disk	Determine which disk to boot your Mac from, if you have more than one disk with Mac OS X installed on it or need to boot from a CD or DVD that contains a system folder (for troubleshooting purposes).

Finding Where Your "Stuff" Is Stored

You are no doubt familiar with the folder structure Windows uses for storing information on your PC. Click on your **Start** menu and select **Computer**, and you will see the disks you have installed on your PC. Open your Local Disk and you will see basic folders such as Program Files (where your applications are stored), Users (folders for each account), and Windows (system files that shouldn't be touched unless you know what you're doing). Open the **Users** folder and you will see folders for each account holder, and within those folders you find others for storing downloads, music, pictures, and the like.

Mac OS X is structured in a similar way. Open a new Finder window and press **⌘-Shift-C** to be taken to the computer level (Figure 2.12).

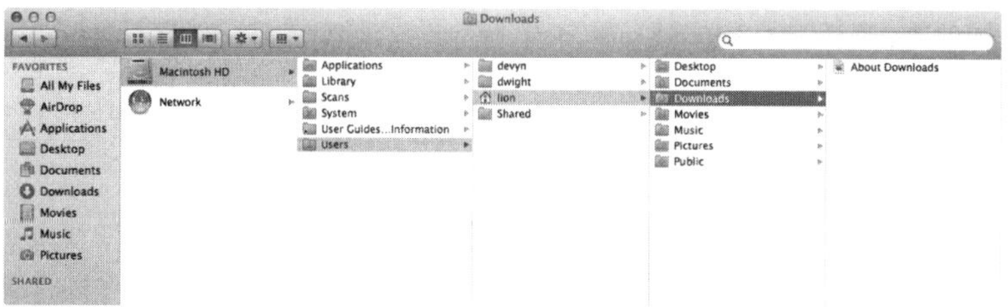

Figure 2.12: *Press **⌘-Shift-C** to see the base computer level of your hard drive.*

Select the **Macintosh HD** icon (equivalent to Local Disk in Windows) to see the folders at the root level of your hard drive. Click on the **Applications** folder (or press **⌘-Shift-A**) to see its contents if you like (Figure 2.13); this is the default installation location for applications that come with Mac OS X and for future applications you may install.

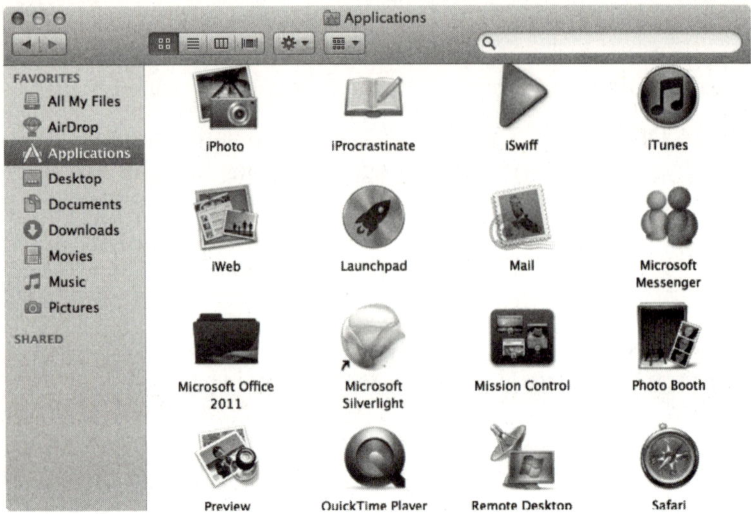

Figure 2.13: *Press ⌘-**Shift-A** to see the contents of your hard drive's Applications folder.*

Stay away from the System folder until you become much more experienced with Mac OS X. In all honesty, there's very little reason for even a seasoned Mac user to poke around in the System folder.

Go to the Users folder and you will see folders for each user account on your Mac. The folder that looks like a house is the home folder for the account that is currently logged in.

Your home folder includes folders for items that only your account has access to, unless you share the folders with other users. Here's a list of the default folders for user accounts:

- Desktop shows all the files and folders that reside on your desktop.
- Documents is the default repository for documents that you create in applications.
- Downloads is Mac OS X's default location for items you download from the internet.
- The Movies folder is where movies you download from iTunes or create with iMovie are stored.
- Music is where your iTunes music library is kept.

- Pictures is where iPhoto and Image Capture store your pictures and scans.
- Public contains a folder called Drop Box. This folder is automatically shared to other users on your computer and over your network. Folks can drop items into your Drop Box, but they cannot see or access items that are in it. All they will see is the Drop Box icon, illustrated in Figure 2.14.

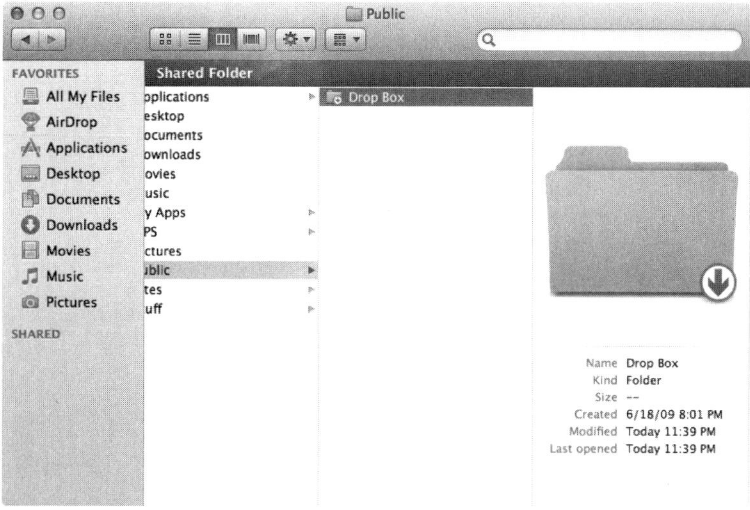

Figure 2.14: *Every user account has a Drop Box that others can use to share files with them.*

Translating Common Explorer Tasks

In today's "show-me-now" society, we tend to want to skip the basics and get to the "good stuff," often failing to recognize that the good stuff doesn't make sense or even happen without the basics. We Southerners understand that you don't get sweet iced tea without water and sugar.

You already know how to perform basic tasks in Windows, such as creating folders and restarting your computer, and now it's time to show you how to do these important base tasks in the Mac world.

Creating New Folders

At the risk of telling you something you already know, folders on a computer act just like folders in a filing cabinet. They are there to help you keep individual documents (and sometimes other items, such as pictures) organized for easy access.

These days, with everybody and their grandmother having a computer, it seems that most of the important inanimate items in our lives reside in folders. From family pictures to tax documents, they're probably stuck in a folder on your computer somewhere. Let's see how to create folders the Mac way, shall we?

The Windows Way

Let's not kid ourselves: this ain't rocket science. The easiest way to create a new folder in Windows is to right-click inside an Explorer window or on the desktop and select **New > Folder** from the resulting contextual menu.

The Mac Way

Once again, there's no lab coat required for performing this action.

Just like Windows, you can right-click (or Control-click) the desktop or within a Finder window and select **New Folder** from the contextual menu.

For those of you who just can't have enough ways to create new folders, you can also simply press **⌘-Shift-N** and a new folder will magically appear in your current location in the Finder.

If you simply enjoy the sound of your mouse clicking, you could also choose **New Folder** from the File menu within the Finder.

Launching Applications

Launching applications is a no-brainer, right? No Mensa membership is required to get an application up and running, but there are multiple ways to do so.

The Windows Way

To launch an application in Windows, you can single-click its shortcut in the taskbar or go to the Start menu, browse the Applications folder, and single-click the icon for the app you are looking for. You could also double-click an app's shortcut on the desktop. Clean and simple.

The Mac Way

Mac OS X can launch apps in a variety of simple ways, too:

- Open a Finder window, browse to the Applications folder, and double-click the app's icon.

- Create an application shortcut in the Dock and single-click it.
- Use Launchpad to browse for and launch your app, much like you would on an iPad, iPod touch, or iPhone.

To create an application shortcut in the Dock, simply open a Finder window to the Applications folder, and then drag-and-drop the app's icon into the Dock (to the left of the divider bar).

Launchpad is accessible in one of two ways: you can click its icon in the Dock (looks like a rocket), or, if your Mac has a trackpad or Apple's Magic Trackpad, you can pinch with your thumb and three fingers to launch it, as shown in Figure 3.1.

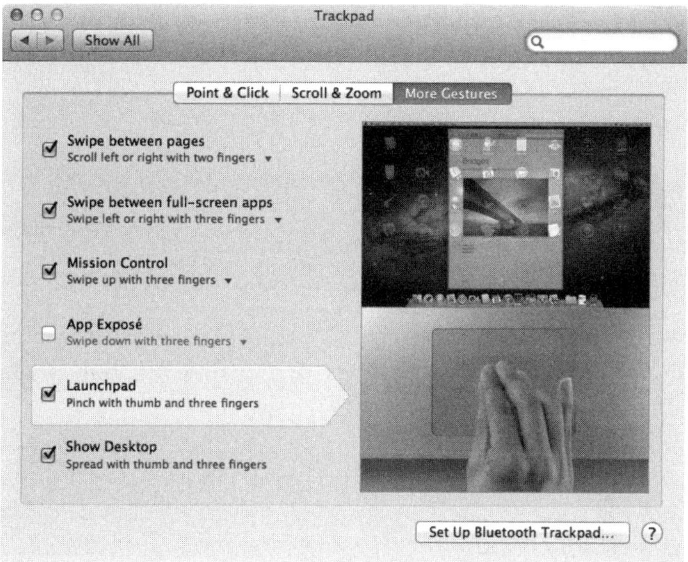

Figure 3.1: *Pinch with your thumb and three fingers on your trackpad to start up Launchpad.*

When Launchpad opens, you will see icons for applications installed on your Mac, as illustrated in Figure 3.2. You can launch any app by simply clicking its icon. If you have more apps installed than will fit on the screen, you will notice small white dots at the bottom of the screen; the number of white dots indicates the number of app screens you have available. To move between app screens, swipe the trackpad to the right or left using two fingers. You can exit Launchpad by spreading (reversing the pinching motion) your thumb and three fingers on the trackpad. Launchpad will automatically close when you launch an app from it.

Figure 3.2: *Click an icon to launch an app.*

Don't fret if you have a Mac without a trackpad. You can still use Launchpad with a mouse by clicking the **Launchpad** icon in the Dock to view your apps, clicking an icon to launch an app, or clicking one of the white dots at the bottom of the screen to view a different app screen. You can also press the left or right arrow key to switch app screens. Click the **Launchpad** icon in the Dock again to exit.

What if App Icons Don't Appear in Launchpad?

App icons will appear in Launchpad as long as the app is installed in the main Applications folder (/Applications) or in your user account's Applications folder (/User/Applications). If the app is installed in a different location on your Mac, its icon will not appear in Launchpad.

You can save real estate on an app screen and make some organizational sense of your apps by combining apps into categories, or folders. Notice the Utilities folder (it actually looks like a square comprised of tiny icons) in Figure 3.3. Several apps are located within the Utilities folder. To launch one of them, you simply click the folder to expand it, and then click the icon of the app you want to launch.

Figure 3.3: *Click a folder to see the apps it contains.*

To create folders, you can click-and-drag the icon of one app onto the icon of another. The two apps will combine into one folder, which you can give a descriptive name of your liking. Don't worry: rearranging icons within Launchpad doesn't monkey with the app's actual location on your Mac.

To remove an app from a folder, open the folder, drag the app's icon from the folder, and then drop it back onto the app screen.

Searching for Items

Finding items on a computer can be an absolute nightmare, especially if you don't know the shortcuts that can help you narrow your search. Basic searches on both Windows and Mac OS X are pretty straightforward, but when it comes to more complex searches, Mac OS X wins this one.

The Windows Way

You can quickly search your PC for an item by clicking **Start** and typing the name of the item you're looking for in the Search programs and files field. If what you want appears in the Start menu, count yourself blessed. If not, then you will want to perform a more narrowed search, and this is where Windows' search feature can be a tad lacking.

To narrow a search, you should open a Windows Explorer window to the hard drive or folder where you believe the file resides. Then type the name of the file you want into the Search field in the upper-right corner. If you are confronted with a multitude of items, you can further narrow the search by choosing a filter from the Search field (click within the Search field to see a list of filters). These filters are very limited, though, and there are even more steps to take if the file is a hidden one. Don't get me started.

The Mac Way

Mac OS X uses a nifty tool called Spotlight to help you find items on your Mac. Spotlight can find everything on your Mac, including items in your emails and websites you've visited. Yep, it's that smart!

To perform a really quick search in Mac OS X, click the **Spotlight** icon (looks like a magnifying glass) in the upper-right corner of your screen and begin typing the name of the item you're looking for. Spotlight looks in every file and folder on your Mac to find text that matches what you are typing. As you type, the search results will display under the Spotlight search field. Once you find the item you want, simply click it, or to see a preview of the item just hold your mouse point over it (Figure 3.4).

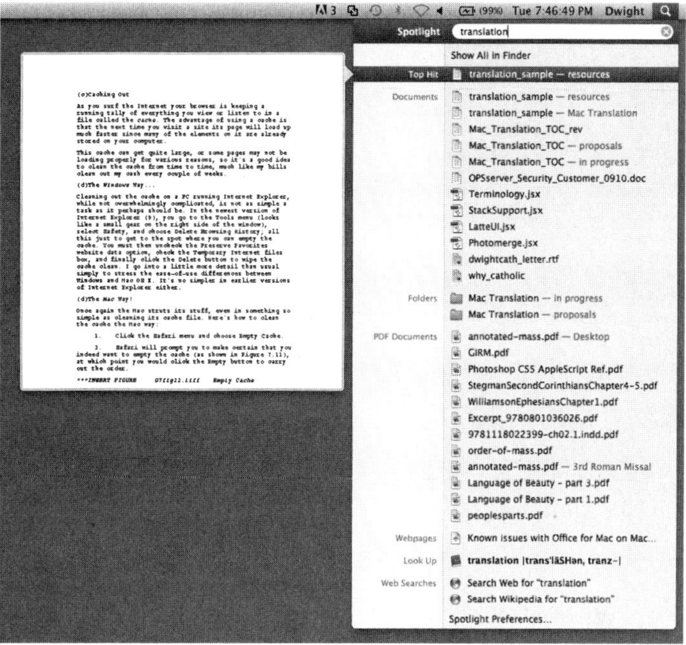

Figure 3.4: *Hover over an item in the search results to preview its contents.*

What if your search results reap a harvest that would take you three days to sift through? Here's where Spotlight has a distinct advantage over searching for items in Windows.

To narrow a Spotlight search:

1. Enter a search term into the Spotlight search field.
2. Click the **Show All in Finder** option near the top of the results list to open a Finder window containing the results.
3. Next to the word "Search:" in the gray Search bar, click **This Mac** to view systemwide results for the search term, or click the name of your user account to only look for matching items in your home folder.
4. Click the **+** button on the right side of the gray Search bar to begin applying filters to your search. Use the options given to customize your filters, and continue clicking the **+** button to add new filters (Figure 3.5). To remove a filter, click the **–** button to its right.

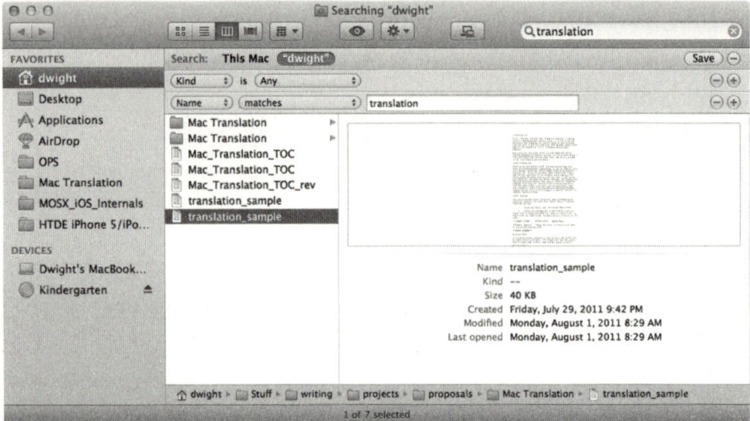

Figure 3.5: *Add more filters to refine your search.*

Need More Filters?

If you don't see the filter you need from the default options, don't worry. Select **Other** in the pop-up menu list and you will see so many filters that your eyes will water.

Taking Screenshots

Taking pictures of items on your display can be useful in very many ways. For example, if you need help troubleshooting an error message that is on your monitor, you can take a screenshot of the message and email it to someone who can help. I've also used screenshots when paying bills online, just to make sure I've got some visual proof in case there is a problem with the payment. There are many more uses than these two I've cited, so let's review the Windows method and then learn how to take screenshots with Mac OS X.

The Windows Way

It's simple enough to take a screenshot in Windows: just press the **Print Screen** key on your keyboard to capture the entire screen, or press **Alt-Print Screen** to capture the currently active window.

If you did this and nothing appeared to happen, that's because Windows simply placed the screenshot in memory; it's now waiting for you to open a document in another application, such as Paint or Word, and paste the screenshot into it. Yuck.

The Mac Way

The Mac way of taking a screenshot holds a big advantage over the Windows way: there's no need to open an app in order to paste the screenshot into it. The screenshot simply shows up on the desktop.

To take a screenshot in Mac OS X:

1. Press **⌘-Shift-3** to capture the entire screen.
2. Press **⌘-Shift-4** to change your mouse pointer into a crosshair, which you can click-and-drag around the area you want to capture (Figure 3.6). You can also press the **Spacebar** to change the crosshair to a camera, which you would then hover over the window you want to capture and click the mouse or trackpad button.

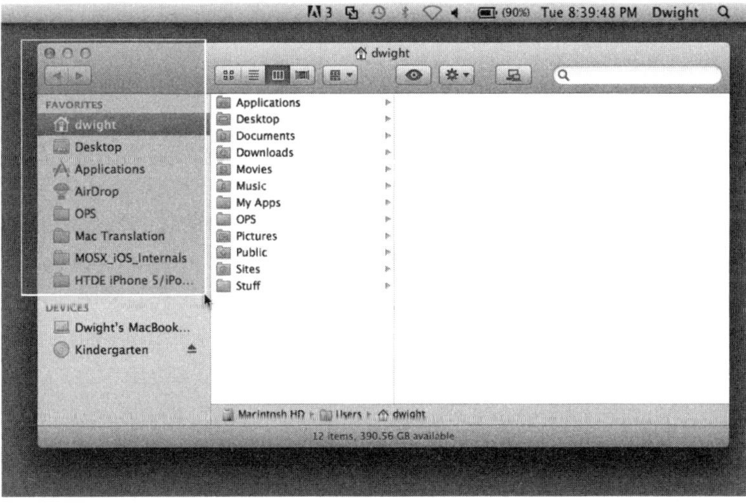

Figure 3.6: *Press **⌘-Shift-4** and then click-and-drag around the area you want to capture.*

Grab is also a nifty screenshot utility that comes with Mac OS X (/Applications/Utilities/Grab). Grab allows you to take captures of a selection, a window, and the entire screen, or you can capture a timed screen (Figure 3.7). When you choose to capture a timed screen, you have 10 seconds to make sure the items you want in the capture are on the screen before Grab takes the screenshot.

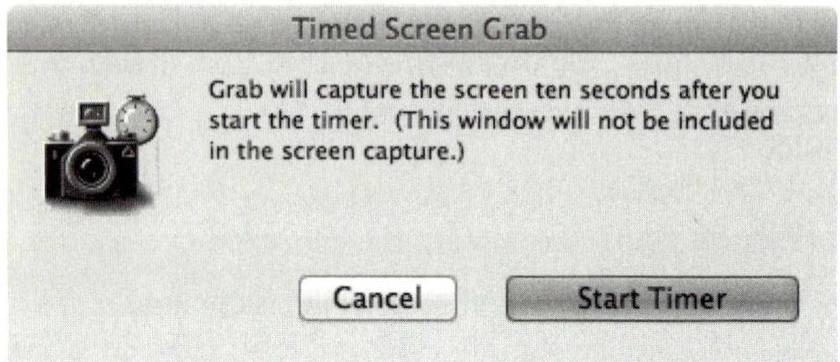

Figure 3.7: *You have 10 seconds to get ready when taking timed screenshots with Grab.*

In the interest of fairness, Windows Vista and Windows 7 both come with Snipping Tool, which is similar to Mac OS X's Grab.

Using Removable Media

Today it's commonplace to use removable media with your computer, such as CDs, DVDs, and USB flash drives, to transport files easily. Generally speaking, you can use removable media with almost any operating system, but there may be some exceptions (for example, a USB flash drive could use a weird file format that only certain OSes can read). This is another one of those topics that doesn't require a doctorate, but when you're stuck trying to safely remove that USB flash drive from your Mac, you'll thank me.

The Windows Way

CDs and DVDs are no problem: insert them in your PC's optical drive, double-click the applicable drive icon to view their contents, and press the **Eject** button on your optical drive to send them packing. Moving files from a CD or DVD is as simple as dragging-and-dropping, but copying data to a writable CD or DVD takes a little more fuss.

USB flash drives are another issue. When you first connect the drive to your PC, you may need to install drivers (which usually happens automatically) in order to use it. Then once you're ready to remove it, you should right-click it and choose **Safely Remove** from the contextual menu to make sure you don't corrupt your data.

Transferring information to and from a USB flash drive is as simple as dragging-and-dropping.

The Mac Way

You handle removable media in Mac OS X much the same way as you do in Windows.

CDs and DVDs simply slide into your Mac's optical drive. To remove them, just drag-and-drop their icons to the Trash (the Trash icon changes to an Eject icon, as shown in Figure 3.8). You could also press the **Eject** button on your keyboard, if so inclined.

Figure 3.8: *Eject a CD or DVD by dragging-and-dropping its icon to the Trash.*

Copying information to or from a CD or DVD is performed with the tried-and-true drag-and-drop. To finalize the copying of data to a CD or DVD, drag its icon to the Trash, which will now change to a Burn icon (illustrated in Figure 3.9). In the resulting window (Figure 3.10), give the disc a descriptive name, choose a Burn Speed and click the **Burn** button.

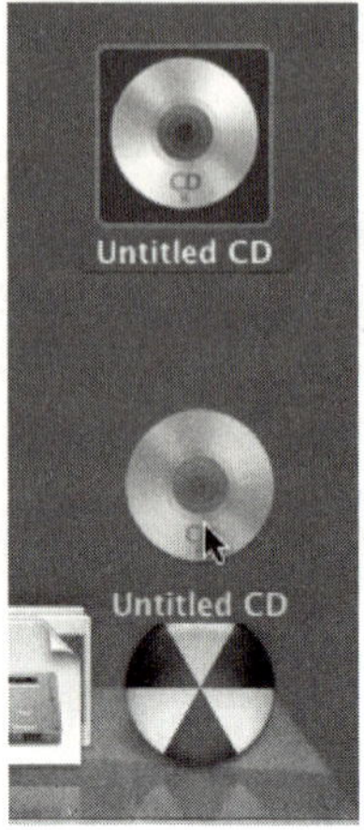

Figure 3.9: *The Trash icon changes to a Burn icon when dragging a writable disc to it.*

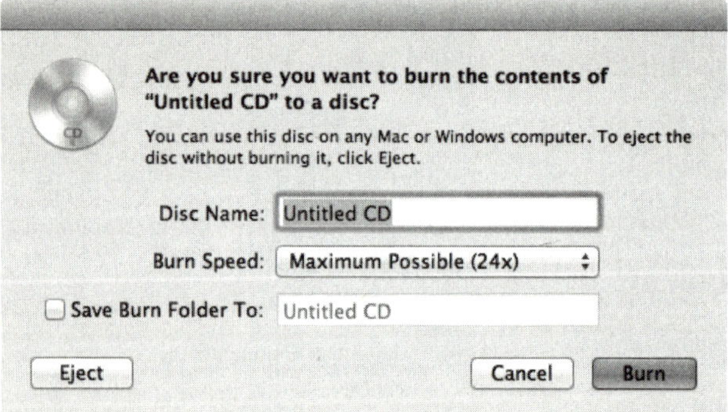

Figure 3.10: *Enter a name, choose a Burn Speed, and click **Burn** to write data to a disc.*

When you connect a USB flash drive to your Mac, Mac OS X places a white drive icon on your desktop and another icon will appear under Devices in the sidebar of Finder windows (both of which are seen in Figure 3.11).

Simply drag-and-drop to move files to and from the USB flash drive.

Be sure that you drag the USB flash drive's icon to the Trash ("ejecting" it as you would a CD or DVD) before unplugging it from your Mac!

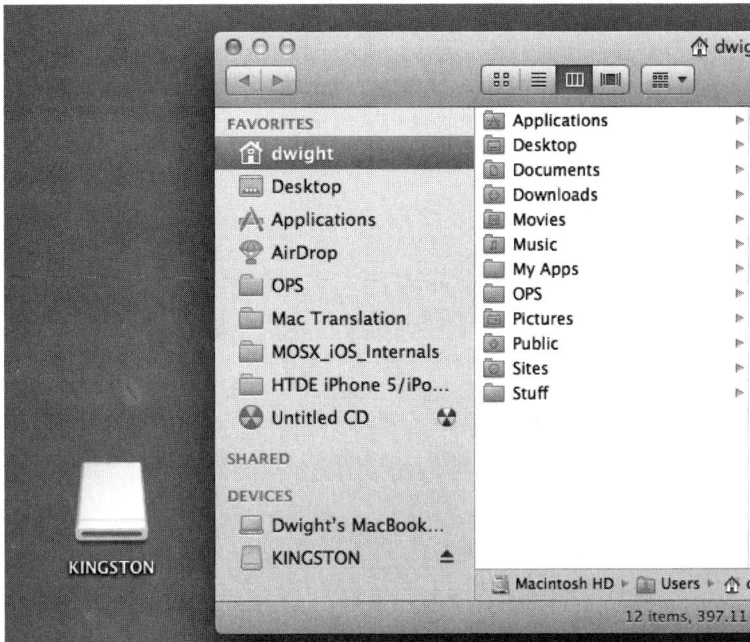

Figure 3.11: *USB flash drive icons appear on the desktop and in the Finder's sidebar.*

Taking Out the Trash

Sometimes a file or folder just simply has to go. It's nothing personal (or maybe it is), but if that file or folder has outlived its usefulness, then it's time to say adios and free up some hard drive space along the way.

The Windows Way

Getting rid of files in Windows is as simple as dragging it to the Recycle Bin and dropping it right in. Ready to empty the Recycle Bin? Just right-click it and select **Empty Recycle Bin**.

The Mac Way

Mac OS X's equivalent to Window's Recycle Bin is the Trash, which is located on the far-right side of the Dock (you couldn't miss it if you tried, and it's a permanent fixture in the Dock). Drag those poor, unwanted files or folders and drop them into the Trash icon. To send them packing, simply right-click (Control-click) or click-and-hold the **Trash** icon, and select **Empty Trash** from the menu. You will then be prompted by your Mac to make sure that you absolutely and unequivocally are certain that you want to empty the Trash, as shown in Figure 3.12. Your answer is up to you, of course: Cancel or Empty Trash.

Figure 3.12: *To empty the Trash or not to empty the Trash?*

If you're like me, you find that warning box almost impossible to tolerate, so you may want to turn it off, unless you have some fascination with frustration. Assuming this isn't the case, here's how to get rid of the warning:

1. Choose **Preferences** from the Finder menu, or simply press ⌘-, while in the Finder, to open the Finder Preferences window.
2. Click the **Advanced** tab.
3. Uncheck the box next to Show warning before emptying the Trash.

No more warnings when emptying the Trash.

Should you decide that you want to retrieve an item from the Trash, simply click the **Trash** icon to open a Finder window displaying items in the Trash. Drag the item(s) you want to remove from the Trash window to their preferred location.

Securely Emptying the Trash

Just emptying the Trash doesn't actually wipe it completely from your hard drive; it simply hides the file from view and allows Mac OS X to write over the file on the hard drive. To truly remove the file from your Mac, you need to securely empty the Trash. To do so every time your Trash is emptied, check the **Empty Trash securely** box in the Advanced tab of the Finder preferences. To do so on an as-needed basis, click the **Finder** menu and select **Secure Empty Trash**.

Shutting Down, Restarting, and Sleeping

Sometimes your overworked computer needs a break (just like you do from time to time), or it may start acting a bit wonky and need to refresh. And then there are other times when installing new software creates a voracious need for your computer to be restarted. For these reasons and more, the engineers of your favorite operating systems have built in the abilities to shut down or restart your computers, or to simply put them to sleep until you need to wake them up again.

The Windows Way

To shut down your trusty PC, click the **Start** button and click the **Shut Down** button in the lower-right of the Start menu. If you simply want your PC to sleep or restart, click the arrow to the right of the Shut Down button and select one of them from the menu.

The Mac Way

Turning off your Mac is every bit as simple. Click the **Apple** menu in the upper-left corner of the screen and select **Shut Down**. Mac OS X prompts you to make sure (Figure 3.13), and even gives you the nifty option of reopening any windows that you have currently open upon logging back in (it's pretty great, so give it a go).

Putting your Mac to sleep or restarting it is just as simple. Click the same **Apple** menu, and this time choose either **Sleep** or **Restart**. Choosing Sleep will simply put your Mac to bed without prompting, but you will be questioned by the OS before it allows you to restart (just like it does with the Shut Down process).

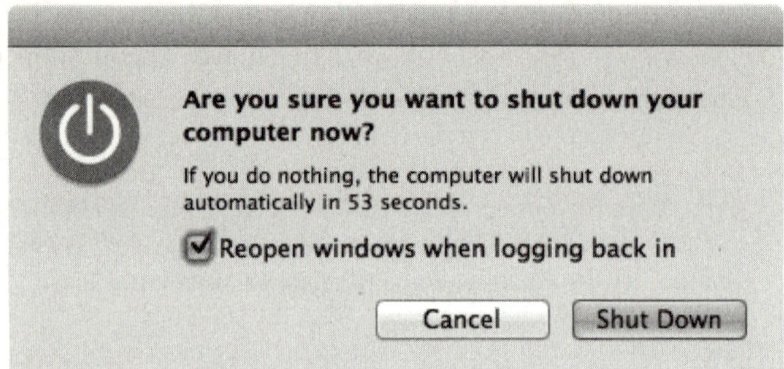

Figure 3.13: *Click **Shut Down** to turn off your Mac completely.*

What if you don't want to be prompted for shutting down or restarting? Simply hold down the **Option** key before you choose Shut Down or Restart from the Apple menu. Are you brave enough to give it a try?

Viewing Information About an Item

When it comes to items on your computer, you can never have too much information. It's a good thing to know the actual size of a file, or which application will open it.

The Windows Way

To get the lowdown on files and folders in Windows, right-click the item and choose **Properties**. A nice little window with lots of info will appear before you, ready to spill the beans on said file or folder.

The Mac Way

Finding out all there is to know about a file or folder in Mac OS X is just as simple:

1. Right-click (Control-click) the item in question and select **Get Info** from the contextual menu, or you could click the item once to highlight it and press **⌘-I**.
2. When the Info window opens (Figure 3.14), you can view General information (kind, size, etc.), More Info (determined by what kind of file or item you're viewing), Name & Extension, Open with (determines which application this

kind of file opens in by default), Preview (just a small preview of the item's icon), and Sharing & Permissions (I'll discuss these more in Chapter 6).

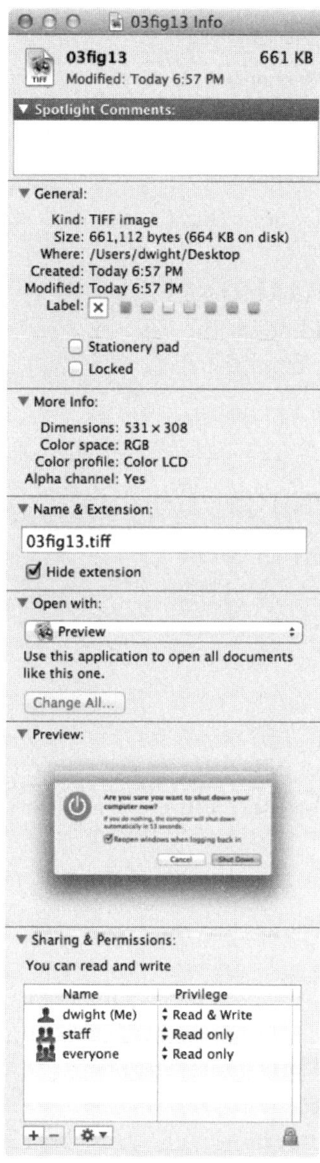

Figure 3.14: *A plethora of information about your files and folders is at your fingertips using Get Info.*

Customizing Your Experience

Your home is a special space that reflects your personality and tastes. From the lava lamps to the leopard-print couch, this is your castle, your refuge, your own Fortress of Solitude. Since your computer is your "cyber home," you will want to customize it to suit your styles and preferences, just as you would your real abode.

Changing Your Desktop Picture

Your home most likely has colorful walls adorned with pictures of family and friends, posters of your favorite movies or sports figures, and other knick-knacks. Your Mac is just as happy to display pictures of your grandkids as your walls are.

The Windows Way

"Hanging a new picture" in Windows is a fairly straightforward job. Right-click the desktop and select **Personalize** from the menu, click the **Desktop Background** link at the bottom of the window, choose a new picture from the immediate offerings or click **Browse** to find one elsewhere on your PC, and then click **Save Changes**.

The Mac Way

I won't pretend that the Mac way of changing your desktop picture is anything revolutionary:

1. Right-click your current desktop picture and choose **Change Desktop Background** from the contextual menu.
2. Select a new desktop picture in one of two ways:
   - Choose one from the folder list on the left side of the Desktop & Screen Saver preferences pane.
   - Click the **+** button in the lower-left corner to browse your Mac's hard drive for a picture. When you've found that oh-so-special pic, click the **Choose** button.
3. Your newly selected desktop picture shows up on the desktop and in the preview window of the Desktop & Screen Saver pane as shown in Figure 4.1. Use options in the pop-up menu next to the preview to change how the picture is displayed on the desktop.

Figure 4.1: *Customize your Mac's desktop with a new background picture.*

My parents have eight grandchildren, and to choose a picture of just one of them as the desktop background for their Mac would cause a mini riot. This kind of situation is easily remedied by allowing Mac OS X to change the picture automatically. If you need to perform a similar feat of family stability, simply do the following:

1. Select a folder containing pictures of all of the grandkids (or any folder of pics).
2. Check the **Change picture** box in the Desktop & Screen Saver pane.
3. Choose a time interval from the pop-up.

To make sure there are no accusations of favoritism, you could also check the **Random order** box to let the Mac choose which picture is displayed at any given time.

New Desktop Pictures on the Fly

There's an even faster way to set a new desktop picture. When you come across a picture file in the Finder that you like, simply right-click (or Control-click) the picture and select **Set Desktop Picture** from the menu.

Selecting a Screen Saver

Screen savers are mainly used for two things on computers these days: eye candy and minimum security. The screen saver not only further personalizes your PC or Mac, but you can also prevent someone from accessing your computer by requiring a password to be entered before disabling the screen saver. It's not Fort Knox, but it does pose somewhat of a deterrent for the curious passerby.

The Windows Way

To select a screen saver in Windows, right-click the desktop and select **Personalize** from the context menu. Next, click the **Screen Saver** link at the bottom of the window and choose a screen saver from the pop-up menu. Click **Apply** for the change to take effect.

The Mac Way

This is almost a carbon copy of the method used to change the desktop picture, but I'm giving Windows the slight edge here. The simplest way to select a screen saver isn't as intuitive in Mac OS X because of the wording in a contextual menu, which I'll discuss in the first of the following steps:

1. Right-click (or Control-click) your desktop picture and choose **Change Desktop Background** from the contextual menu. That's right: it doesn't say "Change Screen Saver," but instead says "Change Desktop Background": this is what I meant by this simplest method not being very intuitive.
2. Select the **Screen Saver** tab in the Desktop & Screen Saver pane.
3. Choose a screen saver from the list on the left side of the pane, or click the **+** button in the lower-left corner to browse your Mac for one (click **Choose** once you've found it).
4. If the screen saver you selected can be configured, you will see the Options button, which you can click to customize the screen saver's behavior.
5. Use the slider at the bottom of the pane to adjust the time your Mac is to be inactive before the screen saver automatically kicks on (Figure 4.2).

Figure 4.2: *Set a screen saver for your Mac.*

Changing the Appearance of Windows

No matter the computer or operating system you are using, at some point you will detect an irresistible calling to change things up a bit to match your style of work/play, especially in the windows you use to access the file system. These windows generally contain methods of quickly jumping to favorite folders or files, arranging the view of items within the windows themselves, and so forth.

The Windows Way

Honestly, there are so many different ways to customize your Windows Explorer windows that I won't attempt to even briefly skim them here. Suffice it to say that Windows does a rather decent job in the options it affords the user when it comes to viewing folders and files, and these options are generally on par with Mac OS X's Finder options.

The Mac Way

There are three main ways with which you can personalize your Finder windows:

- Change the Finder's preferences
- Add, remove, or rearrange items in the toolbar
- Adjust the View Options for individual folders

Let's take a look at each of these three, shall we?

To change the Finder's preferences, click the **Finder** menu and choose **Preferences** (if you're not in the Finder, click your desktop picture or the friendly smiling Mac face on the left side of the Dock to get to it). Once the Finder Preferences window opens, you may select one of the four tabs at the top: General, Labels, Sidebar, or Advanced.

Through the General tab you can:

- Determine which types of items to display on the desktop using the check boxes under the Show these items on the desktop heading.
- Decide the default folder to start from when opening new Finder windows.
- Choose to open folders in a new window.
- Utilize spring-loaded folders and windows. Using spring-loaded folders, you can drag-and-hold an item over a folder and, after the allotted time given in the Delay slider, the folder will automatically open for you to see what other items it may contain. You can continually drill down into more folders until you find the one you desire to place your file into, at which point you would simply release the mouse button or trackpad to drop it right in.

The Labels tab allows you to create custom-color labels that you can assign to files and folders, making it easier to group and identify similar items. For example, you could use one of the labels for work-related items and title it Work. You would then right-click (or

Control-click) a work-related item and assign the appropriate label for it from the contextual menu.

The Sidebar tab of Finder Preferences simply lets you choose whether or not certain types of items, such as hard drives or shared computers, appear in the Finder sidebar. Check the boxes next to the items you want to appear in the sidebar, as shown in Figure 4.3.

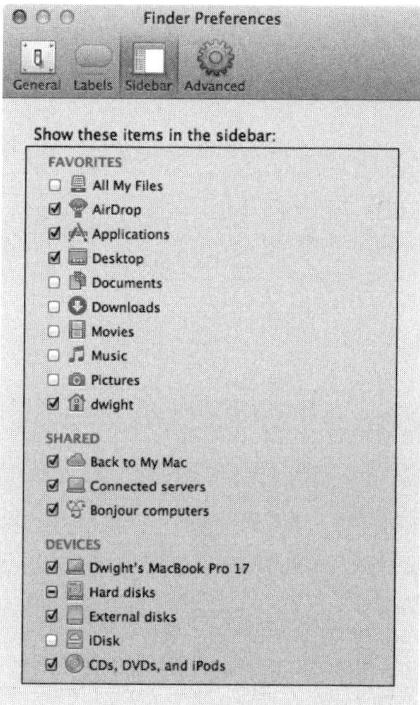

Figure 4.3: *Select the items you would like to appear in Finder's sidebar.*

The items in the Advanced tab are self-explanatory:

- Check the appropriate boxes to see file name extensions for every file, and to warn you of possible issues before an extension is changed.
- Decide whether your Mac should warn you before it empties your Trash, and whether it should do so securely.

Adding, removing, and rearranging items in the toolbar of a Finder window is a cinch.

To add items to or rearrange items in the toolbar:

1. With a Finder window open, choose Customize Toolbar from the View menu of the Finder. The resulting sheet (which is a dialog that extends from a window), shown in Figure 4.4, offers a multitude of items you can add to your toolbar.
2. Drag an item to the toolbar to add it.
3. Rearrange items in the toolbar by simply dragging-and-dropping them to the location you prefer.
4. Click **Done** when you are finished adding items.

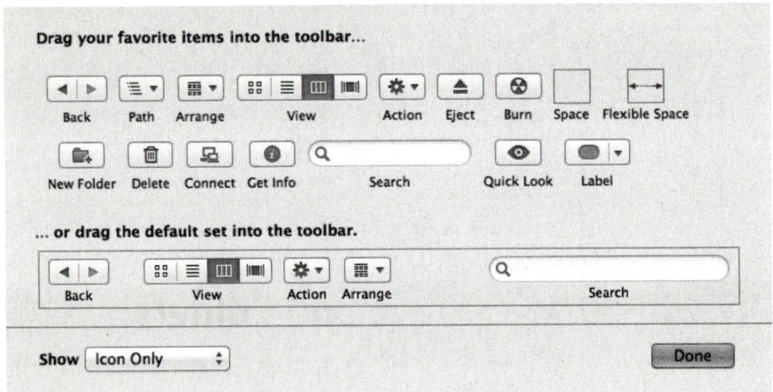

Figure 4.4: *Drag-and-drop items to make them available in the toolbar.*

You can easily remove items from the toolbar, too:

1. With a Finder window open, choose **Customize Toolbar** from the View menu of the Finder.
2. Drag an item from the toolbar and let it go to remove it.
3. Click **Done** to finalize your removal.

Finally, you can apply different view settings to individual folders. For example, you may have a folder whose items you want to view strictly in icon view, or you may want to add a background image to a folder's Finder window.

1. Open a folder within a Finder window. You must be in icon, list, or Cover Flow view to change viewing options.
2. Choose **Show View Options** from the View menu in the Finder, or press **⌘-J**.
3. Make changes to the options available to you when the View Options window opens. The options will vary depending on whether you are viewing the folder's contents in icons, list, or Cover Flow view. These changes will stick with the folder whenever you view its contents.

Adjust Placement of Desktop Items

You can also make adjustments for items that appear on the desktop using View Options. Click the desktop to make it active and press **⌘-J**. You can change the size of icons and adjust the grid spacing using the appropriate sliders. Choose **Clean Up** from the View menu in the Finder to cause items on the desktop to snap into place on an invisible grid.

Choosing Icons for Files and Folders

Many folks like to change the icons of their files or folders to help keep them organized or simply to give them a face-lift.

The Windows Way

Windows does make it just a touch easier to make changes to folder icons than does Mac OS X, but it doesn't afford that same functionality to changing file icons, so we'll call this one a draw.

Right-click a folder whose icon you wish to change and select **Properties**. In the Customize tab, you can add a picture to the default folder icon or you can change the icon altogether. Browse your PC for the picture or icon you want to use, click **Open** (pictures) or **OK** (icons), and then click **Apply** to make the change.

The Mac Way

Changing icons requires a slight bit of work, but unlike Windows you can make these changes to both files and folders.

1. Single-click the source file or source folder whose icon you wish to use for another file or folder.
2. Press **⌘-I** to open the item's Info window.
3. Click once on the icon located in the upper left of the Info window, and press **⌘-C** to copy it.
4. Close the source file or folder's Info window.
5. Single-click the file or folder whose icon you wish to change and press **⌘-I** to open its Info window.
6. Click once on the icon in the upper left of the Info window, and press **⌘-V** to paste the new icon.

Setting Display Resolution

Changing the resolution of your display can help give you more screen real estate or allow you to more clearly see items on the screen. This basic task is pretty simple to perform.

The Windows Way

Windows is hands-down the winner in this task. Simply right-click the desktop and choose **Screen resolution** from the pop-up menu. Make adjustments using the Resolution pop-up menu and click **Apply**. Done!

The Mac Way

While not as lightning fast as changing display resolution in Windows, it's not exactly a painful process in Mac OS X:

1. Click the **System Preferences** icon in the Dock, or choose **System Preferences** from the Apple menu.
2. Select the **Displays** option in the Hardware section of the System Preferences window.

3. Choose a resolution from the list of supported resolutions for your display (left side of the Display tab pane), as shown in Figure 4.5.

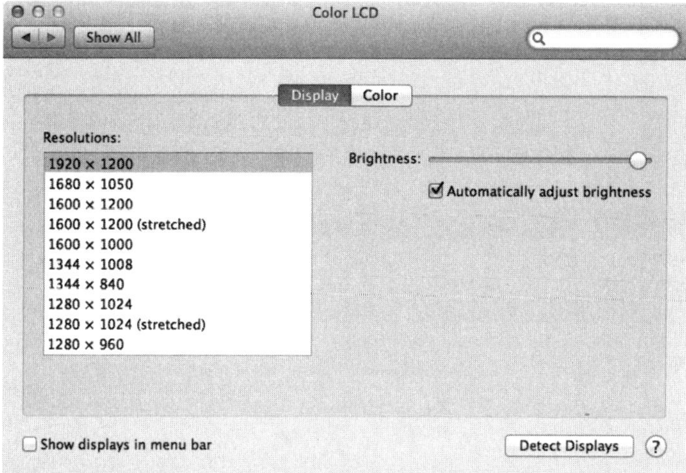

Figure 4.5: *Select a resolution within the Displays preferences pane.*

Managing Fonts

The fonts (not to be confused with the Fonz of *Happy Days* fame) stored on your computer are wont to get a bit unruly unless you have a proper way of managing them in a central location. The font connoisseur will be marginally satisfied working with Windows' default font management, but will be pleased as punch when discovering Mac OS X's Font Book.

The Windows Way

Installing fonts in Windows may be as simple as right-clicking the font file and selecting **Install** from the pop-up menu, but it's not exactly the most intuitive way I've run into. The Fonts control panel is the font "management" tool built into Windows, but only affords the options of previewing, deleting, showing, or hiding installed fonts.

The Mac Way

Font Book in Mac OS X is a true font management utility, allowing you to not only install and delete fonts from a central app, but also to preview the characters as well as gather detailed information on the fonts' characteristics. You can validate fonts to make sure they are safe to use, and even create groups of fonts to better organize them.

Font Book is found in the Applications folder at the root of your Mac's hard drive; double-click its icon to launch it. The Font Book window (shown in Figure 4.6) is simple, elegant, and almost self-explanatory.

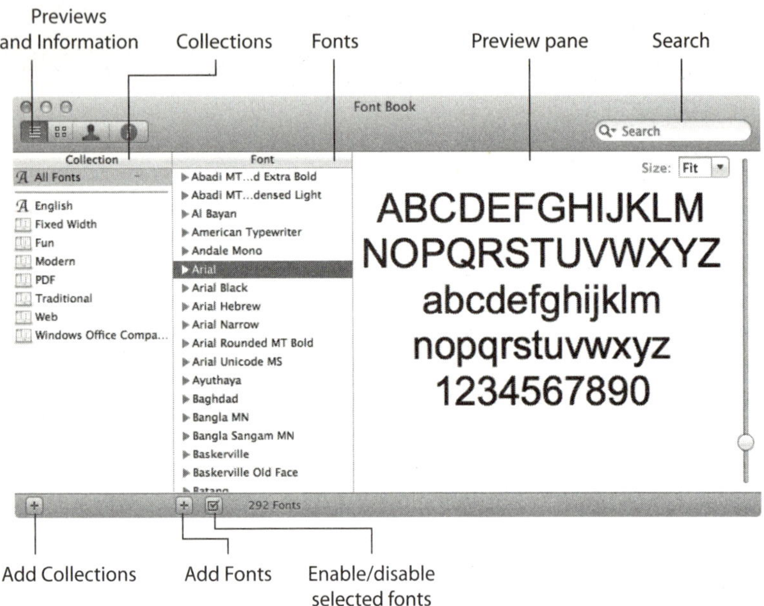

Figure 4.6: *Fonts are easily reined in with Font Book.*

Here are a few of the basic actions you can take within Font Book:

- View a list of all the fonts installed on your Mac by selecting the **All Fonts** collection.
- See which styles are available for a font by clicking the disclosure triangle to the left of its name.

- Adjust the size of characters in the Preview pane by dragging the slider or using the Size pop-up menu in the upper right.
- Add a collection to the Collections column by clicking the + button underneath the column.
- Install new fonts by clicking the + button under the Fonts column, browsing your Mac for the font to be installed, selecting said font, and then clicking **Open**.
- View characters within a font by selecting the font and then clicking one of the Preview buttons in the upper left of the window (you can also select from the Preview menu). Choose the Sample preview to see a sample of the characters, the Repertoire preview to see all the characters available, or the Custom preview to type your own characters into the Preview pane.
- Check out detailed information (such as version, trademark, license, etc.) on the selected font by clicking the **Information** button (blue circle containing a white letter "i") in the upper left of the window.
- Delete a font from the system by right-clicking (Control-clicking) the font and selecting **Remove** "font name" **Family** in the contextual menu.

Tinkering with Power Options

If you're a politician, the title of this section must have excited you, but we're talking about power of the electrical variety, not the political. Managing power for your computer is important, especially if you are using a laptop and want to maximize your battery life. Let's see how Windows and Mac OS X tackle this issue.

If you are someone who wants to deal with the bare basics of power management and not get too bogged down in the details, then Mac OS X will be your favorite in this category. However, should you desire much greater micromanagement of your computer's power handling, then Windows is your champ for this round.

The Windows Way

The Power Options control panel in Windows can be as basic or as detailed as you want to get; therefore, it gets my thumbs-up over the Mac way of power management. You can keep it simple by choosing one of the predefined power plans, or you can dive into the deep end of power management by clicking the **Change Advanced Power Settings** link in the Control Panel window. The Advanced settings allow you to tinker with everything from wireless adapter settings to USB and PCI Express options. You can't fault this approach if you want to truly maximize your computer's power efficiency.

The Mac Way

There's nothing wrong with the way Mac OS X manages power, but there's just not as much to tinker with. To tell your Mac how to best utilize its power sources, click the **Apple** menu and choose **System Preferences**, and then choose **Energy Saver** under the Hardware heading. When the Energy Saver pane opens (Figure 4.7), you will see several options, and which options appear will depend on the type of Mac you have.

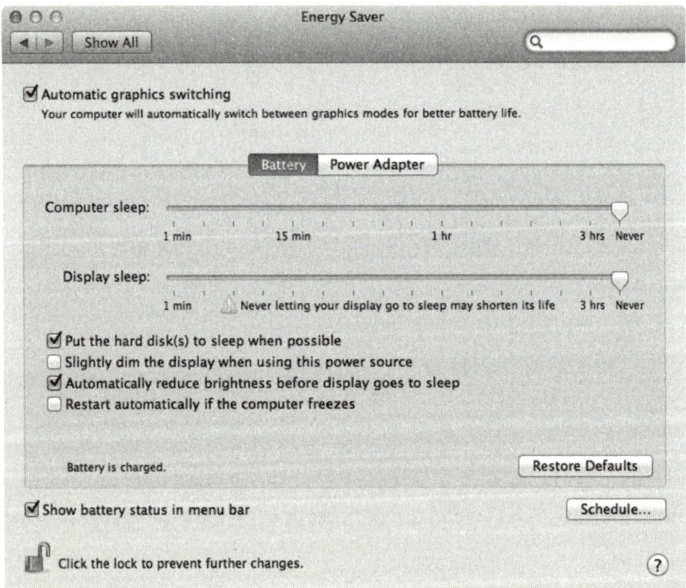

Figure 4.7: *Manage your Mac's power with Energy Saver.*

Table 4.1 affords a brief description of Energy Saver options.

Table 4.1 Energy Saver Options

Option	Description
Graphics	Maximize either battery life or graphics performance.
Automatic graphics switching	Determine when to switch graphics modes. If deselected, the Mac will always run in high-performance mode, meaning shorter battery life.
Battery/Power Adapter/UPS	Manage energy options for a particular power source.
Put the hard disk(s) to sleep when possible	Automatically puts the hard disk to sleep when the Mac is inactive.
Wake for network access	Allow others on your network to access items shared from your Mac (such as printers), even when it is asleep.
Slightly dim the display when using this power source	Display brightness is automatically reduced when using the battery.
Automatically reduce brightness before display goes to sleep	Lowers the brightness of your display a few moments before putting it to sleep.
Start up automatically after a power failure	Should power be interrupted, the Mac will start back up by itself when power is restored.
Restart automatically if the computer freezes	Should your Mac freeze up and become unresponsive, it can automatically restart itself.
Show battery status in the menu bar	Battery life is visible within the menu bar. Pretty handy feature, if you ask me.
Schedule	Set a time for the Mac to automatically turn itself on or off.

Finding and Installing New Apps

Finding new applications in the old days meant having to read the newest tech magazines or websites. Wouldn't it be nice if there was a central location you could go to find new (and old) application offerings for your computer? Wouldn't it be even nicer if you could simply download the application from this central location, install it, and begin using it immediately after download? Some of you can see where I'm going with this, I'm sure ....

The Windows Way

Remember the old days I just mentioned? Well, with Windows, those old days are today. Moving on.

The Mac Way

For those of you in the audience with iPhones or Android-based smartphones, you understand how nice it is to have the App Store or the Android Market on hand to help find the latest and greatest apps for your device. Wouldn't it be cool to have the same kind of experience on your computer? Apple thinks so, and that's why they have created the Mac App Store.

The Mac App Store, shown in Figure 4.8, shows you thousands of the latest app offerings by Apple developers from all over, and even organizes apps by categories.

Figure 4.8: *Thousands of apps are a few clicks away with the App Store.*

Here's a quick how-to on downloading a new app with the App Store:

1. Browse the categories for apps that interest you; you can even search according to price ("free" is where I usually look first).
2. Once you've found an app you simply cannot live without, click the **Free** (or **Buy** if a paid app) button in the upper left (Figure 4.9).
3. Click the **Install App** button.

4. Enter your Apple ID information when prompted and click **Sign In**, or click the **Create Apple ID** button if you don't already have one (don't worry; Apple IDs are free).

5. The download begins; once it is complete, the app will be installed and you can begin using it.

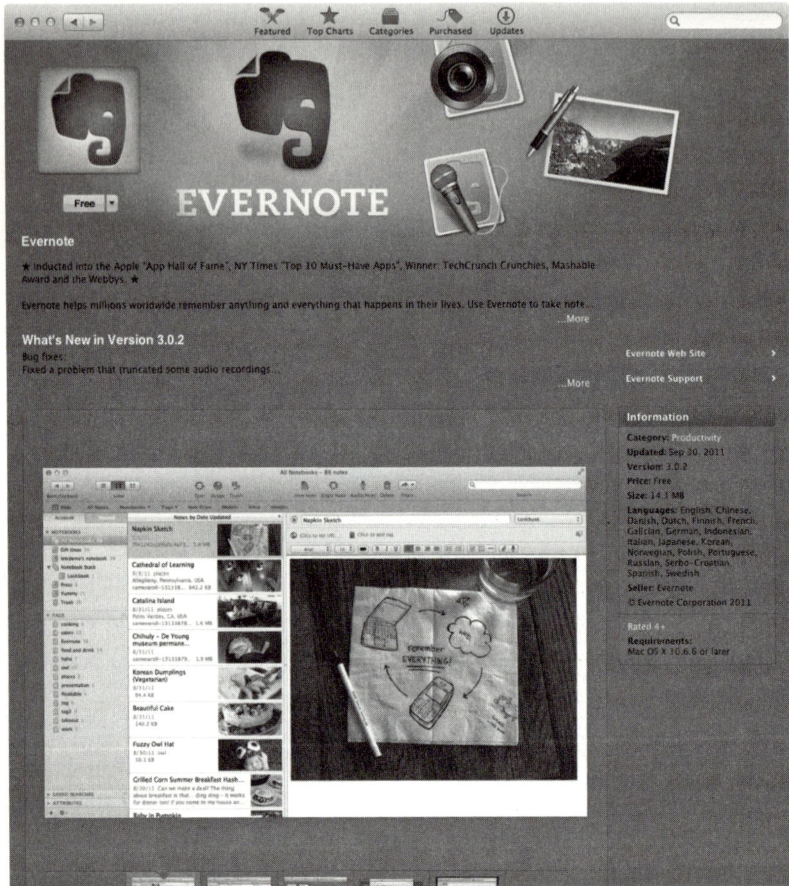

Figure 4.9: *Click the* ***Free*** *or the* ***Buy*** *button to begin downloading your app.*

Click the **Purchased** button at the top of the App Store window to see a list of apps you've bought and their status (installed or not installed).

The Updates button will show you a list of updates that are available for your purchased apps.

Removing Applications

Sometimes that app you thought you couldn't live without just doesn't cut the mustard. Why let it sit there and take up space on your hard drive? Removing an app because you simply don't use it or because it's misbehaving and you need to reinstall it is a reality for all computer users at some point in time (or at least should be).

The Windows Way

Removing an application from Windows can be a harrowing experience. Usually an application will come with an uninstaller, which you can find in the application's folder, but more often than not you will have to completely restart your computer to complete the removal. When that process works well, wipe the sweat from your brow and move forward. When that process doesn't work well, get a few bath towels and buckets handy for collection of said perspiration and get ready to call tech support; you've got a long night ahead of you.

The Mac Way

In most instances, to remove an application from Mac OS X, simply drag-and-drop the app's icon (or folder, if the app comes with a lot of support files, such as is the case with Microsoft Office 2011) to the Trash icon in the Dock and empty the Trash. That's it.

No, seriously, that's it.

The vast majority of the time, the only items left behind in this process are preference files, which are simply text documents that were created by the app so that it could keep up with any custom preferences you may have set within it. These files are text documents and will have no ill effect on your Mac.

Some apps, such as GarageBand, will install files in the /Library/ Application Support folder. These files are okay to leave if you like, but in the interest of freeing hard drive space I suggest you go into the Application Support folder and delete the folder named after the app you're removing.

Once in a blue moon you may run across an app that comes with an uninstaller, but more often than not in those cases you will not have to reboot your system. You may run into a scenario when you need to reboot, but they are very few and very far between. If an app comes with an uninstaller, it usually has stored an item at the system level, such as a printer or scanner driver.

Creating Shortcuts

Everybody loves a good shortcut. Whether trying to beat the rush-hour traffic, catch a movie, or make sweeping changes to an expansive spreadsheet, shortcuts simply make life easier. You can create shortcuts for your favorite folder or application on your computer, too, helping you quickly reach something in one or two clicks that might normally take several.

The Windows Way

Right-click on the item you want to create a shortcut for and select **Create Shortcut** from the contextual menu. The shortcut icon appears; you can tell it's a shortcut because of the little black arrow that's now part of the icon, signifying that this icon refers back to an original. Feel free to place your new shortcut in the place you think provides you the best access, such as the desktop or Start menu.

The Mac Way

Mac OS X can create shortcuts just as easily as Windows, but they are not called "shortcuts," but rather "aliases." To create an alias in Mac OS X:

1. Find the item you want to create the alias for, whether it be an app, folder, or file.
2. Right-click (Control-click) the icon for the item and choose **Make Alias** from the contextual menu.

3. When the alias appears with the little black arrow superimposed (an example is given in Figure 4.10), you may place the alias in a location you deem best for accessing it quickly.

Figure 4.10: *An example of an alias in Mac OS X.*

Networking Your Mac

If you're like me, you remember the good old days when computer networks were rare. Nowadays it's a foregone conclusion that your computer needs to be on a network of some sort that is connected to the internet. It's nearly impossible to do many tasks on the computer that don't require an internet connection. Even some help files that used to come as part of your operating system now can only be seen if you are hooked up to the World Wide Web.

Macs connect to the same networks that PCs do; there is no limitation or restriction to a network based on the operating system you use. If you can connect a PC to your network, you can connect your Mac as well, no problem.

Hooking Up to a Wireless Network

Not all that long ago I would have begun this chapter by showing you how to connect to a wired network, but today wireless is so prevalent I would be doing you a disservice if I didn't cover it first.

Pretty much any computer you buy these days has wireless networking capabilities built right in, whereas just a few years ago you would have needed to add a wireless network card or adapter to your computer to network sans wires.

The Windows Way

Windows knows how to play nice with a wireless network, so you shouldn't run into too much trouble. Simply click the **Network** icon in the notification area to open the Connect to a Network window. Choose a network from the list of those available, enter the security key or password (if necessary), and you will be surfing the net and checking email in no time flat. This is the simplest way to connect, of course. Your mileage may vary if the network is closed or your PC's network adapter is flaky.

A closed network is one that is up and running but cannot be seen by just anyone, which is great for security. You must know the name of the network and its password/security key to access it.

The Mac Way

It's just as simple to join a wireless network in Mac OS X as it is in Windows, assuming the network isn't closed and your Wi-Fi is turned on (which it is by default):

1. Click the **Wi-Fi** icon (looks like ascending radio waves) in the menu bar. If the waves are grayed out, the Wi-Fi is turned off; turn Wi-Fi on by clicking the **Wi-Fi** icon and selecting **Turn Wi-Fi On**.
2. Select a network from the list of those that are available, or at least visible (Figure 5.1).
3. Enter a security key or password for the network, if necessary.

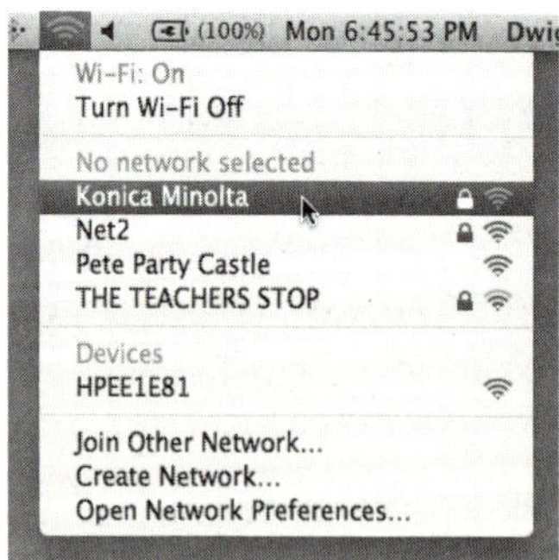

Figure 5.1: *Click the* ***Wi-Fi*** *icon to see available and visible networks.*

The Wi-Fi icon's "radio waves" should go from gray to black, indicating a connection has been made. The more black waves you see, the stronger the connection is.

Joining a closed network is a bit different.

Here's how to join a closed network:

1. Open System Preferences and click the **Network** icon in the Internet & Wireless section.
2. Select **Wi-Fi** from the list on the left side of the Network preferences pane.
3. In the Wi-Fi pane (Figure 5.2), click the **Network Name** pop-up menu and select **Join Other Network**. If the Status reads as Off, click the **Turn Wi-Fi On** button.
4. Enter the exact name of the network in the Network Name field. If you don't know the exact name, contact your network administrator for help.
5. Select the type of security the network uses. Again, contact your network admin if you don't know the answer to this one.
6. Type the security key or password for the network in the Password field.
7. If you want to automatically join this network every time your Mac is within range of it, check the **Remember this network** box.
8. Click **Join** to log in to the closed network.

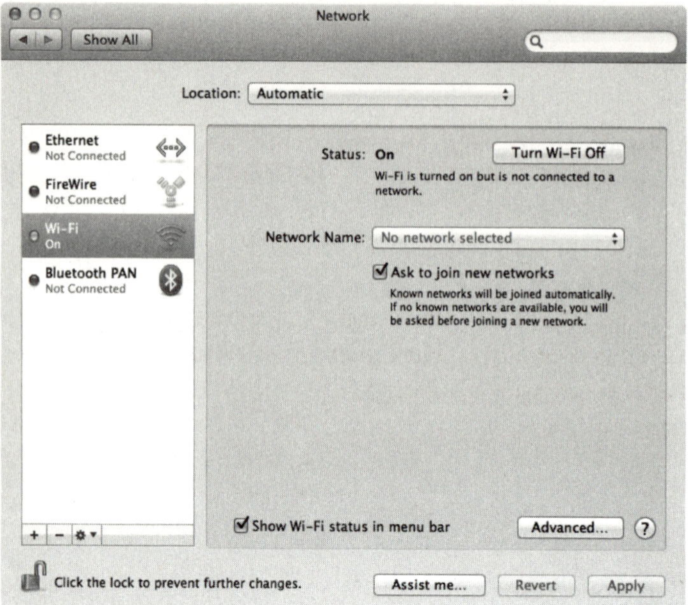

Figure 5.2: *The Wi-Fi preferences pane.*

At this point you should begin cruising the internet with your favorite browser or perusing the shared files and folders offered on your network.

Create a Wireless Network Between Two Macs

Should you find yourself wanting to exchange files with someone but don't want to have to bother with joining a network and finding one another on it, you can create a mini wireless network using two Macs quite easily. Click the **Wi-Fi** icon on the first Mac and select **Create Network**, give the new network a name, and just click **Create** (ignore the other options unless you want to assign passwords and all that other stuff). On the second Mac, click its **Wi-Fi** icon, find the new network in the list, and select it. Boom! An instant network.

Hooking Up to a Wired Network

Sometimes you may not have a wireless network to connect to (not as likely these days as in recent years past, but still possible), or your wireless network adapter may be on the fritz. Should that horror ever be visited upon you, don't fear: your computer has a built-in Ethernet port for just such an occasion (unless you have a MacBook Air).

Let me break it down for you: connecting to a wired network is a no-brainer, no matter the operating system, as you're about to find out.

The Windows Way

I'll try to keep this complicated task as simple as possible, despite the enormous complexity. Here goes: attach one end of an Ethernet cable to your Ethernet network device (hub, router, or switch) and place the other end into the Ethernet port on your PC.

Whew! Glad that's over with.

Honest, that really is it, typically speaking. Your PC will talk to the network device to acquire an address for itself, and away you go. Now, if your network is a large one (for example, a corporate or university network), there may be more steps involved, such as logging into domains and the like, but that's something for your IT department to help out with.

The Mac Way

The Mac is no more complicated than the PC. Plug an Ethernet cable into your Mac and put the other end into a network device … done.

If you want to check up on me and verify you are indeed connected:

1. Choose **System Preferences** from the Apple menu.
2. Click the **Network** icon in the Internet & Wireless section of the System Preferences window.
3. Note the Ethernet icon in the list on the left side. If there is a green button next to it, you're connected (Figure 5.3). If you see a red or yellow dot, something's amiss, and you should try the following:
    - Check to make sure the cables are securely connected.
    - Try using a different cable.

- Try connecting to a different port on the network device.
- Make sure the network device is connected to a power source.
- If all else fails, contact your IT administrator or the manufacturer of your network device.

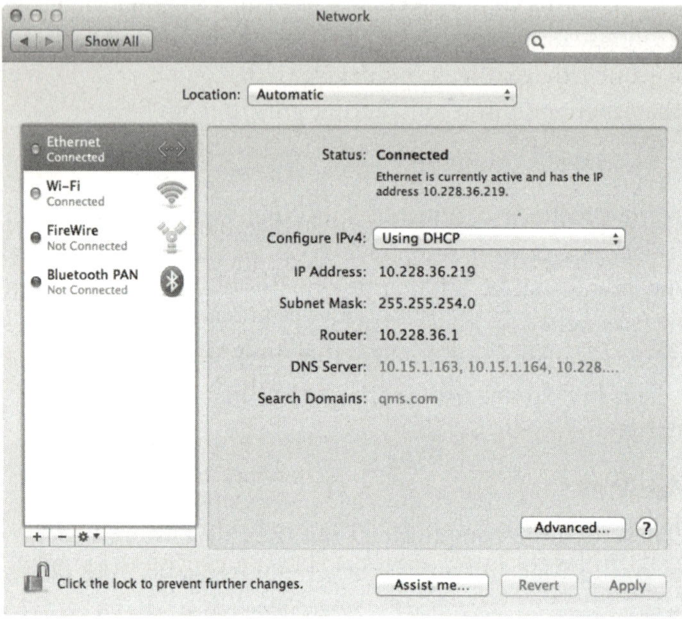

Figure 5.3: *The green light indicates you are connected to your wired network.*

Checking Network Performance

From time to time your network may appear to be running a bit slow, or even seem to not be working at all. Every operating system has a way to allow you to see the status of your network connections. Let's see how Windows and Mac OS X stack up on this one.

The Windows Way

Windows has a very easy way to check out the network speed and connection data, as well as diagnose a problem, but it falls short just by a smidgen to Mac OS X's tool used to do the same.

Go to the Network and Sharing Center control panel. Click the **Local Area Connection** link to open the Local Area Connection Status window. From there you can view your PC's network activity, and if you need more info just click the **Details** button. You can also have Windows attempt to solve a network problem by clicking the **Diagnose** button, but I'm not sure if anyone in history has ever had any real success with it. I'm just sayin'.

The Mac Way

If you've ever had the desire to run a traceroute or a netstat, Mac OS X's Network Utility is right up your alley!

Of course, if you're like the other 99.99 percent of the world's computer-literate population, you may only want to know the status of your Mac's network connection. Luckily, Network Utility can handle that little job, too.

To use Network Utility's … well … network utilities:

1. Open Network Utility by going to the /Applications/ Utilities folder and double-clicking its icon to launch.
2. Click the **Info** tab (seen in Figure 5.4) to see the status of your network connection. Click the pop-up menu to switch between network interfaces, such as your wireless connection or your built-in Ethernet port.

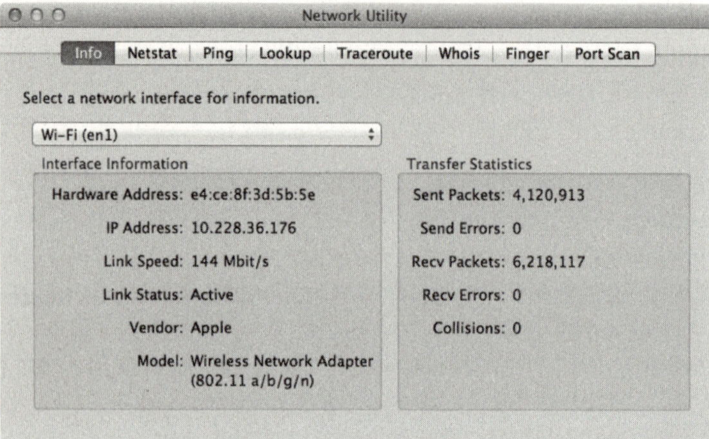

Figure 5.4: *The Info tab of Network Utility will give you the scoop on your Mac's network connection.*

I gave Mac OS X the advantage here because of all the other tools you can use within Network Utility (remember netstat and traceroute that I mentioned a bit earlier?). You can access these utilities, and others, by clicking on their tabs. The one that many of you may be most familiar with is the Ping tab. Ping allows you to send out a signal to another networked computer to see if it will respond to you. The only way to perform this operation in Windows is to execute the ping command from a DOS prompt, so the graphical interface of Network Utility is most welcome.

Modifying Network Settings

Sometimes connecting to a network may not be as cut and dried as plugging in an Ethernet cable or knowing the password for a wireless network. Should that be the case, you will need a way to modify the settings used to make your network connections.

 The Windows Way

To modify the default network settings in Windows, you need to revisit the Network and Sharing Center. Once there, click **Change Adapter Settings** on the left side of the window. Right-click the network adapter (Local Area Connection, etc.) that you want to change and select **Properties** from the contextual menu. Select a network component you want to modify and click the **Properties** button. In the resulting window, make any network configuration mods that you deem necessary. There's a lot of steps involved, and you sometimes have to jump all over the place to get to different settings.

The Mac Way

Mac OS X makes things a good bit simpler than Windows because it tends to keep all the network settings in the same general location, so everything's within relatively easy reach.

Go to System Preferences and click the **Network** icon in the Internet & Wireless section. Select the connection you want to modify from the list on the left, and then click the **Advanced** button in the lower-right corner. From here you can make any changes you need in order to access your network and perform other network-related tasks. If you're not sure what items need to be configured in these options, you should contact your IT administrator.

The Advanced sheet that opens when you click the **Advanced** button gives you pretty much the same options for both wireless and wired networks, with the one exception being the Wi-Fi tab that appears for wireless connections (Figure 5.5).

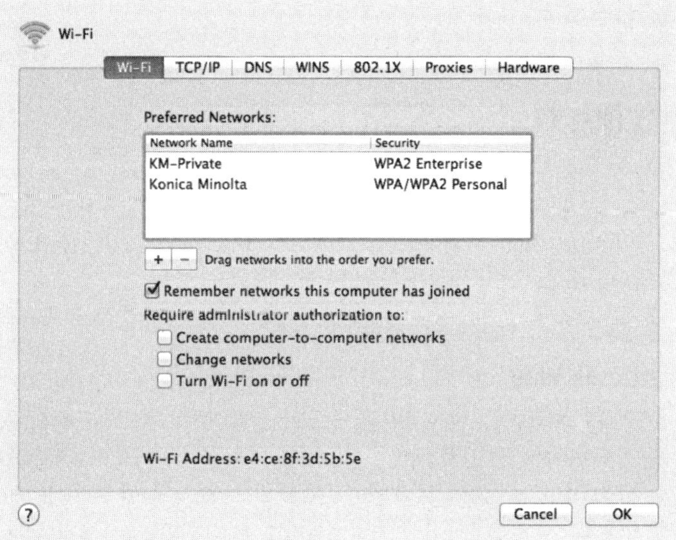

Figure 5.5: *View wireless networks you've connected to from the Wi-Fi tab.*

The Preferred Networks window shows you the wireless networks you've connected to with your Mac. You can click-and-drag the networks into an order you prefer, or you could click the + or – buttons to add or delete networks to or from the list.

The TCP/IP tab lets you see the IP address assigned to your Mac, along with other information about your network connection.

The DNS tab allows you to view, add, or remove DNS servers and search domains that your Mac uses to complete addresses of internet domains you access often.

The WINS tab is where you can go to add your Mac to a Windows workgroup, as seen in Figure 5.6. Click the + or – buttons to add or remove addresses of WINS servers on the network.

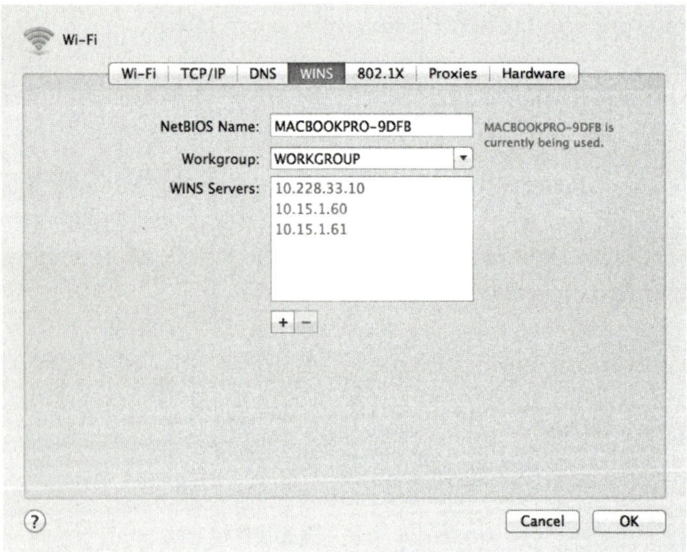

Figure 5.6: *Your Mac can join a Windows workgroup if you provide it with the correct credentials.*

If your network uses 802.1X for enhanced security, you can view information about your 802.1X profile from this tab. If your network does use 802.1X, your IT admin will provide you with a profile that you need to install, which can be done simply by double-clicking it (they'll know this already, so you won't have to remember it). The information from this profile is what you'll be able to see in this tab.

The Proxies tab allows you to configure proxy server settings should you have to connect to the internet through a firewall. Sometimes a firewall can block access to certain types of services on the internet, and these proxy server settings will allow you to reach those services. I should state that proxy server settings are not usually needed for connecting through routers in your home; you're more likely to encounter this in a corporate environment.

The Hardware tab offers the chance to view your MAC address and to configure the network connection speed of your Mac.

Setting Up a Firewall

A firewall can protect you from prying eyes that are lurking on the internet, trying to communicate with your computer against your wishes (most often clandestinely). Enabling the firewall is a good idea if you aren't already behind one; most corporations, universities, and other large networks already employ firewalls that you never even have to think about.

The Windows Way

The Windows firewall is on by default, so there's not much you need to do. However, if you want to turn it off (or back on) or make changes to its configuration, you can access it within Control Panel.

The Mac Way

Unlike Windows, Mac OS X's firewall is off by default. Should you desire to run the firewall, please follow along:

1. Open the Security & Privacy preferences pane.
2. Click the **Firewall** tab.
3. Click the lock icon in the lower-left corner, enter your account name and password, and then click the **Unlock** button.
4. Click the **Start** button to turn the firewall on.

That's pretty much it. You can make adjustments to the firewall's default settings by clicking the **Advanced** button in the lower-right corner, though, should the need arise. The options in the resulting sheet (shown in Figure 5.7) allow you to customize the connections coming into your Mac through the network/internet. If you aren't sure about these, please contact your IT admin or you might be turning off access to items you will need (or letting in little internet demons you'd rather not have to tackle).

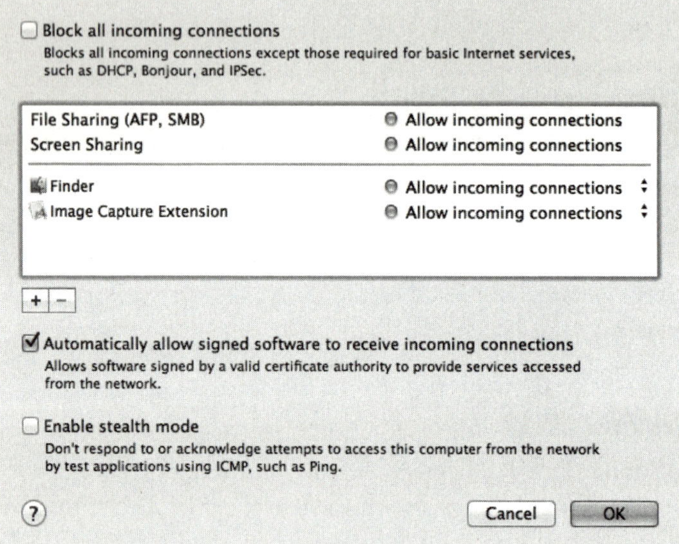

Figure 5.7: *You can customize your firewall settings to match the needs of your network.*

Share and Share Alike

"It's mine!"

"No, it's mine!"

"Give it back!"

"Hey, you!"

"Kids, if you can't share then it's going to be mine!"

If you've ever been in a home or car occupied by two or more children, this exchange will sound painfully familiar. Sharing is something that might not come naturally to some of us, but computers are typically quite good at it. Operating systems that once were unable to share with each other without the aid of expensive third-party software can now extend an olive branch with built-in capabilities. This chapter will cover sharing different aspects of your computer, from sharing files to internet connections to disc drives.

Sharing Files and Folders

The most basic items a computer shares are the files and folders that occupy its space. Sharing documents with work colleagues or sharing pictures with another computer user in the house is a given.

You can typically share items with individual users or with everyone on your network or computer.

The Windows Way

Sharing a folder and its contents in Windows is fairly simple. Right-click the folder you want to share and click **Properties** from the contextual menu. Select the **Sharing** tab, click the **Share** button, and choose users you want to share with (or simply select **Everyone** to share with everyone who has local or network access to the PC). When you have a list of users, click the **Share** button.

Depending on many other variables that we won't go into here, you may need to customize permissions, so in the Sharing tab click **Advanced Sharing** and set to work customizing the permissions for individual users as needed.

The Mac Way

Mac OS X is adept at sharing with Macs and PCs alike, so don't fret if you have a network full of both platforms.

To share a folder and its contents from Mac OS X:

1. Click the **Apple** menu and select **System Preferences**.
2. Select **Sharing** from the Internet & Wireless section.
3. Check the box next to **File Sharing** (Figure 6.1).
4. Click the **+** button under the Shared Folders field.
5. Browse your Mac for the folder you want to share, select it, and click **Add**.

Next, you need to decide whom to share your folder with. By default, a newly shared folder gives the user of the account that owns the folder read and write access, meaning that the user can see and add to the contents of the folder. Mac OS X also gives read-only access to all users on the network, meaning that they can see the contents of the shared folder but cannot change them.

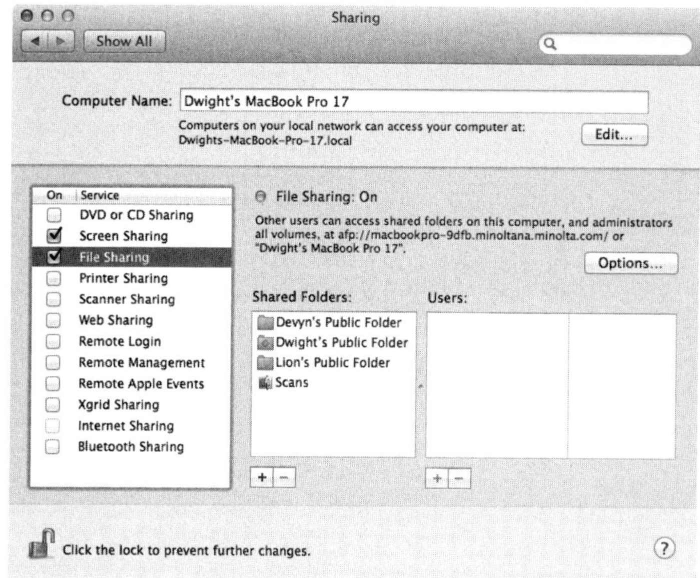

Figure 6.1: *Check the box next to* ***File Sharing*** *to enable the feature.*

To customize the users who can access the shared folder:

1. Click the folder you just added in the Shared Folders section, and then click the **+** button under the Users field to pick someone to share with, as seen in Figure 6.2.
2. Decide who can access your shared folder:
   - To share with a user who already has an account on your Mac, select **Users & Groups** from the list on the left and then select their user account name.
   - To share with someone in your Address Book, click **Address Book** from the list on the left and then choose the name of the person you want to share with.
   - To share with someone else who will not log in to your Mac, you can create a sharing-only account for him or her. Click the **New Person** button and set them up with a user name and password, and then click **Create Account** (Figure 6.3).

3. Click the tiny up and down arrows to the right of the user name in the Users field to set their access permissions to the shared folder.

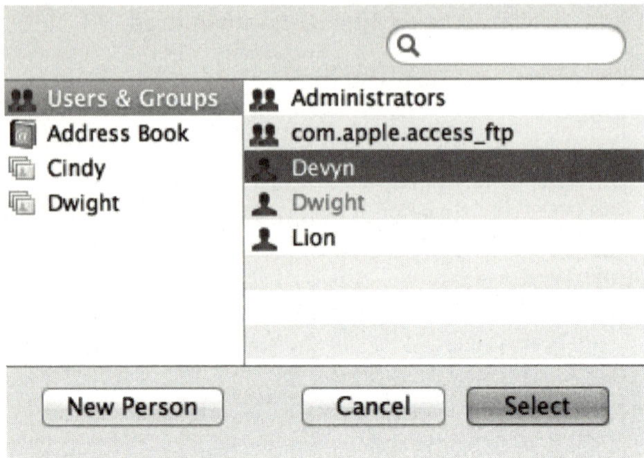

Figure 6.2: *Determine whom to share your folder with.*

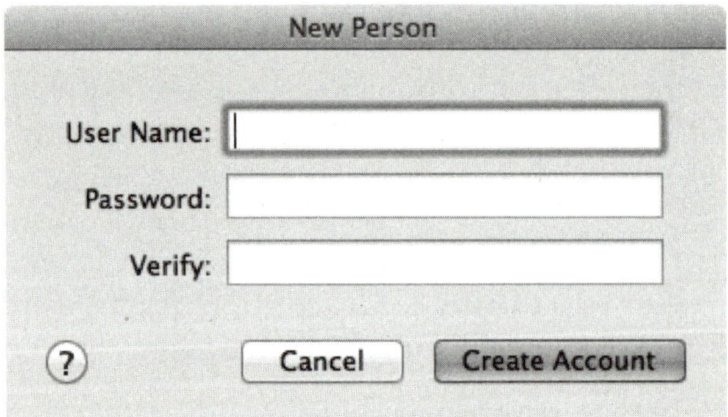

Figure 6.3: *Create a sharing-only account for people who don't have user accounts on your Mac or network.*

If those persons whom you are sharing with are running PCs with Windows, you'll need to take the additional step of enabling Server Message Block (SMB), which is the preferred sharing protocol of Windows.

1. Click the **Options** button in the File Sharing pane.
2. Check the box called **Share files and folders using SMB (Windows)**, as I've done in Figure 6.4.
3. Check the **On** box next to the user to activate their account. Enter the user's password when prompted.
4. Click **Done** when finished.

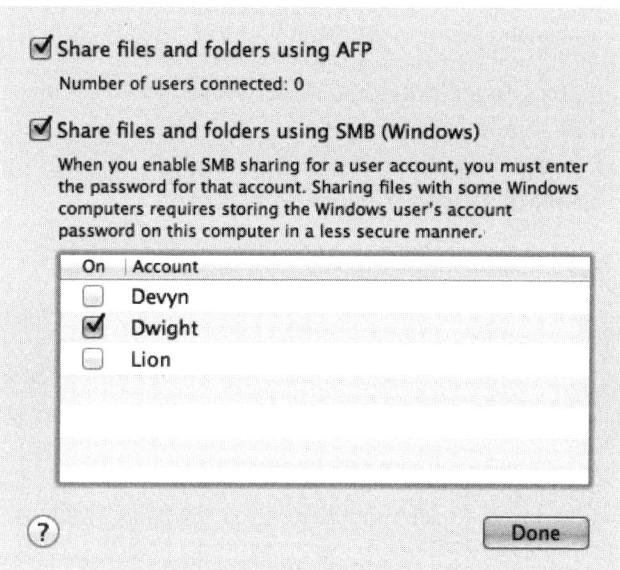

Figure 6.4: *Sharing files and folders with Windows users is a snap.*

Finding and Connecting to Shared Computers

Hopefully you aren't the only one on your network whose parents taught them to share. If there are other folks kind enough to share their files and folders with you, you will need to know how to find them and access their shares.

The Windows Way

Finding shared folders on your network isn't too difficult at all with Windows. Simply click **Start** and select **Network** from the right side of it. The window that opens will show you the network shares available. Double-click the icon for the computer you want to access, and enter a user name and password if necessary.

The Mac Way

Mac OS X can quickly find shared resources on your network, too. Your Mac will see other Macs, as well as PCs running Windows, Linux, and other platforms.

To find and access shared folders from your Mac:

1. Open a new Finder window.
2. Notice the word "Shared" in the sidebar. Hold your mouse pointer over it and the word "Show" will appear to the right. Click **Show** and the sidebar populates with a list of network shares.
3. If you see the share you want in the sidebar, click to access it. If not, click **All** at the bottom of the list to see all the computers sharing files and folders (Figure 6.5).
4. Click the name of the computer you want to access. You will see whatever folders the computer is sharing with all users, but you won't see folders they are only sharing with specific users. If you are one of those lucky few, click the **Connect As** button and enter the appropriate name and password, and then click **Connect** (Figure 6.6).

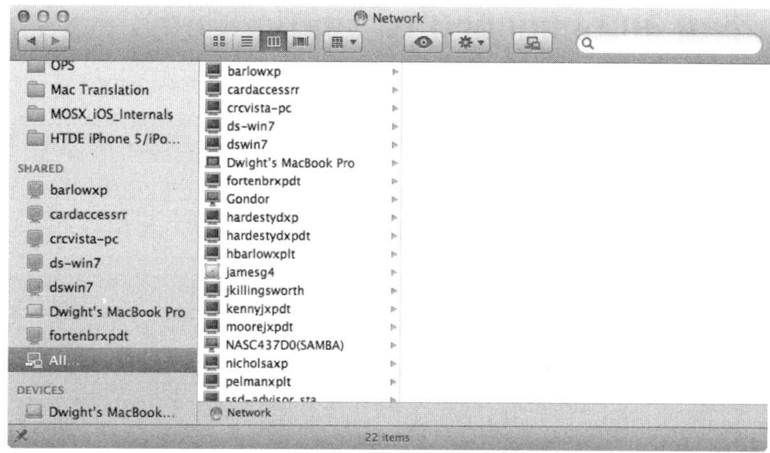

Figure 6.5: *Click* ***All*** *in the sidebar to see all the network shares available.*

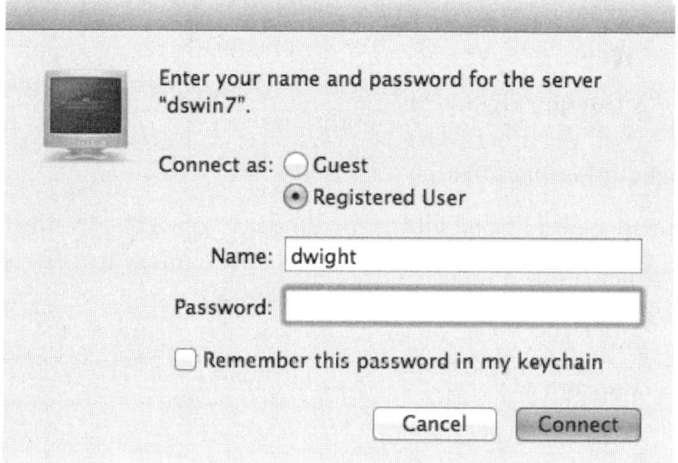

Figure 6.6: *Enter the appropriate user name and password to access a shared computer, if required.*

Using a Domain

If your network uses domain names to log in to computers, you will want to speak to someone in your IT department should you have trouble accessing shared computers. There may be special conventions needed for entering your user name and password.

Manually Connecting to Shared Computers

What should you do if you know darned good and well that a computer is on the network, but for some reason you are unable to see it? Let's find out how to manually get to those stealth servers.

The Windows Way

You can manually access a computer in Windows by entering its name or IP address in the address field of a window. For example, if the IP address of the computer you wanted to access was 10.10.1.9, you would enter the address as \\10.10.1.9 and press **Enter**. At that point you would be asked to enter the user name and password necessary to access the computer.

The Mac Way

It's also simple enough in Mac OS X to manually reach computers on the network. Again, you will need to either know the computer's name or its IP address to successfully connect.

To manually connect to a server:

1. Press **⌘-K** from within the Finder to open the Connect to Server window (you could also select **Connect to Server** from the Go menu), seen in Figure 6.7.
2. Enter the name or IP address of the computer you want to connect to:
    - If the computer you want to access runs a Windows-based operating system, you must indicate this by typing **smb** before the computer name. For example, if the computer's name is dswin7, you would enter **smb://dswin7** in the Server Address field. Note that the two slashes before the name are forward slashes, not backslashes like Windows uses. You may also enter the IP address in place of the computer name.
    - If the computer you want to access is running Mac OS X, you only need to enter the name or IP address of the computer in the Server Address field.

3. Click **Connect** to hook up with the computer, and enter a correct user name and password if required.

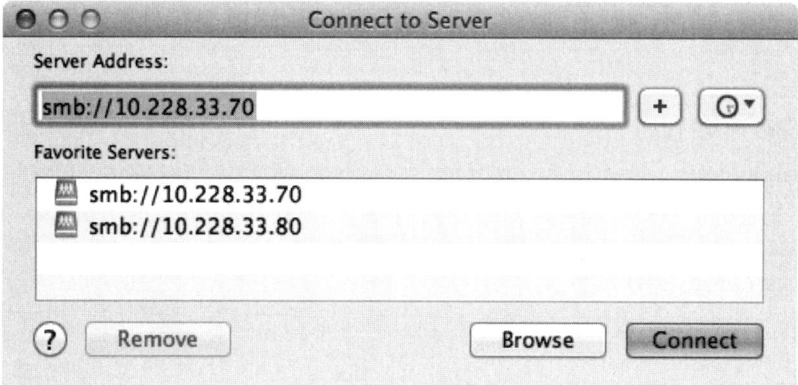

Figure 6.7: *Connect to a computer manually with its IP address or name.*

If you find that you access these servers quite often, you can click the + button next to the Server Address field to add the computer to the Favorite Servers list.

Remotely Accessing Other Computers

How cool would it be to access and use another computer from your own? Windows and Mac OS X allow you to do just that, and it's really a nifty tool to have if you are in a meeting and need to access a computer in your office down the hall, or if you want to keep an eye on what your kids are doing on their computer.

The Windows Way

You must first allow remote connections on the PC you want to remotely connect to. You do this by going to the Remote tab of the system properties and selecting a connection method. Select **Users** for the connection and then click **Apply**.

Next, on the PC you will be using to connect to the remote PC, open Remote Desktop Connection by going to the **Start Menu > All Programs > Accessories**. Enter the computer name, as well as the user name and password needed to connect, and you can use the remote PC as if you were standing in front of it.

This is how you access a Windows-based PC from another Windows-based PC. To remotely access other operating systems, you will need to install third-party software.

The Mac Way

Your Mac can connect remotely to another Mac with the help of a Virtual Network Connection (VNC) and Screen Sharing. Once connected, you can use that remote Mac like you were sitting in front of it. Sweet!

To remotely connect to another Mac, we must first turn on Screen Sharing for that Mac. On the Mac you want to remotely connect to:

1. Open **System Preferences** and go to Sharing.
2. Check the **Screen Sharing** box (Figure 6.8).
3. Click the **Computer Settings** button to set a couple of options (Click **OK** when finished):
    - To allow anyone to request your permission to access your screen, check the box called **Anyone may request permission to control screen.**
    - Require anyone who remotely connects to your Mac to use a password. Check the **VNC viewers may control screen with password** box, and enter a password into the text field.
4. Determine who can access your Mac remotely by choosing **All users** or **Only these users** in the Allow access for window. Click the **+** button to add users to the list.
5. Note the address under the Screen Sharing: On section. The address given is one way in which you can access this Mac remotely, as we will see in a moment.

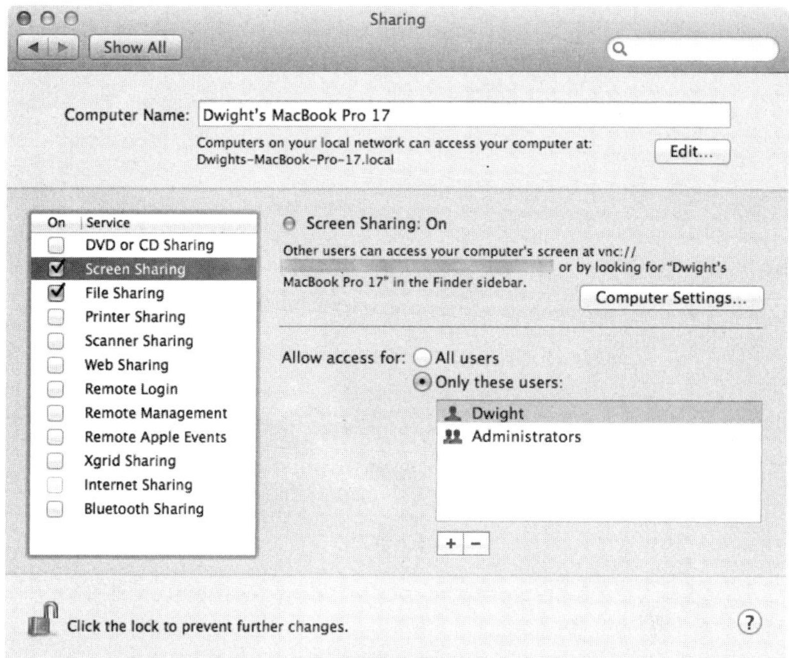

Figure 6.8: *Check the* ***Screen Sharing*** *box so others can remotely access your Mac.*

Now that we have the remote Mac configured, let's find out how to access it. There are two ways to access a remote Mac.

The first way is through the Finder:

1. Open a new Finder window.
2. Click **Shared** in the sidebar and locate the Mac you want to connect to.
3. Select the Mac you want to connect to and click the **Share Screen** button (seen in Figure 6.9).
4. Enter a user name and password if prompted, and then click **Connect**.
5. When the window opens, you can begin using your remotely connected computer, as well as bask in the glory of your latest Mac accomplishment. To end the session, simply close the window.

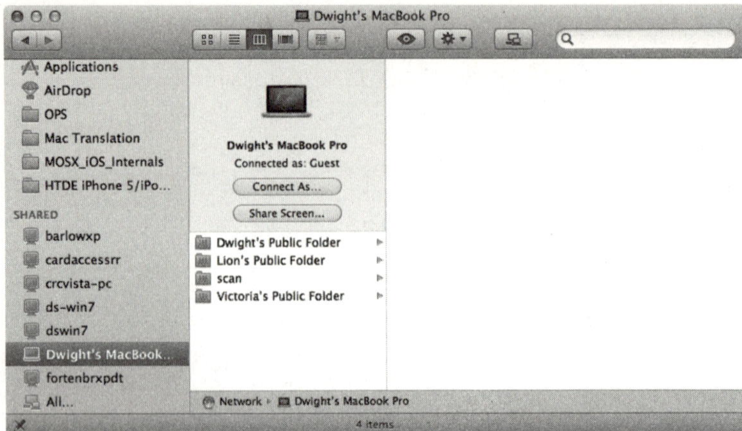

Figure 6.9: *Click the **Share Screen** button to access the remote Mac.*

The second way to access a remote Mac:

1. Open the Connect to Server window by pressing **⌘-K** within the Finder.
2. Remember when I told you to note the address in the Screen Sharing: On section of the remote Mac's Screen Sharing options? Good! You'll need that address to continue. Once you've got the address, enter it into the Server Address field.
3. Click **Connect**, enter the user name and password for the remote Mac when prompted, and away you go.

Remotely Connect to Windows from a Mac

Should you want to remotely connect to a Windows-based PC, you can download Microsoft's Remote Desktop Connection client for Mac. Just visit www.microsoft.com/mac/remote-desktop-client and click the **Download Now** button. As with Windows, Remote Desktop must be enabled on the PC you want to connect to for this functionality to work.

Sharing Internet Connections

Sometimes you might want to share one computer's internet connection with another computer. Normally this wouldn't be the case, as most computers can connect to the internet for themselves, assuming their networking hardware is working correctly, but there are scenarios in which you may want to do this.

The Windows Way

Windows shares internet connections through ICS (Internet Connection Sharing), and there's a bit involved.

You first must enable ICS on the host computer. Go to the Network and Sharing Center control panel and click **Change Adapter Settings**. Right-click the connection you're sharing and select **Properties**. Go to the Sharing tab and check the **Allow Other Network Users to Connect Through This Computer's Internet Connection** box.

You must then make sure that any computers that will be accessing the internet through the one you just configured are set to get an IP address automatically. There's a tad bit more involved, but you get the picture, I'm sure.

The Mac Way

Want to share your internet connection from your Mac? Sure, no problem:

1. Open System Preferences and go to Sharing.
2. Select **Internet Sharing**, as I've done in Figure 6.10.
3. Choose which of your Mac's internet connections you want to share, using the Share your connection from pop-up menu.
4. Check the boxes next to the types of ports the other computers will be accessing your Mac's internet connection with.

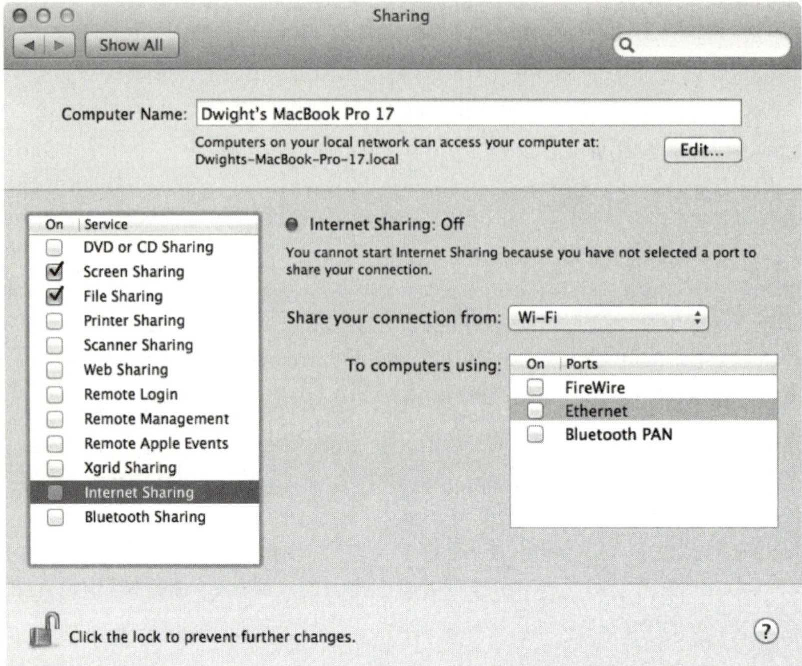

Figure 6.10: *Share your Mac's internet connection with other computers using Internet Sharing.*

Wi-Fi Won't Share with Wi-Fi

You cannot share your Wi-Fi connection with other computers using their Wi-Fi. Alternatively, you could connect your Mac via Ethernet and then share with other computers via Wi-Fi.

Sharing Your CDs and DVDs

Oh, no! Jack's optical disc drive just went up in smoke! He has a huge project due on the boss's desk first thing in the morning, but he has no way of getting crucial information from the CD he burned at the office onto his computer at home. Looks like he'll have to drive an hour across town to go back to the office and work from there.

Wait, what's this? Jill has a heck of an idea! She can simply share her optical disc drive from her computer, allowing Jack to access it through their home network. Brilliant, Jill!

The Windows Way

Windows can easily share an optical drive with another computer on the network. Click **Start** and go to Computer. Right-click the optical drive, hold the mouse pointer over **Share with**, and select **Advanced Sharing**. Next, click the **Sharing** tab and select the **Advanced Sharing** button. Check the **Share this folder** box, give the share a name, and click **Apply**. Others on the network can access the optical drive over the network, just like they would a shared folder. Pretty cool, really.

The Mac Way

Windows was mighty impressive in the last paragraph, wasn't it? Well, Mac OS X won't be outdone on this one!

To share CDs and DVDs from your Mac:

1. Open System Preferences and go to Sharing.
2. Check the box next to **DVD or CD Sharing** (Figure 6.11).
3. Check the box called **Ask me before allowing others to use my DVD drive**. This adds a measure of security for you.

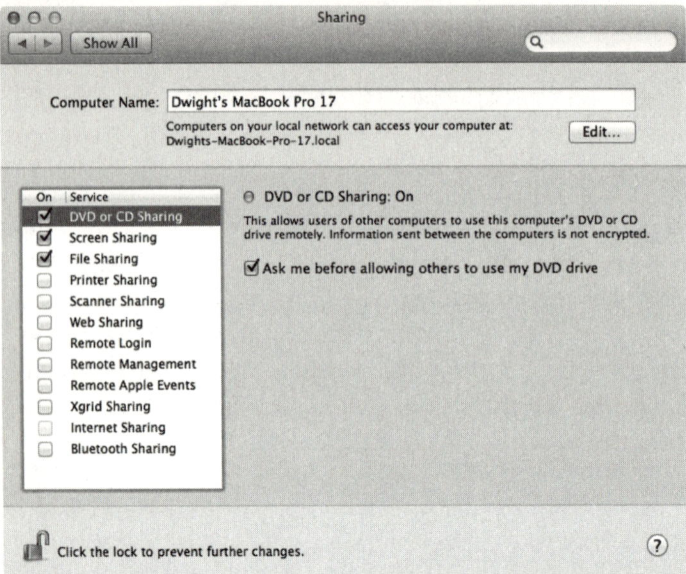

Figure 6.11: *Mac OS X can share your optical drive with others on your network.*

Other folks on your network can access your optical drive with ease:

1. Open a Finder window and locate the name of the Mac sharing its optical drive from the Shared list.
2. Select the Mac that is sharing its drive and click **Connect As**.
3. Enter a correct user name and password to access the Mac when prompted.
4. The title of the shared CD or DVD will appear in the Finder as a shared folder. Click it to access its contents.

Everybody's Gone Surfin'

Today it seems that everyone's a surfer. Not the Bethany Hamilton type, mind you, but the internet variety. From the IT nerd in your family to your great-grandmother, jumping online and cruising for the latest news, shopping deals, or what-have-you is just something that most of us do sometime during the course of a normal day.

Browsing the Web

Thankfully, a website is a website, regardless of which operating system or browser you use to gain access to it (with a minor exception here or there), so going to www.apple.com should yield the same web page whether you're using Windows or Mac OS X.

Cruising the internet requires a web browser, which is essentially a software window into the World Wide Web.

The Windows Way

Every Windows user is familiar with Internet Explorer, and for many (if not most), it isn't exactly a friendly familiarity. To be kind, Internet Explorer is not known by many as the best way to wander the web, and Microsoft has been notorious in the past for trying to tie Windows users to the browser, whether they liked it or not. Although there are a multitude of alternative browsers for the Windows platform, the default experience is with Internet Explorer.

The Mac Way

Let's be honest: if you can use one browser you can use another; it just may take some time to become familiar with where your tools are located. Common tasks like entering URLs (web addresses) are a cinch, but others may not be so intuitive.

Mac OS X comes with one of the best browsers on the planet preinstalled: Safari. Safari has a very clean and easy-to-understand interface, so it's simple to get used to. Open Safari by clicking its icon (looks like a compass) in the Dock.

The Safari interface is exceptionally user-friendly, as seen in Figure 7.1.

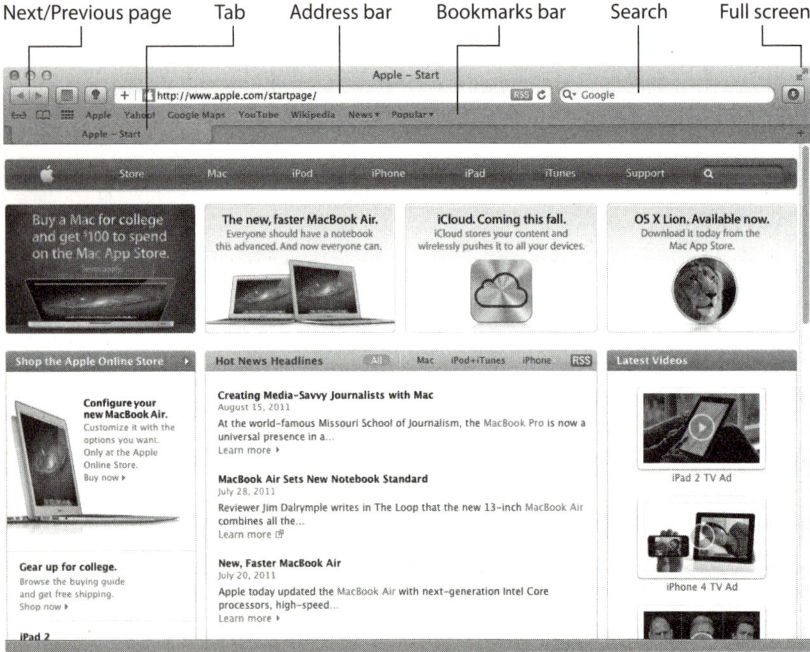

Figure 7.1: *Surfing the net with Safari.*

Although you may know how to use a browser, let's get familiar with how to do a few basic tasks with Safari:

- Enter web page URLs into the address bar and press **Return** to zip to the page.
- Reload (or refresh) a web page by pressing **⌘-R**.
- Press **⌘-[** to move to the previous web page (if you've visited more than one) or **⌘-]** to visit the next web page.
- Click the **Full Screen** button in the upper-right corner of the window to surf the web with no other distractions.
- Enter a subject into the search field and press **Return** to squeeze info from Google.

Safari for Windows

Should you find yourself having to use Windows for whatever reason, you need not leave your new favorite browser, Safari, behind. Apple has a version of Safari just for Windows, and you can get it by visiting www.apple.com/safari from your PC.

Working with Tabs

Sorry, but Safari won't give you a line of credit at your favorite watering hole; that's not the kind of tabs I'm talking about here. Nope, these kinds of tabs are more akin to those found in a filing cabinet, which help you move from subject to subject within the same drawer, as opposed to having a separate drawer in the cabinet for each subject.

Tabs allow you to have multiple web pages open at once, but within one browser window. You can then click on a particular tab to access its wares, while leaving the tabs of other web pages open in case you need to access them quickly.

The Windows Way

Tabs aren't exactly new to web browsers these days, but Internet Explorer was one of the last of the major browsers to implement them for some reason, back in version 7. To create a new tab in Internet Explorer, you would simply click the **New Tab** button that is found immediately to the right of the current tabs and move from tab to tab simply by clicking the one you want.

The Mac Way

Honestly, there's not much to this tab thing. To open a new tab in Safari, you just click the **+** button located on the far-right side of the tab bar, or simply press **⌘-T**. Click from tab to tab to check out each page's contents.

All of this simplicity doesn't necessarily mean that's all there is to tabbed browsing. Here are a few nifty tricks for you:

- Rearrange tabs in the tab bar by clicking-and-dragging the tabs from one spot to another.
- ⌘-click a link to open it in a new tab but still keep the current tab active.
- ⌘-Shift-click a link to open it in a new tab and make it the active tab.
- Drag a tab out of the window to start a new window.
- Drag a tab from one Safari window to another.
- You can easily change Safari's default tab behaviors. Press ⌘- to access Safari's Preferences window and click the **Tabs** button, as seen in Figure 7.2.

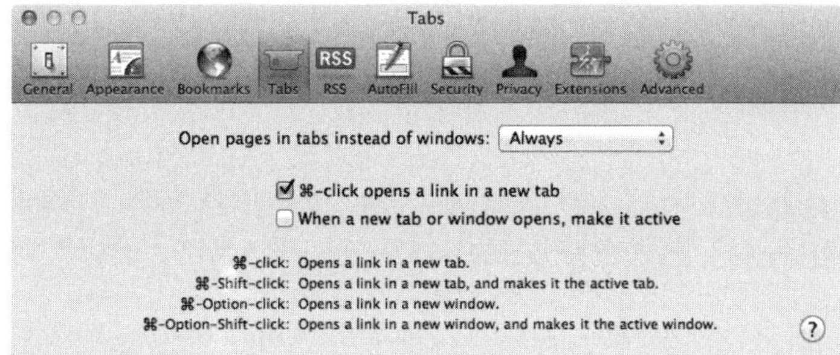

Figure 7.2: *Change Safari's default tab behaviors to suit your needs.*

Setting Your Home Page

There's no place like home, as Dorothy is quick to remind us. Home in this case, though, is your favorite web page, not a geographical location that you harbor special feelings for. You can set a home page for your browser, which will allow you to go straight to your favorite site the moment your browser is launched—no need to bother typing its URL into the address bar.

The Windows Way

To set your surfing home in Internet Explorer, you would click the **Tools** button and choose the **Internet Options** selection. You can then type a URL into the Home page section of the General tab, or click the **Use current** button to set your home page to the site you are currently perusing. Giving Internet Explorer its props, it doesn't get much easier.

The Mac Way

The Safari method isn't much different from the Internet Explorer way when it comes to setting a home page:

1. Click the **Safari** menu and choose **Preferences**.
2. Select the **General** button in the Preferences window.

3. Type or copy-and-paste the URL for your desired home in the Homepage text field, or click the **Set to Current Page** button to do exactly that.

Bookmarking Favorite Sites

In the act of bookmarking a site, you are telling your browser that this site is one of your favorites and you want to access it as quickly as possible—none of that lame typing-in-the-URL stuff for an internet portal that's so near and dear to your heart.

The Windows Way

Internet Explorer is above calling your special sites "bookmarks" like every other browser; it calls them "favorites." To create a favorite, you click the **Favorites** button, which looks like a star, on the right side of the toolbar. In the resulting drop-down window, click the arrow to the right of the Add to favorites button and choose whether to simply add the site to the favorites list or to the Favorites bar.

The Mac Way

There's not much separating Internet Explorer and Safari in this category:

1. With the oh-so-special site open, click the **Bookmarks** menu and select **Add Bookmark**.
2. As shown in Figure 7.3, choose a location for your bookmark using the Add this page to pop-up menu.

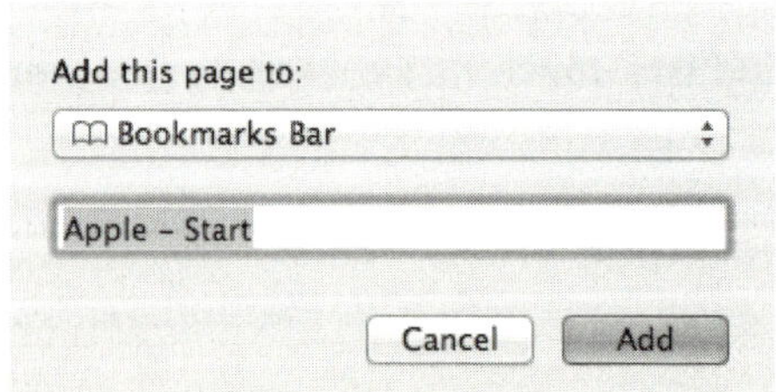

Figure 7.3: *Save your favorite sites as bookmarks to access them quickly.*

To access a bookmarked site, simply click it in the Bookmarks bar or from the Bookmarks menu.

Exporting and Importing Bookmarks

It would truly stink if you had to manually enter the hundreds of favorites you've kept in Internet Explorer for the last umpteen years into Safari. Luckily, the two browsers can play nicely together when it comes to sharing bookmarks, so you can easily import your old Internet Explorer favorites into Safari. When you export your favorites, you are simply saving the list of favorites into an HTML file, which you can then import into any browser.

The Windows Way

Something as seemingly straightforward as exporting or importing favorites is somehow a bit too involved with Internet Explorer. To export your favorites to a file or to import favorites, you must click the **Favorites** button on the right side of the toolbar. In the drop-down window, click the arrow next to the **Add to favorites** button and click **Import and Export**. To export your favorites, click the **Export to a File** button, click **Next**, check the box for **Favorites** and click **Next** again, choose the favorites you want to export, click **Next** yet again, select a destination on your PC for the exported file to reside, and now finally click the **Export** button. Click **Finish** to complete the exhausting task.

To import favorites, select **Import from a File** and click **Next**, check the box next to **Favorites** and click **Next**, type the path where the file you want to import resides on your PC or click the **Browse** button to find it, click **Next**, determine a destination for your imported favorites, click the **Import** button, and at last you may click the **Finish** button. Whew!

The Mac Way

Want to export your bookmarked sites from Safari? Okay, here we go:

1. Click the **File** menu and choose **Export Bookmarks.**
2. Select a destination on your Mac to store the file.
3. Click **Save**.

You may now feel free to import your exported bookmarks into another browser or simply save them as a backup.

Ready to import some bookmarks into Safari?

1. Click the **File** menu and choose **Import Bookmarks.**
2. Browse your Mac for the file, select it, and click the **Import** button.

You can easily access your newly imported bookmarks from the Bookmarks menu.

Blocking Pop-Ups

Advertisements in the form of pop-ups (windows that "pop up" out of nowhere when you visit certain sites or move your mouse pointer over some types of links) are some of the most irritating things ever devised by man, although I'm quite certain Attila the Hun and Vlad the Impaler would have approved of them. Although some sites require pop-ups for purely legitimate reasons, most are just eyesores. Thankfully, today's browsers afford the ability to block those nasty pop-ups from jumping out in front of our favorite sites.

The Windows Way

A tip of the hat to Internet Explorer in this instance. While it isn't as simple to turn pop-up blocking on and off in Internet Explorer as it is in Safari, you can configure Internet Explorer to allow some sites to utilize pop-up windows while blocking others. Selective pop-up blocking is not something that's native to Safari (get with it, Apple!), so I have to give the nod to Internet Explorer on this one.

Block pop-ups in Internet Explorer by clicking the **Tools** button, select **Internet Options**, click the **Privacy** tab, and then check the box titled **Turn on Pop-up Blocker**. To specify how the Pop-up Blocker should work, you can click the **Settings** button, which opens a window that affords options for allowing certain sites to use pop-ups, having Internet Explorer notify you when it blocks a pop-up, or adjusting the level of blocking performed.

The Mac Way

To block pop-ups in Safari, just click the **Safari** menu and choose **Block Pop-up Windows**; a check now appears next to the Block Pop-up Windows option. Allow pop-ups by following the same procedure, which removes the check this time around.

Selectively Blocking Pop-Ups

Don't fret about Safari's inability to allow certain pop-ups to come through the barrier. There are a number of Safari extensions (more on those later this chapter) you can install that do give you the ability to *whitelist,* or allow, selective sites to utilize pop-ups. Better Pop Up Blocker is a good example of these kinds of extensions.

Using and Storing Passwords

As kids, most of us have been part of top-secret clubs that included special knocks, cloak-and-dagger handshakes, and confidential passwords. Well, for grown-ups on the internet, things aren't much different. We have passwords for email accounts, bank accounts, shopping sites, news sites, and many other types of web pages. This plethora of passwords can be a bit daunting to remember, so most browsers offer the option of remembering your passwords for you. While this may be convenient, it's not exactly the safest practice, especially when it comes to your sensitive personal information and finances.

The Windows Way

Internet Explorer simply gives you the option to save passwords or not; there is no way to manage passwords after you've saved them.

Set Internet Explorer to save passwords by jumping through a few hoops: click the **Tools** menu, select **Internet Options**, go to the Content tab, click **Settings** in the AutoComplete section, and finally, check the box called **User names and passwords on forms** (also check the **Ask me before saving passwords** box) in the AutoComplete Settings window. You can clear all stored passwords by clicking the **Delete AutoComplete history** button, checking the **Passwords** box in the Delete Browsing History window, and then clicking the **Delete** button.

The Mac Way

Safari gains the upper hand when it comes to passwords because it allows you to selectively remove passwords as opposed to simply blowing them all away in one fell swoop (although you can do that, too, if you like).

To have Safari store passwords for sites:

1. Choose **Preferences** from the Safari menu.
2. Select the **AutoFill** tab.
3. Check the box titled **User names and passwords**, as shown in Figure 7.4.

Figure 7.4: *Use Safari's AutoFill preferences to store and manage passwords.*

Once you begin storing passwords, you can come back to the AutoFill preferences to delete any that you no longer want to be stored:

1. Choose **Preferences** from the Safari menu.
2. Select the **AutoFill** tab.
3. Click the **Edit** button next to the User names and passwords box.
4. Select the site whose password you want to delete and click the **Remove** button (or click the **Remove All** button to clear all passwords).

Caching Out

As you surf the internet, your browser is keeping a running tally of everything you view or listen to in a file called the cache. The advantage of using a cache is that the next time you visit a site, its page will load up much faster since many of the elements on it are already stored on your computer.

This cache can get quite large, or some pages may not be loading properly for various reasons, so it's a good idea to clean the cache from time to time ... much like my bills clean out my cash every couple of weeks.

The Windows Way

Cleaning out the cache on a PC running Internet Explorer, while not overwhelmingly complicated, is not as simple a task as it perhaps should be. In the newest version of Internet Explorer (9), you go to the Tools menu (looks like a small gear on the right side of the window), select **Safety**, and choose **Delete Browsing History**—all this just to get to the spot where you can empty the cache. You must then uncheck the **Preserve Favorites** website data option, check the **Temporary Internet Files** box, and finally click the **Delete** button to wipe the cache clean. I go into a little more detail than usual simply to stress the ease-of-use differences between Windows and Mac OS X. It's no simpler in earlier versions of Internet Explorer, either.

The Mac Way

Once again the Mac struts its stuff, even for something as simple as cleaning its cache file. Here's how to clean the cache the Mac way:

1. Click the **Safari** menu and choose **Empty Cache**.
2. Safari will prompt you to make certain that you indeed want to empty the cache (as shown in Figure 7.5), at which point you would click the **Empty** button to carry out the order.

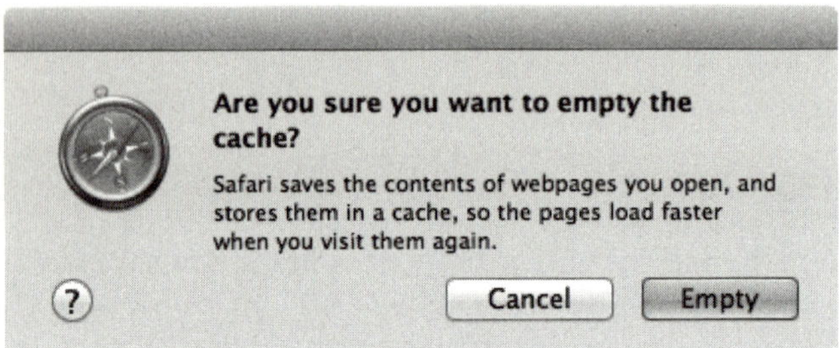

Figure 7.5: *Empty the cache to free up disk space or fix poorly loading sites.*

Secured Sites

If you have trouble accessing a secured site that you've had no issues with in the past, it's a good bet that you simply need to empty your cache to make things copacetic again.

Devouring Cookies

If you're a blue guy with googly eyes and crumbs all over your fur, then the title of this section must hold a special meaning for you. However, you might be bitterly disappointed to discover that we're not talking about Grandma's cookies, but rather files of a certain variety that are stored on your computer when you visit many of the websites on the internet. These files, or cookies, are used by many sites to track your web usage, to remember you and your settings preferences the next time you visit the site, and for many other reasons (some good and others not so good). Ridding your computer of these cookies can restore some measure of privacy back to your browsing, but it is up to you to decide which to remove.

The Windows Way

The procedure for deleting cookies on a PC running Internet Explorer 9 is almost identical to that for clearing your cache. Once again go to the **Tools** menu, move your mouse pointer to Safety, and then select **Delete Browsing History**. You then want to uncheck the **Preserve Favorites** website data option, check the **Cookies** box, and click the **Delete** button. This process is also no easier in earlier versions of Internet Explorer, but truth be told, it's not any simpler when using Safari on a Mac.

The Mac Way

Here's how to delete cookies in Safari:

1. Click the **Safari** menu and choose **Preferences**.
2. Select the **Privacy** button in the preferences window.
3. Click the **Remove All Website Data** button.
4. Safari will ask you to confirm the removal of cookies: click the **Remove Now** button to finally kick those cookies to the curb.

If you don't want to try the nuclear approach, you can click the **Details** button to see a list of all the sites that are currently storing a cookie on your Mac, as illustrated in Figure 7.6.

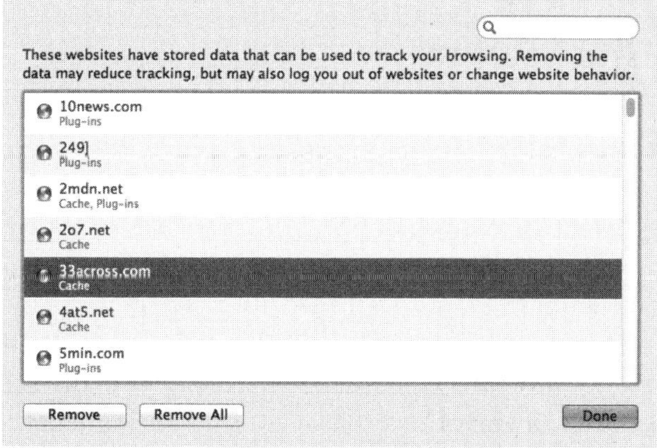

Figure 7.6: *Browse a list of cookies and only remove those you deem less desirable.*

Scroll through the list and remove only the cookies you select (using the **Remove** button), as opposed to just blowing away everything in one fell swoop. Click the **Done** button when you are finished.

Tackling Downloads

Every time you download a file to your computer, your browser keeps a record of it. Any browser worth its salt will also let you manage your downloads.

The Windows Way

Internet Explorer lets you manage downloads by clicking the **Tools** menu and selecting **View Downloads**. From the View Downloads window you can see a list of the files you've downloaded, run the files (if they are executables), set your default location for downloaded files on your PC, open the folder containing a particular download, revisit the page you downloaded the file from, and clear individual or all items from the download list. Pretty good stuff, if you ask me.

The Mac Way

Safari is quite adept at handling downloads, too. Click the **Downloads** button (a dark gray circle containing a downward-pointing light gray arrow) in the upper-right corner of Safari's window to see the list of files you've downloaded, as I've done in Figure 7.7.

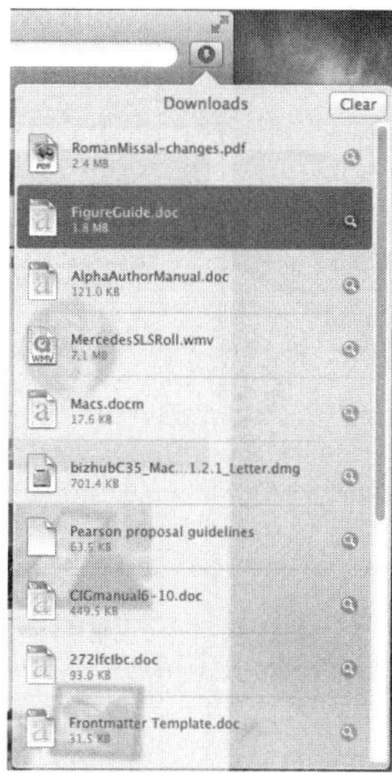

Figure 7.7: *View a list of the files you've downloaded to your Mac.*

From the list of downloads you can right-click (or Control-click) an item in the list to perform the following actions:

- Open the file.
- Show the file's location in the Finder.
- Copy the URL of the site from which the file was downloaded. You can then paste the URL into the address bar to revisit the site.
- Clear the item from the list.

You can also clear the entire list by clicking the **Clear** button at the top of the Downloads list. Once you clear an item from the list, you cannot get it back in. Note that clearing an item from the Downloads list doesn't remove the downloaded file from your Mac.

Disable Automatic Opening of Downloads

By default, Safari will automatically open files you download from the internet. You can disable this feature, if you like: choose **Preferences** from the Safari menu, select the **General** tab in the Preferences window, and uncheck the box titled **Open "safe" files after downloading**. "Safe" files include items like pictures, PDFs, and archived files.

Managing Extensions

No matter how much you love your browser of choice, there's no way that it can do every last thing in the world you want it to do exactly the way you want it done. There will always be a task or two you wish it performed, or at least performed better. That's where extensions come into play. Extensions are (typically) third-party pieces of software that add enhancements and functionality to a browser.

The Windows Way

Internet Explorer allows you to manage extensions and other add-ons (such as additional search providers and toolbars). Click the **Tools** menu and select **Manage Add-ons** to open the Manage Add-ons window, where you can enable or disable extensions as well as find new add-ons.

The Mac Way

Safari is a newcomer to the extensions game (as of version 5), but is quickly mastering it. Here's how to manage extensions in Safari:

1. Choose **Preferences** from the Safari menu.
2. Click the **Extensions** tab to see the options available, as shown in Figure 7.8.
3. Enable or disable extensions browser-wide using the ON/OFF toggle switch.

4. Select an extension from the list on the left side of the preferences pane to make adjustments or set options for its behavior.

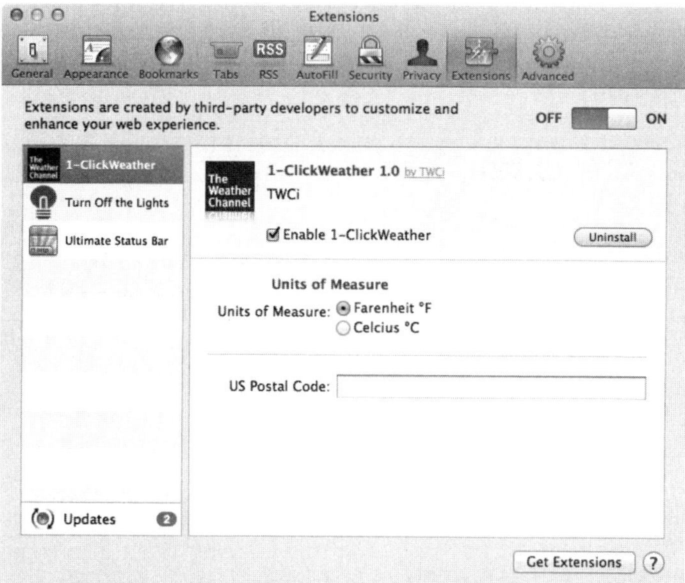

Figure 7.8: *Manage extensions from within Safari's Preferences.*

You can download and install tons of other extensions by clicking the **Get Extensions** button in the lower-right corner of the Extensions preferences pane. Doing so whisks you away to the Safari Extensions Gallery, where you can browse the categories for extensions that suit your needs.

Viewing Your Browsing History

One day you're browsing along when you happen to stumble upon the most useful website—*ever!* The answers to all of life's questions are there, ripe for the picking, but you have to sprint for an appointment. Sure enough, you forgot to bookmark the page and your teenage son used the computer after you left. You come back to discover Facebook instead of your site-of-all-sites. "No problem," you say, "because my browser keeps a history of the sites I've visited in the past!" You are correct, my friend.

The Windows Way

You can sift through your browsing history simply enough with Internet Explorer. Just click the **Favorites** button on the toolbar, select the **History** tab, choose a date, and browse the list of sites you visited. No frills—very simple and straightforward.

The Mac Way

It is every bit as simple to view your history in Safari as it is in Internet Explorer, but the coolness factor is what gives Safari the edge here. To view a list of sites you've visited in the past, simply choose **Show All History** from the History menu. Safari doesn't just list your browsing history, it even shows you the current version of the sites in Cover Flow view, illustrated in Figure 7.9.

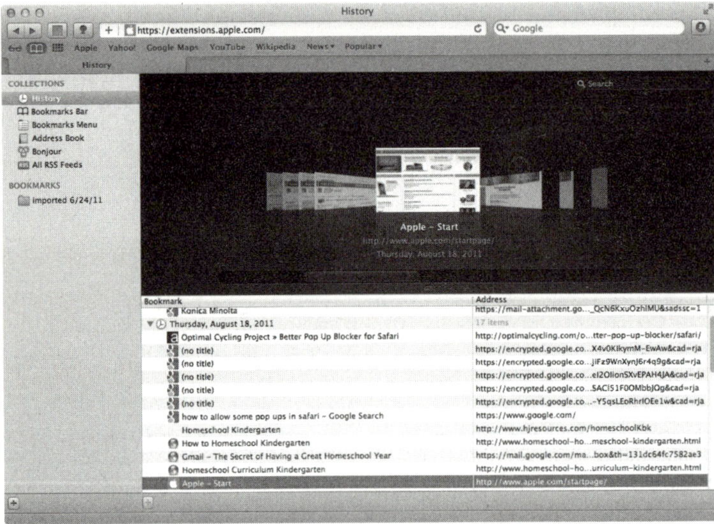

Figure 7.9: *Zip through your browsing history with Cover Flow view.*

Browsing in Privacy

I don't know anyone who wants the world to know all of his or her business, and that includes their internet surfing, too. There are a thousand and one different reasons you might want to keep your browsing private (some good, some not so much), and it is a feature that most browsers have implemented. Browsing the web in private generally means that your browser won't keep any record of the sites you've visited. Nothing is saved in history, no cookies are stored, and the like. Bear in mind that this privacy only extends to your browser; your Internet Service Provider (ISP) is still able to track your surfing habits.

The Windows Way

Internet Explorer's version of private browsing is called InPrivate. You can enable InPrivate simply enough by clicking the **Tools** menu, holding your mouse pointer over Safety, and selecting **InPrivate Browsing**.

The Mac Way

Turning on Private Browsing in Safari isn't exactly rocket science, either. Simply click the Safari menu and choose **Private Browsing**. Safari will prompt you to be sure you want to turn on Private Browsing (Figure 7.10); just click **OK** to begin browsing covertly.

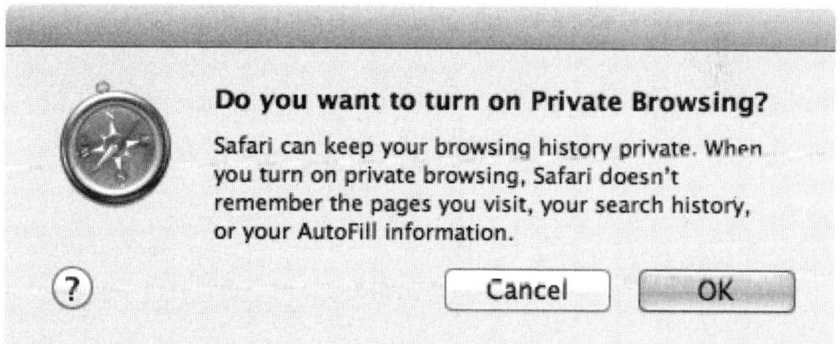

Figure 7.10: *Private Browsing keeps your internet surfing under wraps.*

Discovering Alternative Browsers

Safari's great, but there is simply no such thing as a "one-size-fits-all" browser. Thankfully, there are a multitude of browser choices in the Mac universe, just as there are for Windows.

Here is a list of some of the most popular web browsers for Mac OS X:

- Firefox (www.mozilla.com)
- Opera (www.opera.com)
- Google Chrome (www.google.com/chrome)
- OmniWeb (www.omnigroup.com/products/omniweb)
- Camino (caminobrowser.org)
- SeaMonkey (www.seamonkey-project.org)

There are plenty more, but these should get you going. I suggest downloading some (or all) and giving them a test drive. If you've used Firefox, Opera, or Chrome on Windows, you might want to give them a shot first since you are already familiar with them.

Mail Call

Warning: if you're a postal worker, this will probably be your least favorite chapter in this book.

Most of us these days are quite familiar with email. There's no doubting it's replaced the traditional postal service as our main medium of written communication with friends, family, and co-workers.

Mac OS X is every bit as capable (if not a bit more intuitive) with email as Windows, and I suspect you'll be sending your friends and family the latest jokes and internet urban legends before you know it.

Setting Up Email Accounts

In order to set up an email account, you first need to have one. If you already have an email account, I would advise you to make sure that you have all the connection information necessary to connect to that account before you continue with this chapter. If you don't know the information, contact the provider of your email account for assistance.

If you do not have an email account, you'll need to get one before you dive too deep into this chapter. If you will be using an account provided by your employer, you will need to contact your IT department. If this is your personal email, your Internet Service Provider (ISP) most likely offers email accounts with its service, or if you prefer you can sign up for free email accounts with other providers such as Google and Yahoo!. If you have an iCloud account, you can also use it for email across all your internet-capable devices (go to www.apple.com/icloud for more information).

The Windows Way

Depending on the version of Windows you are familiar with, you've probably been using Windows Mail, Outlook Express, Windows Live Mail, or Outlook (not to mention many of the third-party email apps, such as Mozilla Thunderbird). Some of these are quite good at automatically setting up email accounts for you using a minimal amount of information, which is usually your email address and password. You also have the option (or perhaps the mandate, if your email program isn't the most helpful) of setting up email accounts from scratch, assuming you have all of the necessary information.

Since Windows Live Mail is the newest email client from Microsoft, I'll focus more on it throughout this chapter than the others. However, much of what I explain here will be handled in a similar fashion by the other apps.

The Mac Way

Mac OS X comes with a mighty fine email app called, fittingly enough, Mail. Mail is one of the better email applications I've personally used, and since it's your Mac's native email app, we'll focus on it, although there are many fine third-party email apps out there that I'll discuss toward the end of this chapter.

As with many email clients on Windows, Mail is happy to do most of the heavy lifting for you when setting up new accounts. I'll show you both the easy (automatic) and the slightly less easy (manual) way to set up email accounts on your Mac.

By the way, Mail supports pretty much any kind of email account, including Microsoft Exchange.

Let's start with the easiest first (this way will only work if you've not already set up an account in Mail):

1. Open Mail by clicking its icon (looks like a postage stamp) in the Dock or double-clicking its icon in the Applications folder.
2. In the Welcome to Mail window (shown in Figure 8.1), enter your name, email address, and password.
3. Click **Create** and Mail will contact your email provider and gather all of the information necessary to successfully send and receive email with the account.
4. Mail offers you an Account Summary, as seen in Figure 8.2. If your email provider supports it, you may be asked if you want to set up Calendar and Chat information at the same time. If so, check the appropriate boxes; if not, simply don't check them.
5. Click the **Create** button and your new account will be ready to go.

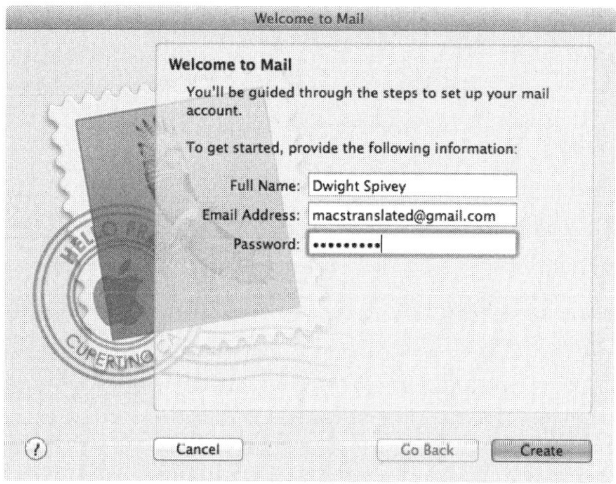

Figure 8.1: *Welcome to Mail!*

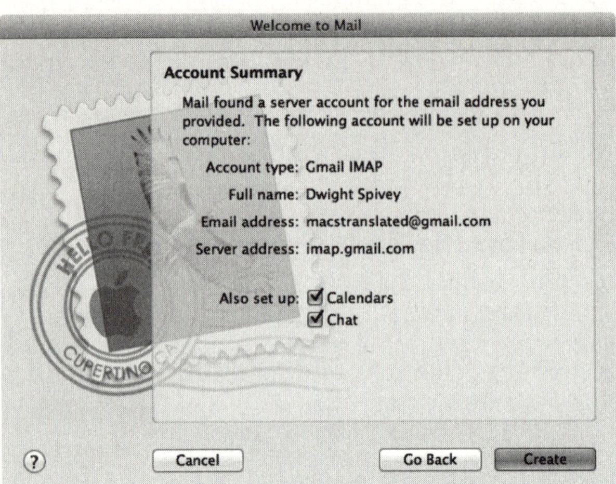

Figure 8.2: *Mail shows you a summary of the account information it's collected.*

Let's say that Mail was unable to pick up the information it needed from your email provider; what now? If that should happen Mail will tell you so, and give you the option of clicking the **Continue** button in the Welcome to Mail window so that you can manually set up your email account. Be sure to have the account information from your email provider handy, such as the mail server and SMTP server addresses (typically in the form: mail.providername.com).

1. Once Mail detects that it is unable to automatically set up the information for you, click **Continue** in the Welcome to Mail window.
2. Select an account type from the pop-up and enter the information for your email accounts' incoming mail server in the appropriate fields of the Incoming Mail Server window, seen in Figure 8.3. Click **Continue**.
3. If your account requires Secure Sockets Layer, check the box and select the type of authentication needed using the pop-up menu. Click **Continue**.
4. Next, enter the correct information in the Outgoing Mail Server window (Figure 8.4). Click **Continue**.

5. Once Mail has all the information it needs, you will see the info in the Account Summary window. Click **Create** to begin using Mail.

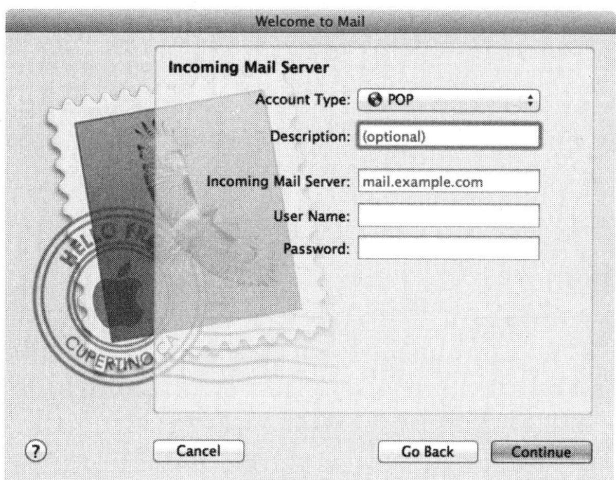

Figure 8.3: *Select an account type and enter the incoming mail server information.*

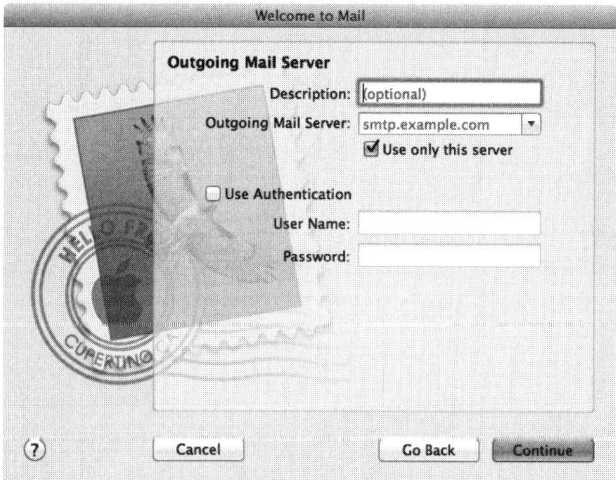

Figure 8.4: *Enter the outgoing mail server information to be able to send email.*

Receiving New Email

Don't you love that giddy feeling when you get a new email? Who could it be from? The subject line has just enough detail to be really intriguing, but not quite enough to give away the contents completely. There could be almost anything in this newest message from what's-his-name!

If that sounds like you, I would advise you to switch to decaf. Once that's taken care of, follow along and I'll tell you how to go about receiving new messages in Mail.

The Windows Way

In all honesty, this isn't a difficult task, whether in Windows or Mac OS X. Typically, an email application will have a set default time sequence for checking on new messages, or an account may be the kind that can receive pushes, meaning that when the email provider receives a new email for you it pushes a notification to your computer automatically.

If you're the impatient type (like me), you will most likely find a Send/Receive button in the toolbar of your email application, and clicking it will force your email app to tap your email provider on the shoulder to see if there is any mail available. If there's new email, your email app will download it for you.

The Mac Way

It pains me to say, but out of the box, Mail makes it just a shade more difficult to manually check for new messages than most email apps. Instead of there being a button in the toolbar, you must either press **⌘-Shift-N** or click the **Mailbox** menu and select **Get All New Mail**.

Nah, I'm just kidding! See the button with the envelope in it in the upper-left corner of Mail's window? That's the Get Mail button. Simply click it to get the newest messages from your email provider.

You can tell Mail how often it should check for new messages with your email provider:

1. Press ⌘-, or select **Preferences** from the Mail menu.
2. Click the **General** tab in the Preferences window to see Mail's General preferences (Figure 8.5).
3. Change the Check for new messages pop-up to whatever time period suits you.

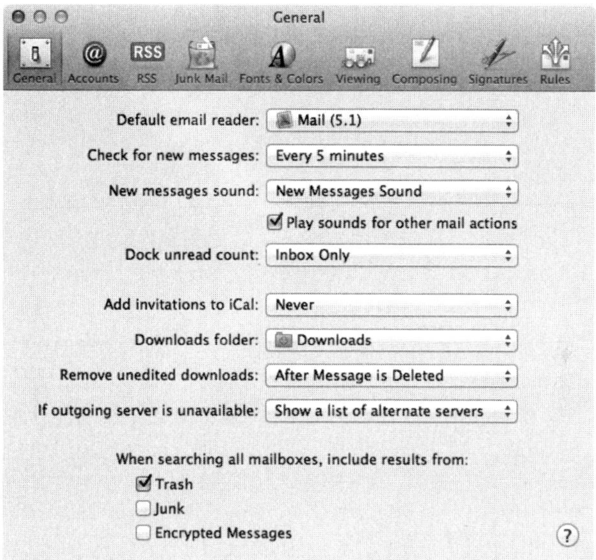

Figure 8.5: *Change the amount of time it takes Mail to check for new messages.*

By the way, new messages will appear in your Inbox, whose contents are viewable on the left side of Mail's main window, as shown in Figure 8.6. When you select a message from the Inbox, its contents are displayed in the message pane, also seen in Figure 8.6.

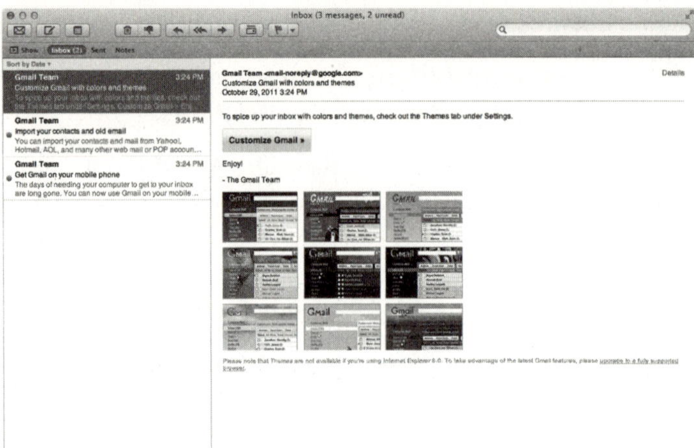

Figure 8.6: *The Inbox in Mail's main window.*

You can reply to or forward messages by clicking the **Reply** (left-pointing arrow) or **Forward** (right-pointing arrow) buttons in the toolbar (if you wish for your reply to go to all the folks copied on the email, you should use the **Reply All** button). You can also toss an email in the garbage by clicking the **Trash** icon (guess what it looks like).

New and Unread Message Notification

You might be working away on some other project and not be keeping up with your emails, but you can get a quick look as to whether you have any new or unread emails. Whenever there are new or unread emails in Mail, the Mail icon in the Dock will display a red circle with the number of unopened messages.

Creating and Sending New Messages

Here comes the fun part! Reading email is nice, but creating and sending your own is what makes you a true email professional. It's time for you to prove your mettle as an email aficionado by typing out the funniest joke you've heard in years and sending it to all your buds instantly. Just imagine: when all of your friends forward your creation to their other friends, and their other friends do likewise, your email could circle the globe and come right back to you before you know it.

The Windows Way

In Windows Live Mail, click the **Email Message** button to open a new email message window. Type in your recipient's email addresses, enter your subject into the Subject field, and type your content. When you're ready, click the **Send** button to zip your email across the internet.

The Mac Way

Mac OS X's Mail makes it just as simple as Windows Live Mail to create new email messages.

1. Note the Compose new message button (looks like a piece of paper with a pencil about to write on it) in the upper-left corner of Mail's main window: click it to open a new email window (Figure 8.7).
2. Enter the email addresses of your recipients in the To field, and any others you may want to copy on the message into the Cc field.
3. It's good practice to enter a subject into the Subject field, and then enter the text for the body of the email.
4. Click the **Send Message** button (looks like a paper airplane) in the upper-left corner of the New Message window to send your email.

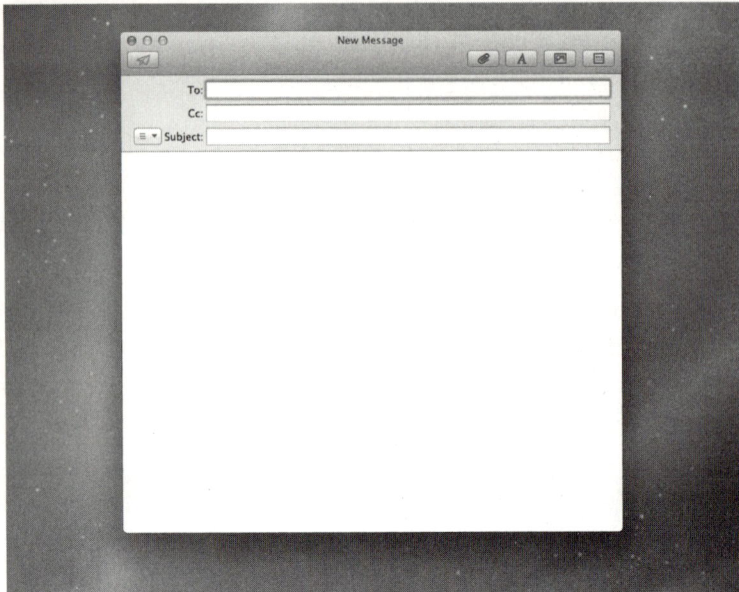

Figure 8.7: *The New Message window is where you begin your new emails.*

Adding Attachments to Messages

Sometimes you may want to send a document or other item to a recipient, and these items are called attachments. Sending attachments with your emails is akin to placing a brochure into an envelope along with your original letter.

The Windows Way

In Windows Live Mail, click the **Attach File** button in the toolbar of a new message window, browse your hard drive for the file you want to attach, select the file, and click **Open**. Done.

The Mac Way

Not much different here:

1. Open a new message or reply to a message in your Inbox.
2. Click the **Attach** button, which looks like a paper clip.

3. Browse your Mac for the file you want to attach and select it.
4. Click **Choose File** to attach it to your email.

Sending Attachments to Windows Users

If the recipient of your email happens to be running Windows, check the **Send Windows-Friendly Attachments** box at the bottom of the window. This is generally a good practice no matter what operating system your recipient is currently running, to be honest. In some cases you may not know for certain what operating system they are running, so it's best to cover your bases.

Saving Attachments from Messages

Let's say that someone sends you an attachment: what do you do with it? Well, if it's important enough to you, you will most likely want to save it, no?

The Windows Way

Saving attachments with Windows Live Mail is a snap. Open the email containing the attachment, right-click the attachment, and select **Save As** from the contextual menu. Find a suitable place on your PC's hard drive for the attachment to reside and click **Save**. Simple.

The Mac Way

Mail makes it pretty simple to save attachments, too. However, some attachments, such as PDFs and image files, will usually show up in the message in their entirety. If all you need to do is see the attachment, there may not be a need for you to save it past this point.

Should you want to save the attachment, however, here's the way to do it:

1. Click the **Details** link (in blue) in the upper-right corner of the message.

2. Click the **Save** button and select the attachment you want to save (Figure 8.8).
3. Select a location for the attachment on your Mac's hard drive and click **Save**.

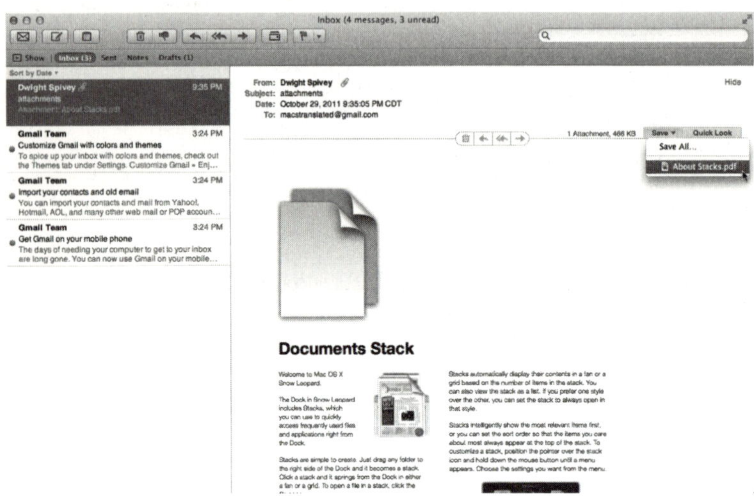

Figure 8.8: *Click the* ***Save*** *button and choose the attachment to save.*

Okay, it's time for me to confess: I just gave you the "difficult" way of saving an attachment. To tell you the truth, you could simply drag an attachment from an email and drop it right onto the desktop. That's great if you only want to save it to the desktop and perhaps move it to another folder later, but if you want to place it straight into a folder the first method I described is the best way.

Customizing Your Messages

Sending a plain text message to someone is about as exciting as using a slide rule for mathematical equations. It's just so 1980s. Today we like to add a little pizzazz to our messages, to give them a little pep and really catch someone's attention. Let's see how to give those boring old messages a little style!

The Windows Way

Windows Live Mail is pretty good with the basics of changing up fonts and font colors. Oh, and you can also change the justification of your text. Wow. I'm afraid that while the basics are covered, there's not much else you can do to really spice up your emails.

The Mac Way

Mail excels at adding an extra "Oomph!" to your messages, as you're about to find out.

First, I'll cover the aforementioned basics of font customization. Second, I'll cover adding photographs to your emails (not as attachments, but as actual contents). Thirdly, we'll get to the really good stuff, which is a little thing Mail likes to call Stationery.

Is the text in your email not quite fancy enough for the occasion? You can spiff up the text with ease:

1. Open a new message or reply to another message.
2. Click the **Show Format Bar** button (looks like a capital A) in the toolbar to display the format bar underneath the toolbar, as seen in Figure 8.9.
3. Highlight the text you want to change and perform one or all of the following:
    - Choose a new font from the Font pop-up.
    - Select a size for the font from the Size pop-up.
    - Choose a new color from the Font Color pop-up.
    - Make the text bold, italic, or underlined using the buttons provided.
    - Change the justification of the text to left, center, or right.
    - Insert a bulleted or numbered list.
    - Adjust indentation.

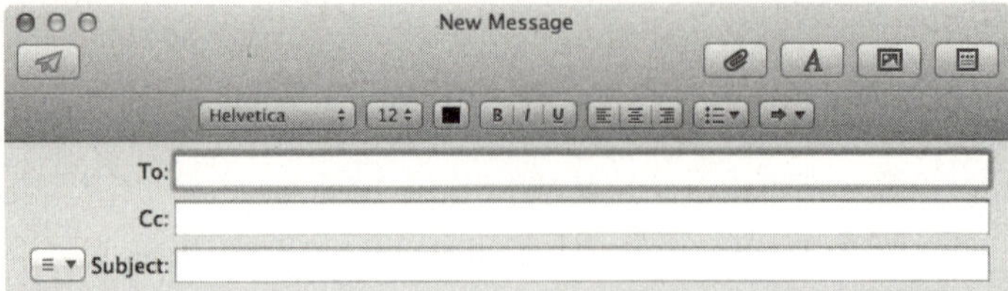

Figure 8.9: *The format bar appears underneath the toolbar.*

Next, let's see how to insert a picture into your messages:

1. Again, open a new message or reply to an existing one.
2. Click the **Photo Browser** button (looks like a miniaturized painting of a mountain and a celestial body—don't know which) in the toolbar.
3. Find a picture you want to add to your message.
4. Drag the picture from the Photo Browser into the message window (Figure 8.10).
5. You can change the size of the picture in the image using the Image Size pop-up menu in the lower-right corner of the screen.

Figure 8.10: *Drag pictures from the Photo Browser to the message window to insert them into your message.*

The Photo Browser is cool, for sure, but Stationery is even better, at least in my humble opinion.

Stationery is Mail's way of making the ordinary email invitation or letter extraordinary. Apple has provided some really nice templates for you to use in your emails, and these templates are the Stationery to which I keep referring. Each template contains text placeholders that you can modify to your needs. Many of the templates also contain picture placeholders; use the Photo Browser to drag-and-drop your own photos into the template.

Let me show you how to incorporate Stationery into your emails:

1. Create a new message or reply to an existing one.
2. Click the **Stationery** button (looks like a piece of paper with words on it, sort of) to open the Stationery pane under the Subject field, as shown in Figure 8.11.
3. Choose a template from one of the subject choices on the left of the stationery pane: Birthday, Announcements, Photos, Stationery, or Sentiments. The message pane of your email will fill with the template you've selected.
4. If the template you chose only includes placeholders for text, you may click the placeholder text and enter your own.
5. If the template you chose includes picture placeholders, open the Photo Browser and drag the pictures you want to use into the picture placeholders (Figure 8.12). You can adjust the picture size by clicking the picture to highlight it and then dragging the size slider. You can also move the picture within the placeholder by clicking-and-dragging it.

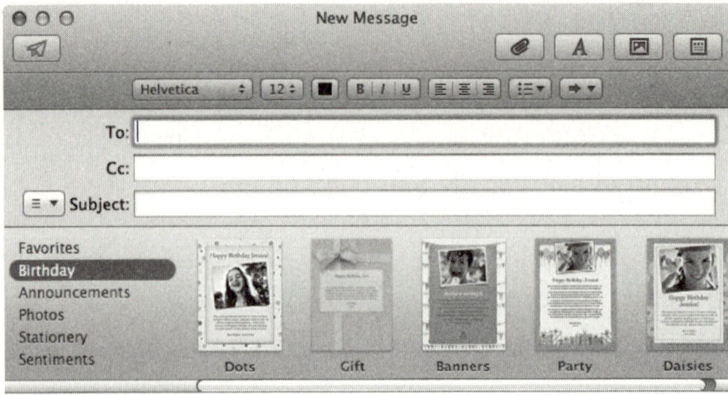

Figure 8.11: *The Stationery pane appears under the Subject field.*

Figure 8.12: *Add your own pictures to templates by dragging them from Photo Browser into the placeholders.*

Adding Favorite Templates

Should you find yourself using certain templates more than others, you can drag the popular templates and drop them onto Favorites in the Stationery pane. Next time you need them, just click on **Favorites** instead of drilling through all the templates.

Finding Alternative Email Apps

There really is no "Windows Way" or "Mac Way" for this topic, so I'll just break it down.

As with Windows, there are multiple other email applications in the world of Mac that you can use, should Mail not suit your needs or tastes for whatever reason.

Here is a list of the most popular email apps for Mac OS X (I've used each one, so I can personally vouch for them all):

- Mozilla Thunderbird is my personal favorite (after Mail, that is). Thunderbird can be downloaded from Mozilla's website at www.mozilla.org/en-US/thunderbird. One of the reasons Thunderbird is so popular is because of the multitude of add-ons you can install for it, which add a great deal of customized functionality. Oh, yeah, one more thing: it's free.
- Microsoft Outlook is also a very good email application, especially for long-term users of Outlook for Windows. Of course, Outlook comes as part of the Microsoft Office suite of applications for Mac (such as Word, Excel, and PowerPoint), so you'll have to spring for the whole enchilada to get it. Give it a look at www.microsoft.com/mac.
- Sparrow is one of the newest email clients for Mac OS X, and it's very good if you are a Gmail user due to its integration of labels. The Facebook Connect aspect of Sparrow is pretty nifty, too. Take a gander by visiting sparrowmailapp.com.

There are other apps out there, but these three should whet your appetite for now. If you're a true email client geek, keep your eyes peeled; there seems to be new email apps popping up quite often these days.

Disco Mac

Put on your platform shoes, drop the mirrored ball, crank up the lighted dance floor … it's time to get the party started with the help of your Mac!

Music has evolved from the days of radio and vinyl records, although some would say that's not entirely a good thing (I, for one, kind of miss making the weekly trips to the "record store"). Like it or not, the best place to find new music today is right on your computer.

Importing Music to Your Computer

You could stream music via the internet to get music on your computer, but what about the (literal) wall of CDs you acquired back in the 1980s and '90s? You can't just toss that kind of a collection! Of course, you and I both know that there is another option: import those CDs (and digital music files) into a music player on your computer.

The Windows Way

There are several media players for Windows, just as there are for Mac, but we'll concentrate on Windows Media Player since it comes as part of a Windows installation.

Open Windows Media Player and press **Ctrl+M** to add the classic menu to the toolbar. Click **File**, go to Manage Libraries, and select **Music**. From here you can select a folder that contains music files for Windows Media Player to pull in content.

You can also add music from CDs by inserting the CD into your PC. The CD will appear in Windows Media Player's sidebar. Select the CD and click the **Rip CD** icon to copy the CD's contents to your computer's hard drive.

The Mac Way

iThis, iThat, iEverything. It seems like Apple is on a roll with the iNames, and one of the first products to tout this naming convention was the venerable iTunes. iTunes was once a simple music player, but it has evolved into a full-blown entertainment hub. For the most part, though, in this chapter we will concentrate on its musical roots.

When you first fire up iTunes, there's not much music to play (there's none, actually), as seen in Figure 9.1; you've yet to import your music into iTunes' Library.

You can import digital music files or you can bring music in directly from CDs. I'll show you how to import music files first, but first you'll want to know what music file formats iTunes supports.

Here is a list of music file formats that you can import into iTunes:

- MP3
- AIFF
- WAV
- MPEG-4
- AAC
- Apple Lossless

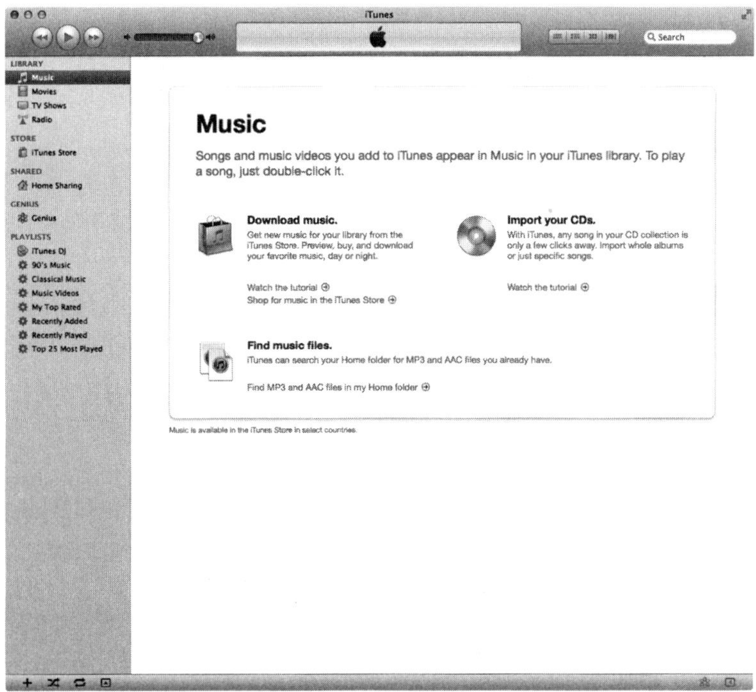

Figure 9.1: *The initial iTunes screen.*

To get a music file into your iTunes Library:

1. Open iTunes by clicking its icon in the Dock or double-clicking its icon in the Applications folder.
2. Press **⌘-O** or choose **Add to Library** from the File menu.
3. Browse your Mac, as I'm doing in Figure 9.2, to find the folder that contains the music file(s) you want to add to the Library.
4. Select the desired folder or a single file, and click **Open**.
5. The newly added songs appear in iTunes in the Music section of the Library (Figure 9.3).

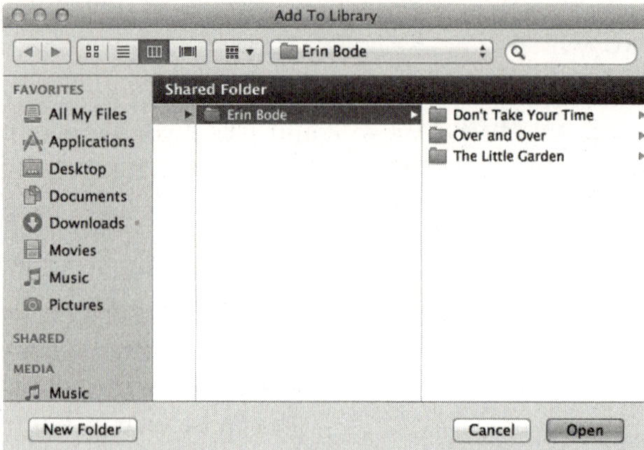

Figure 9.2: *Browse your Mac to find the folders containing music files you want to import.*

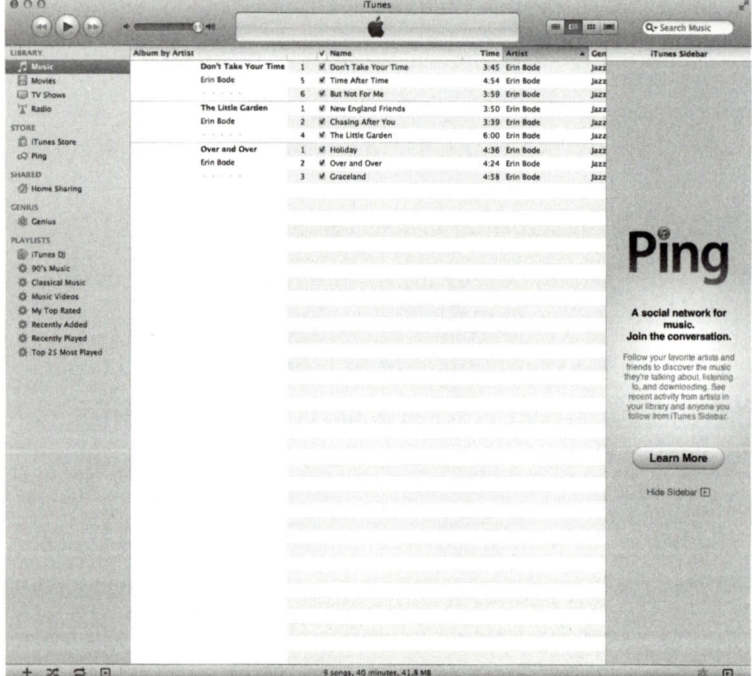

Figure 9.3: *New music files are added to the Music section of the Library.*

You can also import music from your CD collection:

1. Open iTunes, if it's not open already.
2. Insert a CD into the optical drive of your Mac.
3. iTunes recognizes the CD and asks if you want to import songs from it, as shown in Figure 9.4. Click **Yes** to begin the import.
4. iTunes shows you the progress of your import. Songs already imported have a green circle containing a white check box to their left. Songs that are currently being imported have an orange circle containing a white wave to their left. Both imported and importing songs can be seen in Figure 9.5.

Figure 9.4: *iTunes asks if you want to import songs from CDs.*

Figure 9.5: *Imported songs are represented by green circles, while importing songs have orange circles.*

Importing an iTunes Library from Windows

If you have used iTunes on Windows to sync music and other entertainment with your iPhone or iPod, you can copy those iTunes Libraries to your Mac and not skip a beat. Visit this page on Apple's support site for instructions on how to move your iTunes Library in a variety of ways: http://support.apple.com/kb/HT4527.

Once you have songs in your iTunes Library, you can create playlists of your favorites so that you can quickly access them.

1. Choose **New Playlist** from the File menu.
2. The new playlist will appear under the Playlists heading in the sidebar. Be sure to give it a descriptive name.
3. Drag-and-drop songs from the Music Library to the new playlist. Simple, huh?

Listening to Your Tunes

What good is having music on your computer if you don't listen to it? Most music player apps are controlled in pretty much the same standard way, so there won't be much groundbreaking information here, unless you've never listened to music on your computer.

The Windows Way

To listen to your tunes in Windows, open Windows Media Player, select **Music** in the left sidebar, highlight the song you want to play, and click the **Play** button at the bottom of the screen. Again, the controls aren't eye-popping, just your standard play, rewind, fast-forward, etc.

The Mac Way

iTunes works much the same way as other music player apps, so there's not much to rave about—yet (I'll show you something cool in a bit—just keep reading).

To play music in iTunes:

1. Open iTunes if it's not already opened.
2. Select **Music** on the left sidebar under the Library heading.
3. Browse the playlist to find the song you want.
4. Select the song and click the **Play** button in the upper left of the iTunes window (Figure 9.6).

Figure 9.6: *Playback controls in iTunes.*

Should iTunes be in the way of other items on your screen, or if you just want a simple and fast way to control playback, click the green button in the upper left of the iTunes window to switch to the miniplayer, shown in Figure 9.7.

Figure 9.7: *Switch to the miniplayer to minimize the iTunes window to just the playback controls.*

Okay, so now that the music's pumpin' and the house is jumpin', there are a couple of other things I want to show you about playing your tunes.

The first is Cover Flow in full-screen mode, which is shown in Figure 9.8.

1. To enter Cover Flow, click the **Cover Flow** button in iTunes' toolbar.
2. To enter full screen mode for Cover Flow, click the full screen button (looks like two small arrows facing away from one another) that is found just to the right of the progress bar that is displayed under the album art.
3. Browse your Library by clicking through the songs in Cover Flow, or if you have a trackpad you can simply flick the trackpad to the left or right to fly through your songs. Click a song to play it.
4. Press the **Esc** key when you're ready to exit full screen mode.

Figure 9.8: *Fly through your songs using Cover Flow in full screen mode.*

Another cool playback feature in iTunes is the Visualizer. The Visualizer is a really neat graphical representation of the musical notes (think of crossing the lights on an equalizer with a nebula). Figure 9.9 gives you an example of the Visualizer, which you can enable by pressing **⌘-T**. To exit the Visualizer, just press the **Esc** key.

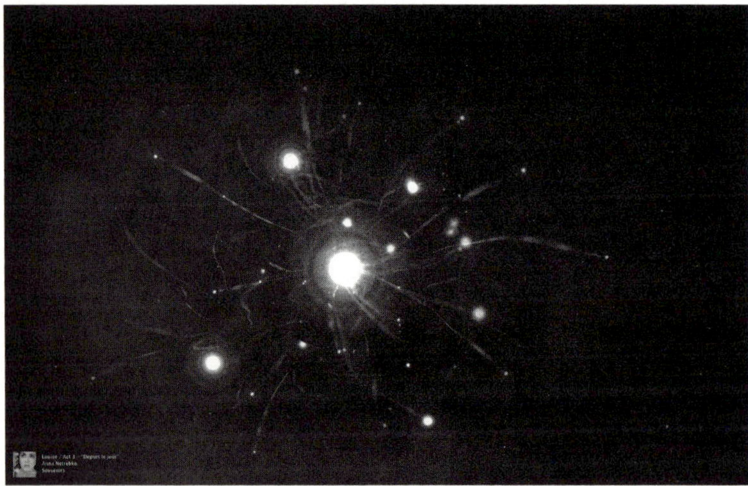

Figure 9.9: *The Visualizer is a graphical representation of a song's musical notes.*

If you really want to wow the guests at your next party, connect your Mac to your television and run the Visualizer on a really big screen.

Purchasing New Music (and More)

As I mentioned earlier in the chapter, I miss the days of going to the local music store and flipping through the seemingly endless collection of vinyl records and cassette tapes. I especially enjoyed the hole-in-the-wall stores that you found (and still can find) on college campuses, where some of the rarest of records could be discovered. Those days are pretty much gone, though, with the advent of online music stores, such as iTunes, Amazon, and more.

The Windows Way

Windows Media Player can help you go to online stores to download music (as well as video and audiobooks), but Microsoft doesn't have a store of its own. This makes purchasing new music on a PC a third-party venture, and not something that is built into the player itself.

To purchase new music in Windows Media Player, if you see the Online Stores button in the lower-left corner of the window, click it to see a list of online stores where you can purchase music. If you see the Media Guide button instead, click the arrow to the right of Media Guide and choose to browse online stores.

Of course, you could just download and install iTunes for Windows ....

The Mac Way

The iTunes Store has become the de facto standard of online music and media stores. Apple has become a massive player in the digital media market, and it won't be losing ground to any competitor for the foreseeable future.

To access the iTunes Store, as I've done in Figure 9.10, simply click the **iTunes Store** link in the sidebar.

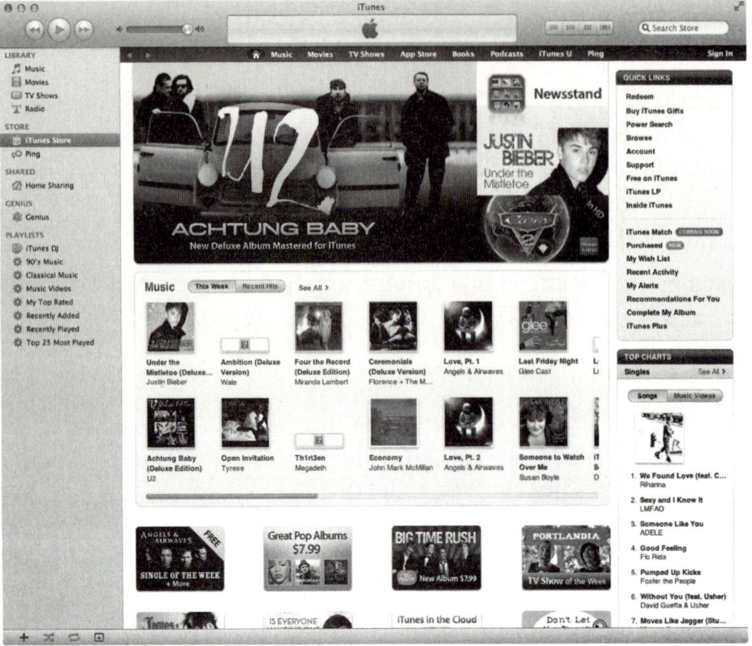

Figure 9.10: *The iTunes Store is a one-stop shop for all digital media.*

The iTunes Store is divided into several different sections, much like a department has different sections for clothing, shoes, appliances, etc. Here's a list of the types of digital media you can access in the iTunes Store:

- Music
- Movies
- Movie trailers
- TV shows
- Apps for your iPhone or iPod
- Books

- Podcasts, which are essentially recordings of your favorite audio shows, such as those heard on the radio or found online.
- iTunes U, which is an online learning repository, with audio and video instruction on a multitude of topics, provided by some of the top colleges and universities in the world.

That's quite a list of digital media items that you can download from the iTunes Store, and what's more, many of them are free.

You can sync items that you purchase in the iTunes Store with your portable devices, such as your iPhone or iPod.

Before you can purchase anything from the iTunes Store, you must have an Apple ID, which is just an account with Apple. An Apple ID allows you to not only access items in the iTunes Store, but also from the Mac Apps Store and iCloud (for more information, visit www.apple.com/icloud).

To obtain an Apple ID from within iTunes:

1. Click the **iTunes Store** link in the iTunes sidebar.
2. Click the **Sign In** link in the upper-right corner of the iTunes Store window.
3. In the resulting window (Figure 9.11), click the **Create New Account** button.
4. Click **Continue** in the iTunes Store window.
5. Agree to the terms and conditions by checking the box in the lower-right corner of the window, and then click **Agree**.
6. Follow the instructions provided for associating an email address with your account, entering your personal contact and billing information, and the like. When you're done, you'll be able to log in to your Apple ID account using the email address and passwords you provided.

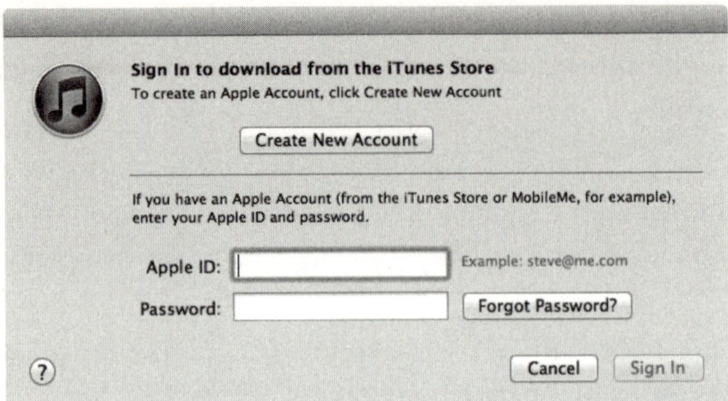

Figure 9.11: *Get an Apple ID by clicking* ***Create New Account****.*

Now that you have an Apple ID, you can purchase items from the iTunes Store.

To purchase a song from iTunes:

1. Open the iTunes Store link in the sidebar, and then click the **Music** tab at the top of the window.
2. Browse the selections provided in the iTunes Store window, such as checking out items in the charts (on the right side) or by choosing one of the items under the Music Quick Links section. Once you find an artist or album you're interested in, give them a click.
3. On the album page, you can choose to buy the entire album (click the **Buy Album** button in the upper left, as seen in Figure 9.12) or to buy single songs from the album (click the **Buy** button to the right of the song title). You can also hear a preview of a song by double-clicking it in the list, or hear previews of all the songs by clicking the **Preview All** button at the bottom left of the song list.

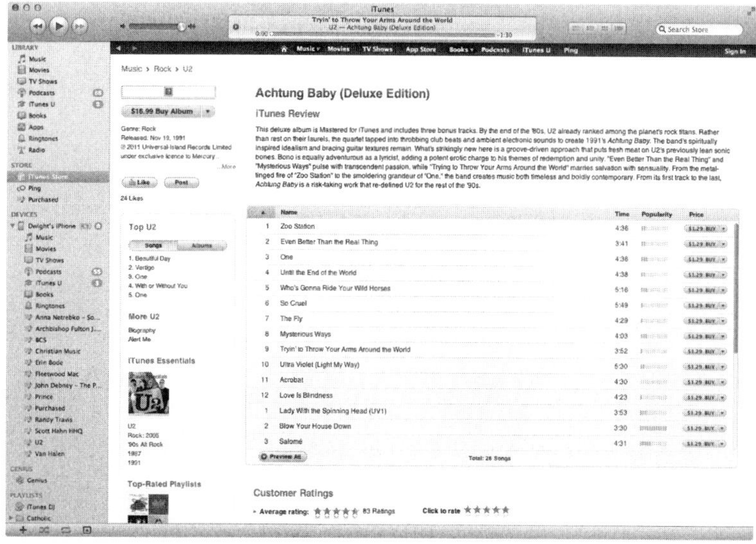

Figure 9.12: *Buy an entire album or just individual songs from the album.*

Burning Audio Discs

Many of us still like to listen to CDs in our cars or homes as opposed to wearing a set of earbuds everywhere we go. Burning songs to a CD is also a good way to have a hard-copy backup, although if you have an extensive music library in your music player you may end up spending the next week of your life burning stack after stack of CDs.

The Windows Way

To burn songs to CD using Windows Media Player, click the **Burn** tab, and then the **Burn Options > Audio CD**. Next, insert a blank CD into your computer's CD burner. If an AutoPlay dialog box opens, just close it. Click the **Clear List** button to remove songs from any previous burn sessions. Locate items, such as songs or playlists, in your Windows Media Player Library that you want to burn to CD. Drag these items from the details pane to the Burn list pane. When your list is ready, click **Start Burn**. Now, remember to breathe again after all that activity!

The Mac Way

iTunes is a master at burning your audio files to CD for your computerless and iPhone- or iPod-less listening pleasure.

To burn an audio CD in iTunes:

1. Create a playlist consisting of the items you want to burn to CD.
2. Right-click (or Control-click) the playlist and select **Burn Playlist to Disc**.
3. Set up your preferences for burning the CD and click **Burn** (Figure 9.13). Select the **Use Sound Check** box if you want the volumes of the songs on your CD to be relatively the same.
4. Insert the blank CD and iTunes handles the rest, and in pretty short order, too.

Figure 9.13: *Set the burn options before burning your audio CD.*

Sharing Music Files (Legally!)

Yes, you can share your music files, as long as you keep the sharing on the up and up. Now, by sharing I don't mean you can give copies of your purchased music to others who haven't purchased it. I mean others can listen to your music files by you sharing access to them.

The Windows Way

Windows Media Player will allow you to stream your audio library with others on your network. However, you must go to the Network and Sharing Center control panel to enable media streaming. Once you've enabled media streaming, you must select which devices on your network can access the streaming media from your PC.

The Mac Way

The Mac is good at sharing, and so is iTunes. iTunes will happily share your media files with up to five computers on your network. While others may be able to play items you share from your iTunes Library, they will not be able to copy those items, hence legality is firmly established.

To share items from your iTunes Library:

1. Press ⌘-, to open iTunes' preferences, or choose **Preferences** from the iTunes menu.
2. Click the **Sharing** tab, shown in Figure 9.14.
3. Check the **Share my library on my local network** box.
4. Select **Share entire library** to do just that, or choose **Share selected playlists** to share only the playlists you deem worthy.
5. You can provide a little security by requiring those who connect to your shared library to use a password of your making.
6. Click **OK** to begin sharing your digital media with the rest of the world (at least the part of it that is connected to your private network). iTunes will give you a little advance warning (Apple calls it a "reminder") that sharing is for personal use only, at which point you would just click **OK**.

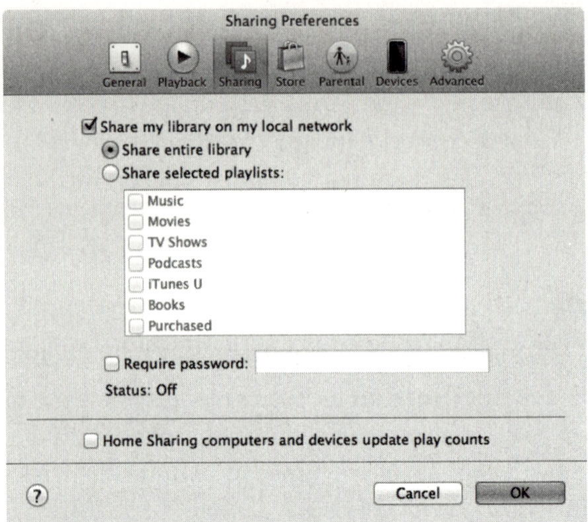

Figure 9.14: *Share your iTunes library with others on your network.*

Of course, to turn off sharing, simply uncheck the **Share my library on my local network** box. If there are folks connected to your shared iTunes Library, you will be warned that you are kicking them off; you can select **Yes** or **No** at this juncture. In upcoming versions of iTunes, if the connected user kicks up a fuss, iTunes will drag them outside and pummel them into submission. Okay, I'm just kidding about the last one.

Right, now what if you desire to connect to a shared library? Easy enough:

1. When others are sharing their iTunes Libraries, you will see the name of their share in the sidebar under the Shared heading. Click the name of the share to see the items being shared.
2. Double-click the items you want to listen to.

Wasn't that hard?

Syncing Music with an iPhone, iPad, or iPod

I love the convenience of taking my music and other digital media with me using my iPhone, iPad, or iPod. The ability to connect my iDevice to a computer and synchronize its content is a must, and the easier the sync the better.

The Windows Way

Windows Media Player cannot sync with an iPhone, iPad, or iPod on its own. iTunes for Windows is by far your best bet, but if you have an allergy to iTunes there are several other media players for Windows that will allow synchronization with an iPhone, iPad, or iPod. However, none is as elegant a solution as iTunes.

The Mac Way

iTunes is the tool Mac OS X uses to synchronize media and other information with your iPhone, iPad, and iPod.

I'll concentrate on syncing music with your devices, but syncing other information and media is performed in a very similar fashion.

If you haven't already set up your device with iTunes, you will see the Setup Assistant upon connecting the device to your Mac with its USB cable. Enter a name for your device, and then check or uncheck (depending on your preference; I recommend unchecking it) the box next to **Automatically sync songs with my device**. However, if you have more music in your iTunes Library than your device can hold, iTunes will automatically create a random playlist of songs that will fit on your device. Of course, this list can be edited at some other time, but who needs the hassle?

Here's how to sync music with your iDevice using iTunes, if you've previously connected your iDevice:

1. First things first: open iTunes and then connect your iPhone or iPod to your Mac.
2. iTunes will recognize the device and display it in the sidebar. Click the device name in the sidebar to see its information and settings summary (Figure 9.15).

3. At this point you have two options: manually sync music and videos (which I recommend), or allow iTunes to handle syncs automatically upon connection of your device to your Mac. To sync manually, continue with step 4; to sync automatically, jump to step 7. I recommend manually syncing because it puts you in control instead of iTunes. Should you accidentally delete a song from iTunes, you won't want it to be removed from your device upon syncing.
4. Scroll down to the bottom of the summary window and check the box next to **Manually manage music and videos**. Click **Apply** to make the change stick.
5. Go to the Library heading in the iTunes sidebar and click **Music**.
6. Drag individual songs or entire playlists and drop them onto your device in the sidebar. iTunes will copy your music to your device. Skip to step 11 to finish.
7. Scroll down to the bottom of the summary window and make sure the box next to **Manually manage music and videos** is unchecked.
8. Click the **Music** tab at the top of the summary window and select the **Sync Music** check box. If prompted whether you are sure, click the **Sync Music** button.
9. Check the **Sync Music** button and select the items you would like to sync, such as your entire Library (could take all day) or only playlists and artists that you select.
10. Click the **Apply** button to begin syncing your music.
11. When finished, click the **Eject** button next to the name of your device in the sidebar to safely remove it from your Mac.

Figure 9.15: *Click your device in iTunes' sidebar to see a summary of its information and settings.*

These same basic steps can be taken when syncing movies, television shows, podcasts, and the like.

Hollywood on Your Mac

10

The excitement of the latest summer blockbuster, the smell of fresh popcorn ... there's nothing quite like a night out at the movies. Especially if you're the type who enjoys spending $15 on a ticket, sitting in broken chairs, and having to pry your shoes off the sticky theater floor with a crowbar after the show's over.

In spite of a few potential negatives, a night at the movies can be good fun, but why not bring movie night to your house? Or, for that matter, why not make your own movies from time to time?

Watching Digital Movie Files

Watching a movie at home once meant pushing a cassette tape the size of a small paperback book into the slot of a large black box that sat near your television set. Now you can open your laptop and double-click a movie file to enjoy its contents while you're sitting on the couch, lying in bed, swinging on the front porch, or working in the garage.

The Windows Way

Windows Media Player is the de facto media player of Windows (hence the name). Simply double-click a video file of the proper format (it supports many popular formats, such as AVI and MPEG-4) and

Windows Media Player will be happy to afford you some fine digital entertainment.

Also, there are a multitude of other video players available for Windows, including Apple's own QuickTime.

The Mac Way

Macs have always been known as the favorite computers of Hollywood types, and for good reason. No other computing platform fits the needs of filmmakers and other artists quite like the Mac. From advertising agencies to photographers to musicians, if it has to do with creation or design, the Mac has historically been the go-to machine. Ease of use, a history of faster and more reliable hardware, and better color control and font management are just a few of the reasons for this.

QuickTime is Mac OS X's native video format, and it is the favorite in Tinseltown. Like Windows Media Player, QuickTime supports many different video and audio formats, including, of course, its native format, MOV.

QuickTime Player can be launched by double-clicking the icon for a movie file (as long as it's of a supported format), or you can go to the Applications folder and double-click the **QuickTime Player** icon.

If you double-clicked a movie file to open QuickTime Player, you will see the movie's window and the playback controls, as shown in Figure 10.1.

Everything but the Action button is self-explanatory. The Action button allows you to upload your video to a number of the most popular internet video-streaming sites, such as YouTube and Vimeo. You can also choose to trim a video, which is a pretty neat tool.

Figure 10.1: *QuickTime Player's playback controls aren't foreign to anyone who's used a DVD player.*

To trim a video:

1. Click the **Action** button in QuickTime Player's playback controls and select **Trim**.
2. The frames of the video appear where the playback controls were, wreathed in yellow, shown in Figure 10.2.
3. Drag the yellow handles left or right to encompass the frames you want to keep.
4. When satisfied with your edit, click the **Trim** button.

Figure 10.2: *You can trim videos by dragging the yellow handles around the frames you want to keep.*

Playing DVDs

I remember when the only way to see a movie, at least within some reasonable amount of time after its release, was to go to the theater. It could be years before one of the big three television networks picked up a movie, especially if it was a big hit at the box office. And then one day, the magic of Betamax and VHS made movies available for watching at home, but again, usually only years after release. Nowadays it seems that a month after a movie leaves the cinema, its DVD is sitting on a shelf at the local store or it can be downloaded via iTunes.

The Windows Way

Windows Media Center or Windows Media Player will work for you if you want to watch a DVD on your PC. Controls for playback work just like your actual DVD player, and menu items can be accessed just the same, too. This one's a cinch.

The Mac Way

Mac OS X's DVD Player is exactly what you need to view the latest DVD releases, as well as old favorites:

1. Insert the DVD into your Mac's optical drive.
2. DVD Player will automatically open. As a matter of fact, it will go straight into full screen view. If you move the mouse, you will see the playback controls for full screen mode at the bottom of the screen (Figure 10.3). Click on an option in the DVD's main menu screen to work with your DVD, just as you would on a television.

Figure 10.3: *Move your mouse to see the full screen playback controls.*

Personally, I don't care to be launched into full screen mode the moment I insert a DVD. To change this behavior:

1. Press the **Esc** key to exit full screen mode, if you are already in it.
2. Press ⌘-, or choose **Preferences** from the DVD Player menu.
3. Click the **Player** tab.
4. In the When DVD Player opens options, uncheck the box next to **Enter Full Screen mode** (Figure 10.4).
5. Click **OK** to exit the DVD Player preferences.

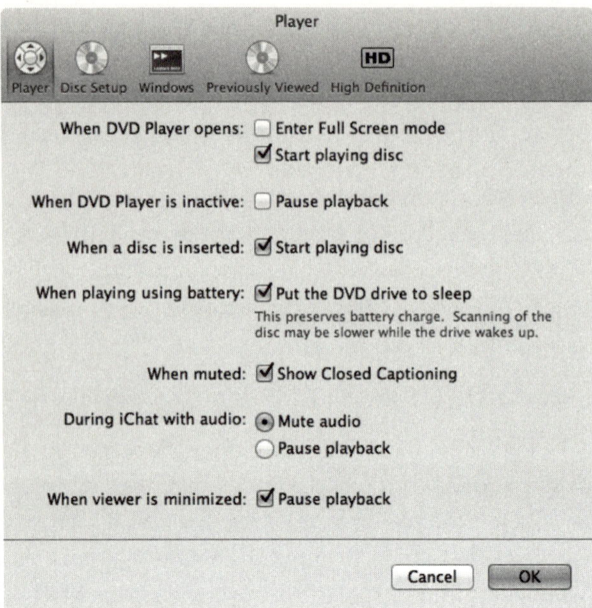

Figure 10.4: *Uncheck* ***Enter Full Screen mode*** *on the DVD Player preferences.*

Should you determine to watch a DVD in windowed mode, you will see a full set of playback controls near the lower-left corner of your screen (seen in Figure 10.5). The windowed controls also allow you to do a few more options than the full screen controls. Note the dark gray icons on the right side of the controls; this dark gray area is called the drawer. The buttons in the drawer allow the following options:

- Slow motion
- Enable or disable subtitles
- Moving frame by frame
- Controlling audio

Figure 10.5: *Windowed playback controls work just the same as those for full screen, with a few more features added.*

Streaming Videos via the Internet

Does anyone reading this remember having to go to the video store to rent a movie? It really wasn't that long ago when video stores dotted nearly every major intersection of a city. Now the latest video releases can be downloaded right over the internet to your computer or television. But there's more to video on the internet than movie studio releases, as you probably well know. The internet has become one of the best ways to share personal videos, and is a great way for companies to remotely train employees.

The Windows Way

Windows is quite adept at playing streaming video of all types. If you want to watch video on YouTube, Vimeo, or the like, simply go to their websites. Should you want to watch QuickTime video, however (such as movie trailers on Apple's site, www.apple.com/trailers), you will need to download and install QuickTime from Apple. If you have an iPhone or iPod and already use iTunes, you most likely have QuickTime installed already. The reason for needing QuickTime is that it installs QuickTime extensions and plug-ins for your web browser, so that the browser will recognize the QuickTime format and play the files.

The Mac Way

You already have QuickTime installed, so there isn't a need to download and install it. Also, as with Windows, pretty much any browser on the Mac will allow you to play content from sites like YouTube.

However, there is one format that turns the table on Mac users and requires them to download a third-party player: Windows Media. Windows media audio and video files won't natively play in Mac OS X, but thankfully there is a way to get them to work.

1. Open a web browser and go to www.microsoft.com/download/en/details.aspx?id=9442.

2. Click the **Download** button to download the Windows Media Components for QuickTime. The file may expand automatically after download is complete, but if not simply double-click the file to manually expand it.
3. When the file expands, double-click the **Flip4Mac WMV.mpkg** file.
4. Follow the instructions from there to install the Windows Components for QuickTime (Figure 10.6).
5. Once the installation is complete, restart any web browsers you may have had open.

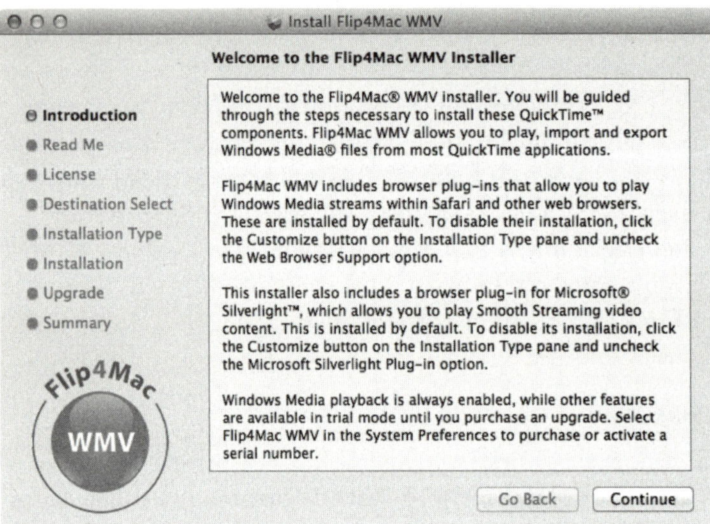

Figure 10.6: *Install Windows Components for QuickTime so you can play Windows media on your Mac.*

Now, whenever you run across Windows media while browsing the web, your browser will be able to play it. Also, if a friend sends you a Windows media file, you will be able to open and play it back using the stand-alone QuickTime Player.

Creating Your Own Movies

One of my favorite pastimes with my parents is when we break out the ancient movie projector and watch old home movies. The sound of the projector certainly brings back good memories. I sometimes think it's rather unfortunate our own children won't be able to experience those kinds of memories. Today, home movies can be watched directly on a computer or television, or even a cell phone for that matter, and it seems to remove the necessary element of proximity to family since the movies can be so easily shared via the internet. But while the familial trade-offs are a definite possibility, the benefits of technology do provide a balance. While I bemoan the fact that we don't need to be in a family group setting to watch things like home movies these days, I wholeheartedly cheer that we can send a soldier halfway around the world video of his first child's birth.

The Windows Way

For a good while the Mac had the definitive upper hand when it came to making movies on a computer, but Windows has made some nice strides forward in the last few years. Windows Live Movie Maker is a good program for compiling and editing movies, but still lacks the polish that some of the third-party movie-editing applications possess.

The Mac Way

iMovie is the application from Apple that makes home movie making a breeze. iMovie is part of the iLife suite of digital lifestyle apps, and it most likely came with your Mac. Go to your Applications folder and double-click the **iMovie** icon to open it.

iMovie's interface is designed to make movie making as simple and intuitive as possible. Figure 10.7 affords a bird's-eye view of iMovie.

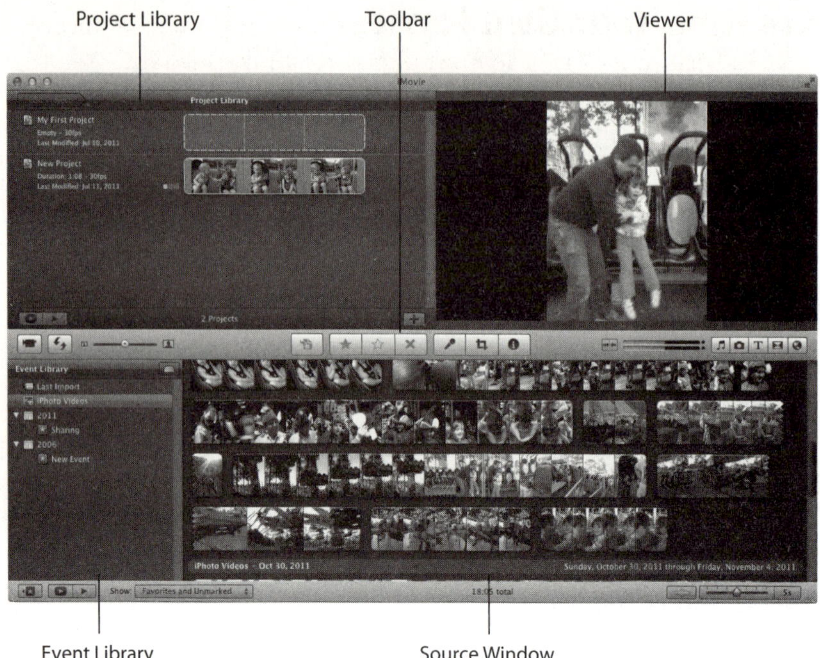

Figure 10.7: *The iMovie interface is simple and intuitive.*

What Is an iMovie Event?

Videos that you import into iMovie are kept in the Event Library. These imported videos are called Events, and they are used to help you organize your video collection based on names you supply for them. You can add or remove video clips to and from Events.

iMovie can import video from digital video cameras, as well as import movie files, such as MOV, MPEG-4, and many other formats.

Importing with a camera is the typical way to import video into iMovie. There are two types of digital video cameras:

- Random Access Devices (RADs) are cameras that are not tape-based. They use media such as DVDs, hard disk drives, or flash memory. Since they connect to computers via USB, iMovie refers to them as USB devices. RADs allow you to import video clips selectively. Video-capable cell phones, including the iPhone, are also RADs.

- Tape-based digital video cameras use FireWire to connect with your Mac. You must play through the recording to import video, even if only importing sections.

To import video from a RAD:

1. Set the camera to computer mode and connect it to your Mac, and the Import window will open.
2. Select **Import All** to import all the video clips. You can also import selections by choosing **Manual** from the left side of the Import window and checking the boxes next to clips you want to import.
3. Select a location to save the clips.
4. Choose to create a new Event or add the video clips to an existing Event.
5. If you want iMovie to analyze the video clips for people or stabilization issues, use the After import analyze for pop-up menu.
6. Click **Import** to begin importing your video (this may take a while).

To import video from a tape-based camera:

1. Set the camera to Play or VCR mode.
2. Connect the camera to your Mac with a FireWire cable, and the Import window will open.
3. To import all the video on the tape, set the option on the left side of the Import window to Automatic, and then click **Import**. To import sections of the video, change the option to Manual. Use the controls in the Import window to rewind or fast-forward the tape to the section of video you want to import, and click the **Import** button. Click the **Stop** button to stop the import.
4. Select a location to save the video.

5. Choose to create a new Event or add the video clips to an existing Event.
6. Click **OK** to complete the import.

To import a movie file:

1. Choose **Import > Movies** from the File menu.
2. Browse your Mac for the movie file you want to import.
3. Select the movie file to import and select a drive from the Save To destination if necessary.
4. Choose to create a new Event or add the video clips to an existing Event.
5. Use Choose a size from the Optimize video pop-up menu if the movie is in the HD format.
6. Choose whether to copy the movie files or move them from their original location (Figure 10.8).
7. Click **Import** to import the movie.

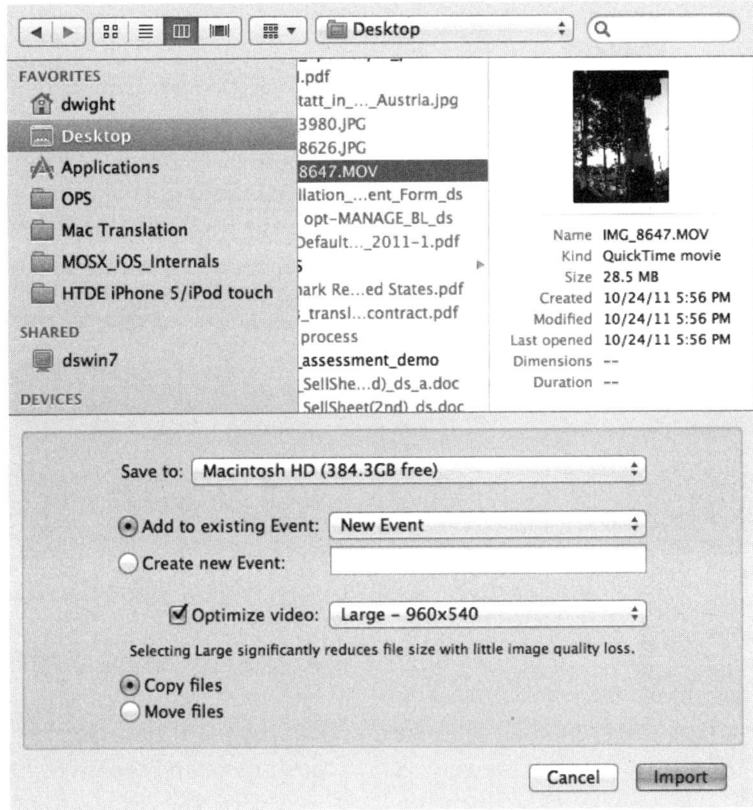

Figure 10.8: *Easily import movie files into iMovie.*

A new Event will show in your Event Library after you finish an import. Click an Event and its video will appear in the source window (Figure 10.9). These are video clips and they contain all the audio and images (called frames) from your recordings.

Figure 10.9: *Imported video can be seen in the source window.*

Drag your mouse pointer over a clip: you can see each frame and hear the audio; this is called skimming. You can play the entire clip by clicking a point within it and pressing the Spacebar. To select a portion of video to work with, click anywhere within a video clip and a yellow border box surrounds a four-second section of the clip. You can shrink or expand this border by clicking-and-dragging the selection handles on either side (Figure 10.10). Hold down the Option key when clicking the clip to select the entire clip in one fell swoop.

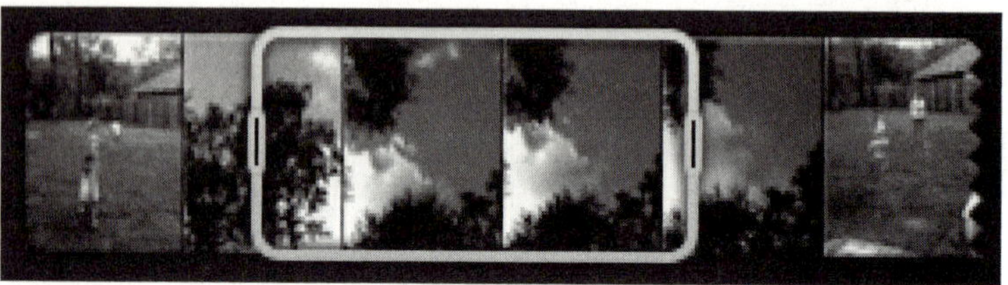

Figure 10.10: *Drag the yellow handles on either side to shrink or expand a video selection.*

Next, you need to create a new project with your imported video clips. Press **⌘-N** or click the **+** button beneath the Project Library window to start a new project. Name your project and then select a theme for it (No Theme is the default). Select an aspect ratio for the project (Standard, iPhone, or Widescreen) and click **Create.**

Time to add video to your project:

1. Choose an Event from the Event Library, and make a selection from the clips associated with it.
2. Click the **Add to Project** button in the toolbar to add your choice to the project, or you can drag-and-drop the selection into the Project window. Continue with this step until you have all the clips you need for your project.
3. Drag-and-drop clips to any position in the Project window to arrange them.
4. Click the **Play Project** button under the Project Library to see a preview of the project.

Adding music and sound effects to your project gives it extra pizzazz. Open the Music and Sound Effects pane (Figure 10.11) in the lower-right corner by choosing **Music and Sound Effects** from the Window menu.

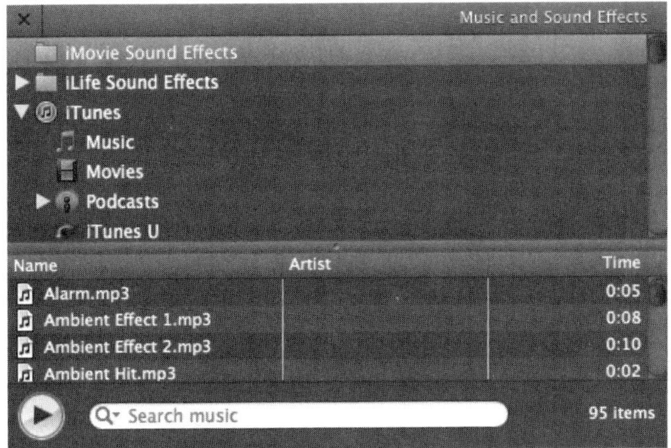

Figure 10.11: *Choose music or sound effects to add to your project.*

Choose music or sound effects from any of the sources listed. Drag a selection to the background of your project, making sure you drop it into the background, not onto the clip. A green box represents the music or sound effect.

That's it for creating a very simple movie. You can do much more, like adding transitions, fades, special effects, and titles to your movies.

A Darkroom on Your Desk

I used to think that film would never be replaced by digital when it came to taking pictures, at least not by the serious photographer. Oh, how wrong I was! Photographic film has gone the way of the vinyl record, and I for one think we're all the better for it, both from a convenience and financial standpoint (among other reasons). My wife is the kind of picture taker who likes to take 10 snaps of the exact same pose before she decides to move on to the next subject. Needless to say that digital has been a financial godsend, since we no longer have to develop a roll of film that contains 24 pictures of only two different subjects.

Digital cameras have become the norm for both Windows and Mac users. In this chapter, I'll show you Windows users how to use your digital camera with a Mac, and perform the tasks that you are used to carrying out with your cherished pictorial memories.

Connecting a Camera to Your Computer

In order to get pictures from your camera to your computer, you will need to get them to talk to one another. A USB cable is the typical mode of communication between a digital camera and a computer, so you might want to go ahead and have one handy, particularly the USB cable that came with your camera. Your camera may need to be set to a particular mode in order to connect with your computer; check with the manufacturer to find out, if you don't know how to do this.

How About Using a Camera Phone?

If your cell phone has a camera, you can use it to connect to your Mac, just as you would a normal camera. If your cell phone doesn't have a camera, you should ask your pals Fred Flintstone and Barney Rubble to give you a lift to the nearest cell phone store for a seriously needed upgrade.

The Windows Way

Connect the camera's USB cable to a USB port on your PC, and then turn on the camera (if it's not already on). Windows will recognize the device automatically and ask you what you want to do from that point.

The Mac Way

As with a PC, connect the camera's USB cable to your Mac (with the other end connected to your camera, of course). Your Mac will recognize the camera (assuming it's turned on), but may or may not automatically perform an action, such as opening an app to begin importing pictures; this depends on the settings made in applications, such as iPhoto and Image Capture (which I'll cover later in this chapter).

Importing Photos from Your Camera

The camera's connected: now what? If you have pictures you'd like to move from the camera to the computer, please follow along. Typically, you can import all photos from your camera or just a selection of them.

The Windows Way

Once you connect the camera to your PC, Windows will recognize the device and ask if you want to import the pictures. Tell Windows to import the pictures, and after you provide a tag (or description) for them, they are automatically imported to your My Photos folder. You can also use an application such as Windows Photo Gallery to import pictures.

The Mac Way

Mac OS X can import pictures from your camera using apps such as iPhoto and Image Capture. Both apps typically come with most newer Macs, but only Image Capture is included with Mac OS X (iPhoto is part of Apple's iLife suite of digital applications). I'll explain both, just in case you don't have iPhoto, or if you simply want to know how to use Image Capture (for example, if you want to quickly get a single photo from your camera without having to go through the steps of importing into iPhoto).

Since most folks will use iPhoto, though, let's start there.

1. If iPhoto opens automatically when you connect your camera, good for you. If not, click its icon in the Dock, or double-click its icon in the Applications folder, to launch.
2. iPhoto will show your camera in the sidebar on the left side of the window, and display pictures it contains, as shown in Figure 11.1.
3. iPhoto considers the date you took your pictures as an Event, so it offers you the option of naming your Event before importing pictures. Type the Event name in the upper-left corner of the iPhoto window if you so desire. You can also check the **Split Events** box to separate pictures into different Events automatically.
4. You have two options at this point:
    - Click the **Import Photos** button to import all the photos on your camera in one fell swoop.
    - Select individual pictures by clicking them (hold down the ⌘ key to select multiple pictures), and then click the **Import Selected** button.

5. When iPhoto is finished importing your pictures, it asks if you want it to delete the original photos from your camera, as shown in Figure 11.2. This is up to you, but my advice is to say “no, thanks” (click the **Keep Photos** button), just to make sure that the pictures have been correctly imported before you delete them from your camera. You can always come back and do that later on the camera itself.
6. Your newly imported pictures will show up in iPhoto, ready for you to view, organize, and edit.

Figure 11.1: *iPhoto will display images that are on your camera.*

Figure 11.2: *To delete or not to delete ….*

Automatically Open iPhoto When Connecting a Camera

You can have iPhoto open automatically when you connect your camera. Click the **iPhoto** menu and select **Preferences**, select the **General** button at the top of the preferences window, and change the Connecting camera opens pop-up to iPhoto.

Should you choose to import pictures with Image Capture:

1. If Image Capture opens automatically when you connect your camera, you're golden. If not, double-click its icon in the Applications folder to launch it.
2. Your camera will appear under the Devices section in the sidebar on the left side of the window, and display pictures it contains, as illustrated in Figure 11.3.
3. Choose a location to import the pictures onto your Mac's hard drive using the Import To pop-up menu at the bottom of the window.
4. Decide which pictures to import:
   - Click the **Import All** button to import all the photos on your camera at once.
   - Select individual pictures by clicking them (hold down the ⌘ key to select multiple pictures), and then click the **Import** button.
5. When Image Capture is finished importing your pictures, it will display a green circle with a check in the lower-right corner of the picture's icon.

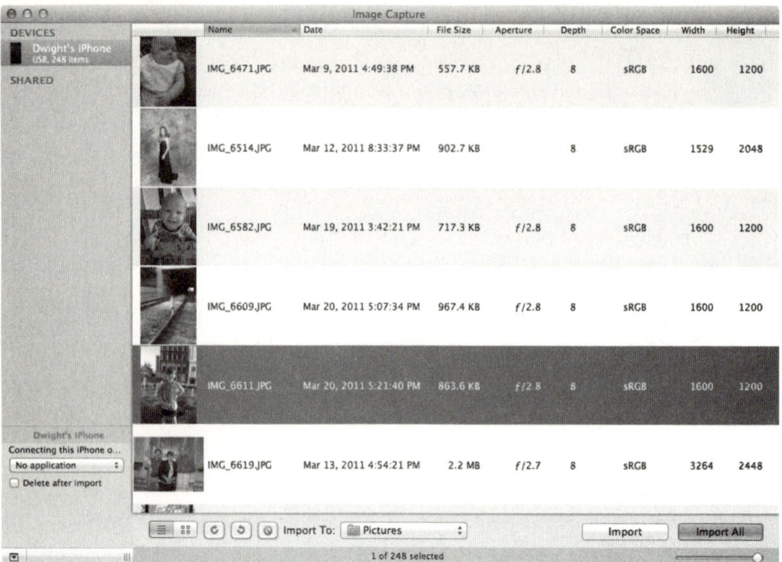

Figure 11.3: *Your camera will show up under the Devices section of the sidebar in Image Capture.*

Automatically Open Image Capture

You can also have Image Capture open automatically when you connect your camera. Click the **Device Settings** icon (looks like a square containing a small black arrow) in the very lower-left corner of the window to see the settings options. Choose **Image Capture** from the Connecting this camera opens pop-up menu. If you want to automatically delete pictures from your camera once Image Capture imports them (not recommended!), place a check in the **Delete after import** box.

Organizing and Working with Photos

Getting pictures onto your computer is only half the battle: organizing them is key (unless you're the type who would just toss pictures into shoeboxes back in the day, instead of using photo albums).

The Windows Way

There are multiple ways you can organize your pictures in Windows. The Windows Photo Gallery allows you to rename pictures, create folders, and the like, all from one central location. You can also use the Windows Picture Library, if you're running Windows 7. The Picture Library affords you an aggregated view of pictures that may reside in multiple locations on your PC.

The Mac Way

If you import your pictures using Image Capture, you will have to simply use standard folders within a Finder window to organize them. However, if you use iPhoto, you are in for an organizational treat.

iPhoto helps you organize your pictures in four distinct ways:

- Events view (Figure 11.4) organizes your pictures according to dates. You can also create new Events if you have multiple pictures taken on the same date that you don't want to group together. When viewing Events, you will only see one of the photos it contains; this photo is called the key. Double-click an Event to view all the photos it contains.

Figure 11.4: *Events view in iPhoto.*

- Photos view will show you each individual photo contained within an Event (Figure 11.5).

Figure 11.5: *See individual pictures with Photos view.*

- Faces view, shown in Figure 11.6, actually lets you see photos based on the faces of their subjects. When you first visit Faces view, you are allowed to view faces of subjects in your pictures and assign names to them. This can yield some hilarious results when assigning names to faces, such as when it asks you to name faces of toys and statues, as illustrated in Figure 11.7.

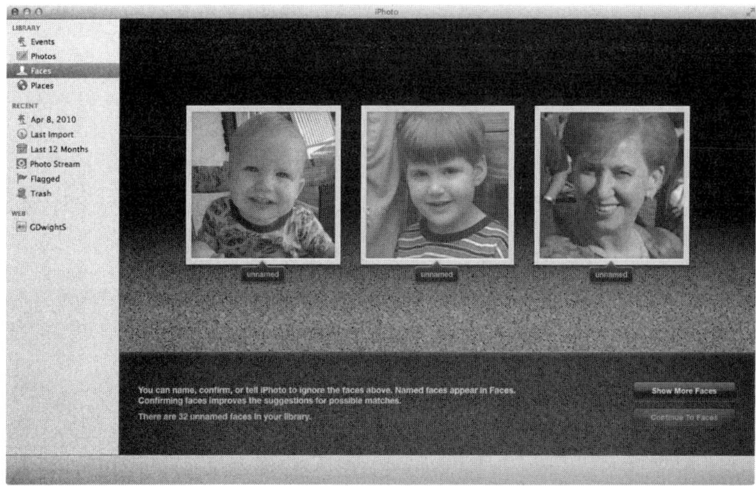

Figure 11.6: *Faces view lets you find photos based on the faces of subjects in them.*

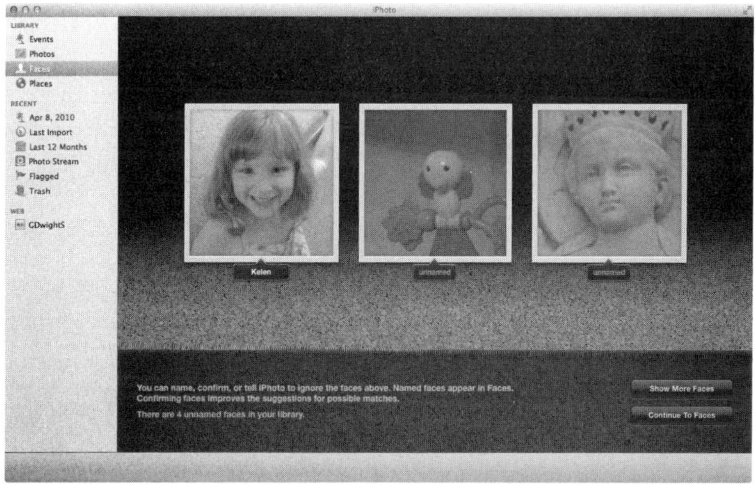

Figure 11.7: *Faces view lets you assign names to faces in your pictures, even those of inanimate objects.*

- If your camera contains a GPS, it can attach location information to a photo. Places (seen in Figure 11.8) lets you view pictures based on the location in which they were taken. Click on one of the drop pins on the map to see photos taken in that location.

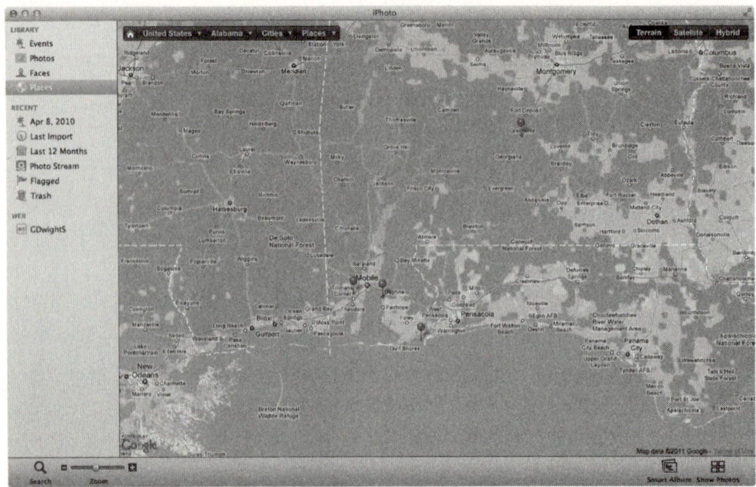

Figure 11.8: *Use Places view to see pictures based on the locations in which they were taken.*

Simply choosing a view isn't all there is to organizing pictures.

Go to Photos view and hold your mouse pointer over a picture. Notice the small white circle containing the black arrow in the lower-right corner of the picture (Figure 11.9)? Click that white circle to see a few quick things you can do with it, such as:

- Click **Rotate** to rotate the picture counterclockwise by 90 degrees, or Option-click to rotate clockwise.
- Click **Hide** to hide the picture from view without deleting it.
- Click **Trash** to chuck that picture into iPhoto's Trash. This doesn't completely delete the picture from your Mac; it just places it in iPhoto's Trash until such time as you decide to empty it.
- Give a picture a star rating by clicking the stars.
- Cut, copy, or paste a picture for use in other applications.
- Click **Show Event** to open the Event that this picture is assigned to.

Figure 11.9: *Perform some quick actions with photos.*

You can also flag a photo for use later. Again, hover your mouse pointer over the picture and click the flag that's found in the upper-left corner.

Empty iPhoto's Trash

When you send a picture to the Trash in iPhoto, it isn't instantly deleted from your Mac. The unwanted picture is placed in the Trash, which you can view by clicking **Trash** in the sidebar on the left side of iPhoto's window. To empty the Trash, which deletes the pic from your Mac, click the **Empty Trash** button in the top-right corner of the window. You can also rescue pictures from the Trash by dragging and-dropping them onto Photos or Events in the sidebar. Be sure to empty iPhoto's Trash periodically, as the pictures stored here can unnecessarily take up quite a bit of space on your hard drive over time.

Select a picture from your collection and click to open it. Once there, click the **Info** button in the lower right of the iPhoto window to view detailed information about the picture (Figure 11.10). From here we can make several changes to the picture's information that will help with organization.

Figure 11.10: *The Info button gives you the scoop on many elements of a picture.*

- You can view information about the device that took the picture, the picture's resolution, its file type, and more, in the upper-right corner.
- Notice the name of the picture in Figure 11.10: it's called "IMG_0100." This is the name given the picture by my iPhone; your camera will give your pictures a similar name. You can change these names by clicking the current names and typing a new one.
- Give a picture a star rating by clicking one of the stars to the right of the picture's name.
- Click **Add a description...** to do just that.
- You can assign a name to the faces of subjects in the picture, if they don't already have one. Click **Add a face...**, move the resulting square over the face you want to assign a name, and then type the desired name (Figure 11.11).

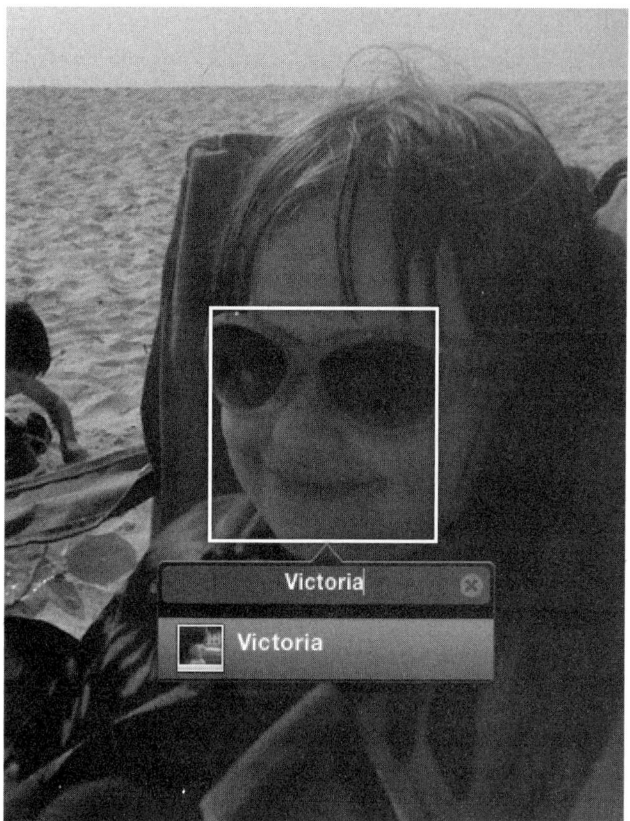

Figure 11.11: *Add names to the faces of your photos subjects from within the Info section.*

- If your camera has added location information to your picture, you will see the location in the map at the lower right of the iPhoto window.

Making Color Adjustments to Photos

Sometimes no matter how hard you try or how fantabulous your camera is, the colors in your pictures may not always come out just like you want them to. That's another benefit of digital pictures: you can adjust the colors of your images quickly and easily with photo editing software.

Now, if you're a photographer and are looking for top-of-the-line photo editing, Photoshop is your best bet. But us regular folks can get the basic job done on our PCs or Macs without having to get a second mortgage on our home to afford Photoshop.

The Windows Way

Once again, it's Windows Photo Gallery to the rescue. With Windows Photo Gallery you can automatically adjust elements of the picture, change the exposure, adjust the color, apply noise reduction filters, and add special effects. Of course, you can also rotate the picture and revert to the original file if the changes don't suit you.

The Mac Way

Image Capture doesn't allow for any color correction, but you can rotate pictures. That's not such a big deal, so we'll move on to iPhoto.

iPhoto is a whiz at quick and easy color correction, but some of the options it affords may surprise you in their detail. Let's check it out.

Figure 11.12: *iPhoto gives you a list of quick and easy fixes to apply to your pictures.*

Select a picture to play with and double-click to open it. Next, click the **Edit** button in the lower-right corner of the iPhoto window to access the editing options.

First up is Quick Fixes, as denoted by the tab in the upper-right corner of the iPhoto window (Figure 11.12). Here's a rundown of each option:

- Click **Rotate** to rotate the picture counterclockwise by 90 degrees. Hold down the Option key while clicking the **Rotate** button to rotate 90 degrees in the clockwise direction.
- Click the **Enhance** button to let iPhoto make automatic adjustments. Figure 11.13 shows an original image on the left, and the adjusted image on the right (after clicking the **Enhance** button). iPhoto compensated for the darkness of the original and enhanced the bright colors.

Figure 11.13: *Quickly adjust colors in an image with the Enhance button.*

- Click the **Fix Red-Eye** button to make your picture's subjects look a little more human than demonic. You can let iPhoto handle the job automatically, or you can make manual adjustments. To manually remove red-eye, simply click the pupil you want to humanize and drag the Size slider to match the size of the red area.

- If a picture is a bit out of kilter, you can right it by clicking the **Straighten** button. Drag the Angle slider to straighten the image, using the yellow grid to help with horizontal and vertical spacing (Figure 11.14).

Figure 11.14: *Get an image back in line with the Straighten tool.*

- You can clip an image using the Crop button. Click the **Crop** button and then drag the handles that are found in the corners of the image to clip parts of it you could do without. You can also keep the cropping proportional by selecting the **Constrain** check box and setting its dimensions using the pop-up menu. Click **Reset** if you don't like the hatchet job you just performed.
- The Retouch button lets you touch up blemished areas in your pictures. Click the **Retouch** button, move the mouse pointer—which now becomes a dashed circle (as seen in Figure 11.15)—over the blemished area, and click the mouse or trackpad button to smooth the blemish. If the circle isn't the proper size for the blemish, simply drag the Size slider to accommodate. If the blemish is a small one, you may want to use the Zoom slider (found in the lower-left side of the iPhoto window) to zoom in on the area of the picture

where the blemish is found. You can see where you are in the picture using the Navigation window that pops up on the screen (also seen in Figure 11.15).

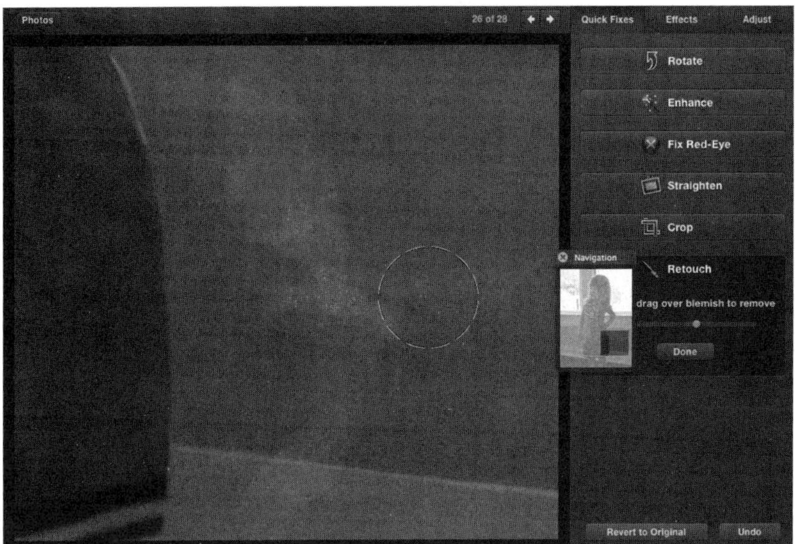

Figure 11.15: *Remove blemishes from your pictures with the Retouch tool.*

iPhoto allows you to add a number of special effects to your images, too. Click the **Effects** tab in the upper-right corner of the iPhoto window to see several effects you can apply to your picture (Figure 11.16). Simply click an effect to apply it, click **Undo** to remove the applied effect, or click **Revert to Original** to bring the picture back to its untainted state.

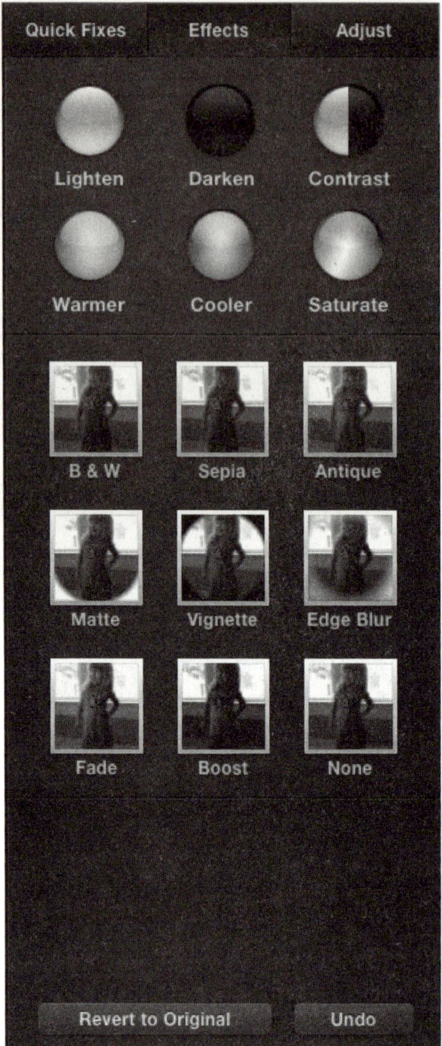

Figure 11.16: *Add special effects to your special memories.*

If making the basic changes isn't good enough for you, you can really get your hands dirty with the options available in the Adjust tab (Figure 11.17). From here you can manually adjust color levels, exposure, contrast saturation, and much more.

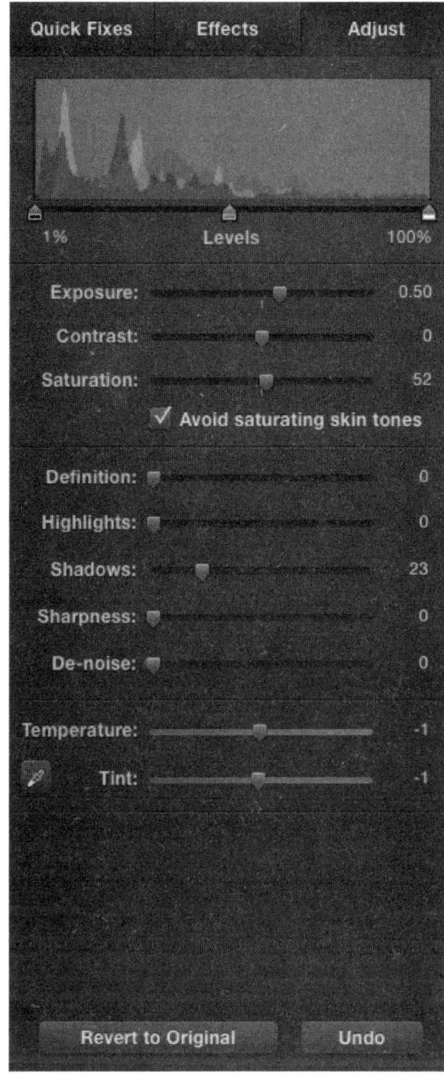

Figure 11.17: *iPhoto lets you get hands-on with detailed adjustments.*

Getting Your Gutenberg On

Printing and the use of paper were things that were supposed to be ushered out the door by the onslaught of the digital age, but many would argue that the reverse is true. People with computers use printers to print everything from tax forms to grocery lists to family photos, so I don't see the pulp industry going belly-up anytime soon. In spite of today's digital book readers, there's still nothing like the heft and feel of a heavy book in your hand, and the sound of turning pages.

Your Mac can work with most printers on the market today, including laser and inkjet printers, and most likely whatever printers you have already been using with your Windows PC. Be sure to look for the Mac OS X logo on the box of the printer to make certain it's compatible with Macs, or if in doubt, contact the manufacturer. That being said, let's see how to get the most out of your printer using Mac OS X.

Installing Printer Drivers

Your printer will likely come with a driver CD in the box, or you can visit the manufacturer's website to download the latest drivers for your operating system. Getting the latest and greatest driver is always a good idea.

Install Drivers Before Connecting Your Printer

Be sure to install drivers for your printer before you connect it to your Mac. If you connect the printer first, the world won't suffer some sort of natural disaster, but your Mac will automatically create a printer queue (more on those in just a bit) using generic drivers, which may rob you of some of the printer's functionality.

The Windows Way

When you install the CD for your printer, Windows will (by default) open the CD's installer application, at which point you would follow the prompts to install the driver. Simple enough.

If you download a driver, you will have to extract the installer from the downloaded file, unless your browser does it for you. Double-click to launch the install file and follow the prompts.

The Mac Way

Should you choose to install the driver using the printer's CD:

1. Insert the CD into your Mac's optical drive. If your Mac doesn't have an optical drive, skip to the next paragraph for instructions on downloading drivers.
2. If the installer begins automatically, great. If not, open the CD by double-clicking its icon on the desktop or by selecting it in a Finder window. You should see an installer file, which you should double-click to launch. If you have trouble locating the file, consult the documentation that came with the printer or contact the manufacturer's technical support.
3. Follow the prompts in the installer to complete the driver installation. At some point you will be prompted to enter your user name and password as a security measure, which you should do if you're serious about installing the driver.

Downloading the driver from the manufacturer's website is the best way to go, in my humble opinion, ensuring you have the most up-to-date files.

1. Visit the printer manufacturer's website, locate the driver files for your particular printer model, and download the files. These files are compressed and are typically disk images (files with .dmg extensions), but some may be .zip files.
2. Once the download is complete, the file should automatically decompress if you are using Safari (and haven't messed with its defaults). If you're using a different browser or if Safari doesn't decompress the file, locate the file and double-click it to decompress it. A window containing the installer package should open for you.
3. Double-click the installer package and follow the prompts (similar to those in Figure 12.1) to install the driver.

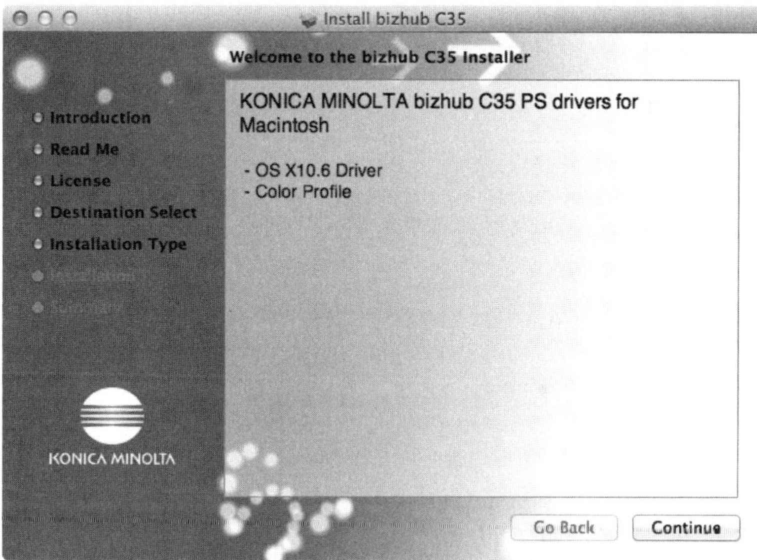

Figure 12.1: *Follow the installer's prompts to install your printer driver.*

At this point the drivers are now installed on your Mac, but you still need to create a print queue—which is conveniently our next topic.

Creating a Print Queue

A print queue is a visual representation of your printer, and is where your print jobs go before your computer routes them to your printer. You can view jobs and manage them from within a print queue, but I'll tackle that subject in a bit. For now, suffice to say that a print queue must be created before you can begin printing to your printer.

The Windows Way

If your printer is attached via USB, creating a queue is typically as simple as connecting it to your PC after the drivers have been installed. Windows should recognize the type of printer it is, find the appropriate driver, and create a print queue without you having to so much as lift a finger.

Should the printer be on a network, well, that's a whole different ball of wax. You have to invoke the magic of the Add Printer Wizard to create the queue for a network printer, and it's not always as simple as it may seem. If you know your printer's IP address, you'll be okay, but if not, well, tech support is a mere phone call (and a 30-minute hold) away.

The Mac Way

As with Windows, if you are connecting your printer with USB, you are golden after you connect the printer to your Mac (assuming you've installed the driver prior to doing so, that is). The printer's queue should show up just as pretty as you please in the Printers list on the left side of the Print & Scan preferences pane (Figure 12.2). What's that? How do you get there, you ask?

1. Choose **System Preferences** from the Apple menu.
2. Click the **Print & Scan** icon in the Hardware section of the System Preferences window.

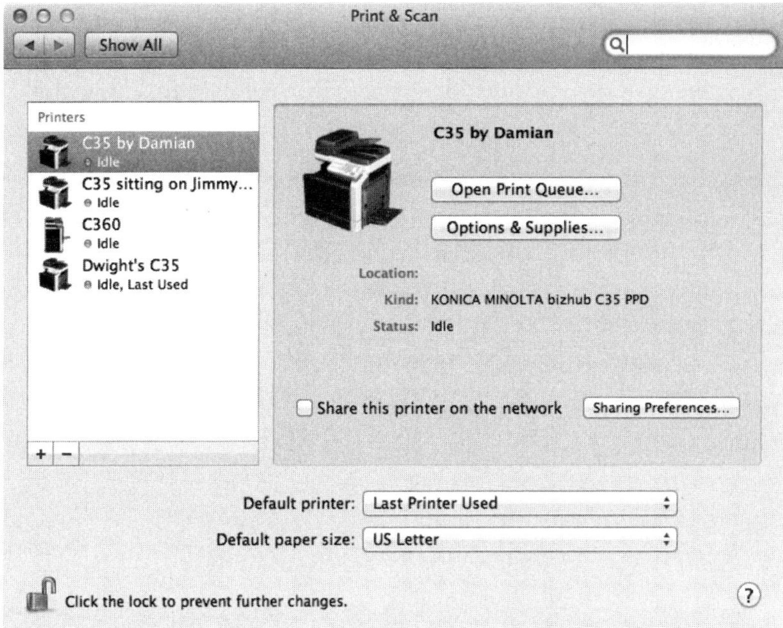

Figure 12.2: *Printer queues appear in the Print & Scan pane's Printers list.*

If your printer is a network device, fear not: you may be able to install it easily, even if you don't know the printer's IP address, using a little gem known as Bonjour.

Bonjour is a network protocol built into Mac OS X that makes it incredibly simple to connect devices that are running it. Devices running Bonjour broadcast their names over the network, and other devices running Bonjour simply find them (or the printer) and begin talking. If your printer is fairly new (manufactured sometime in the last four to five years), Bonjour is most likely running on it by default.

To add a network printer using Bonjour:

1. Open the Print & Scan preferences pane.
2. Click the **+** button underneath the Printers list.
3. Click the **Default** button in the Add Printer window, if it's not already active. If your printer is running Bonjour, you will see it in the Printer Name column, as seen in Figure 12.3.

4. Select the name of your printer. The Print Using pop-up menu should reflect the make and model of your printer, assuming you've installed the driver before beginning this process (shame on you if you haven't!).
5. Click the **Add** button, prompting your Mac to query the printer for information about its configuration (Figure 12.4). For example, your Mac is looking to see if your printer has any options added to it, such as a duplexer or extra paper trays. Set the configurations as needed and click **OK** to add the printer queue to the Printers list. If you're not sure, click **OK** anyway and I'll show you in the next section of this chapter how to configure your printer queue after the fact.

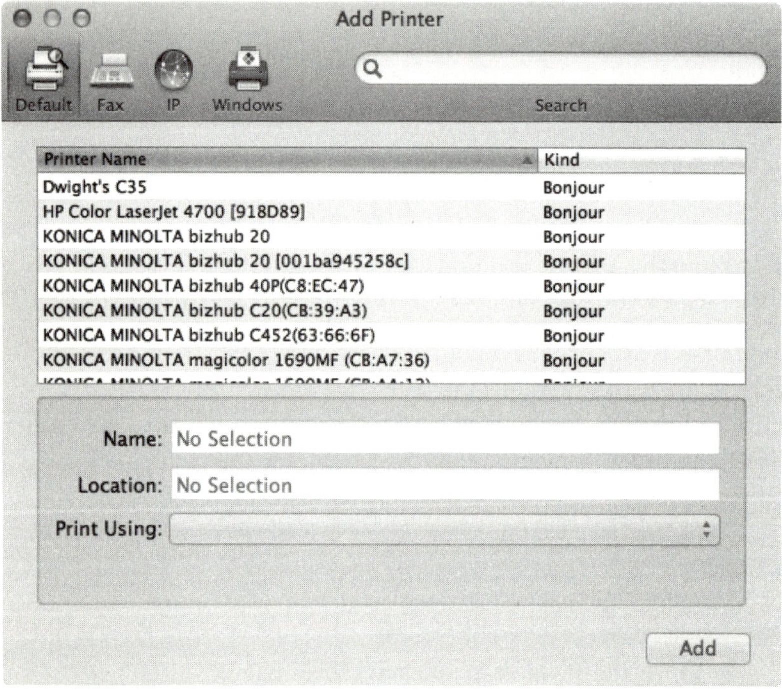

Figure 12.3: *Find your printer's name in the Add Printer window.*

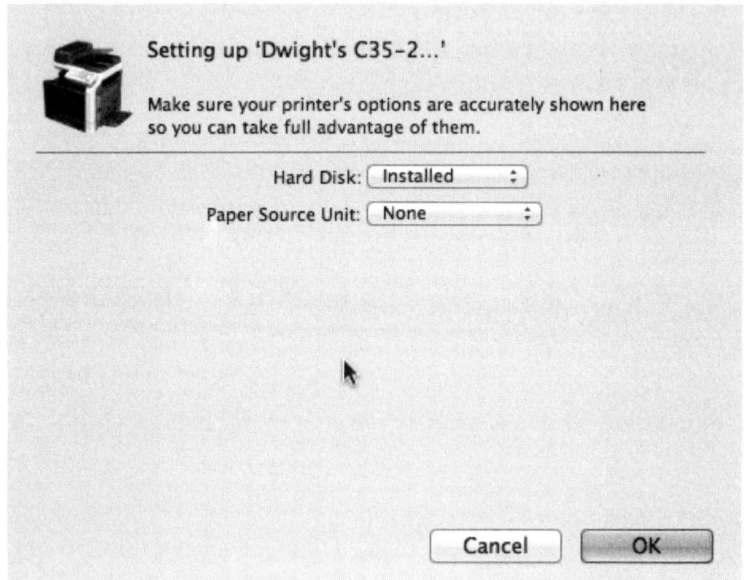

Figure 12.4: *Configure your printer's options and click **OK** to add it to the Printers list.*

If your printer doesn't support Bonjour, you can still install it using its IP address. Be sure to get the IP address for the printer before beginning these steps: print a configuration page from the printer by perusing the network settings on the front panel of your printer, or by contacting your IT department or the printer manufacturer's tech support.

To add a printer using its IP address:

1. Open the Print & Scan preferences pane.
2. Click the **+** button underneath the Printers list.
3. Click the **IP** button in the Add Printer window.
4. Select a protocol from the Protocol pop-up menu. Line Printer Daemon (LPD) is the default; consult your IT department or the printer manufacturer's tech support if you're not sure or if LPD doesn't work after completing the remaining steps.

5. Enter the printer's IP address into the Address field, and populate the Queue field if necessary (again, consult IT or tech support if you don't know).
6. Give the printer a descriptive name and enter a location to help you know where the printer is physically located.
7. If the driver is installed, the Print Using pop-up menu should already be populated with the correct make and model, as illustrated in Figure 12.5. If not, click the pop-up menu, choose **Select Printer Software**, and browse the list of drivers to find the one that corresponds to your printer.
8. Click **Add** to add your IP printer to the Printers list.

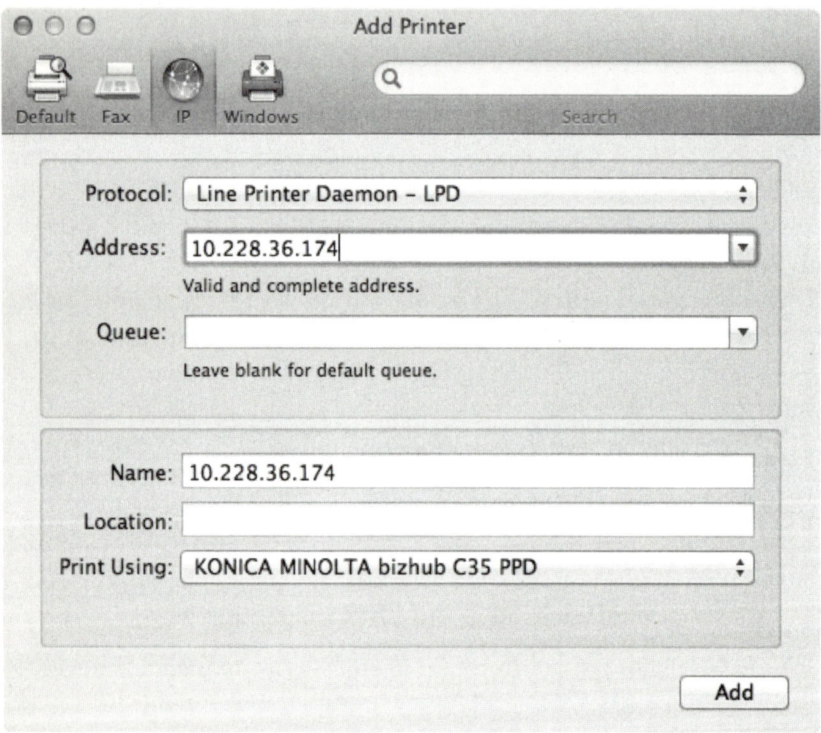

Figure 12.5: *Be sure that the Print Using pop-up displays the correct make and model of your printer.*

Delete a Printer Queue

Deleting a printer queue is as simple as highlighting the printer in the Printers list and clicking the – button underneath. The queue is dispatched to printer queue heaven (unless it was a bad printer queue, of course).

Configuring Printer Options

Now that you've got printers added to Print & Scan, you're ready to print, right? Well, maybe not. What if, during the course of creating the queue, you forgot to tell your trusty computer that your printer had an optional hard drive installed in it? Or what if you later add an optional paper tray (or some other option) and need to tell the computer about the latest addition to your printer?

The Windows Way

To update a printer's configuration in Windows, go to Control Panel and open Devices and Printers. Once inside, right-click the icon for the printer you want to monkey with and select **Printer Properties**. You're on your own from there, as the number of options and where they are located is up to the printer manufacturer and vary from printer to printer.

The Mac Way

Changing a printer queue configuration on a Mac is a tad simpler than on Windows. That's not to say that manufacturers can't try their darned-tootin' best to make it difficult, but for the most part they stick to the keep-it-simple principle.

To configure your printer's options:

1. Open the Print & Scan preferences pane.
2. Click once to highlight the printer that you need to configure in the Printers list.
3. Click the **Options & Supplies** button.

4. In the resulting sheet, click the **General** tab to see the version of your installed printer driver and to rename the printer if necessary (you're renaming the printer queue on your Mac, not the actual name of the physical printer). If your printer has a built-in web page for remotely monitoring or making settings changes, you can view the web page by clicking the **Show Printer Webpage** button.
5. Click the **Driver** tab to change the driver assigned to your printer and to make changes to its hardware configuration. This is particularly handy if you're one of those readers who consistently ignored my pleas to install the driver before creating a print queue; now you can go in after the fact and choose the appropriate driver (after you install it, of course).
6. If your printer supports this feature, click the **Supply Levels** tab and see a graphical representation of the remaining life of your printer's supplies (shown in Figure 12.6).
7. Click **OK** when finished making your changes.

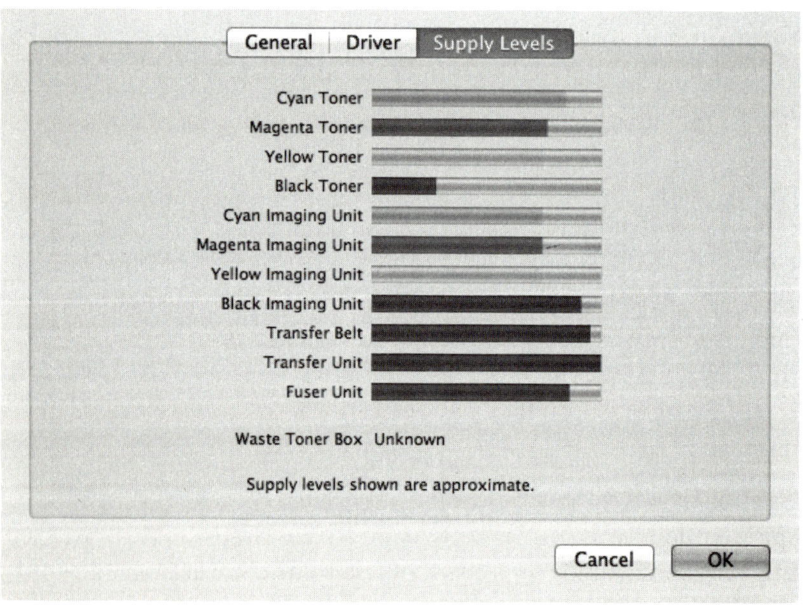

Figure 12.6: *View your printer's supply levels without leaving your chair.*

Printing Documents

At last, we get to the crux of the matter! It's time to put some toner (or ink) to paper (or vellum, or transparencies, or … well, you get the picture).

For the most part, whether on a Mac or PC, printing steps and options are pretty universal. However, on occasion, an application's developer can get a wild hair and really muck up the printing process with a million print options of its own. I can't help you with those kinds of issues (that's why application developers have tech support, too), but I can give you the basics.

The Windows Way

Printing a document or picture (or whatever else you can conjure) in Windows is just as simple as it is on a Mac. Typically, you will choose **Print** from the File menu, or you may even have a printer icon in the application's toolbar that you can click to access the printing options. Select a printer from the list (if the printer you want to use isn't the default), go to Preferences if you need to make adjustments to your print settings (such as for paper size or print resolution), and click **Print** to send your job on its merry way. There is usually quite a bit more involved than what I've listed here, but this is a book about learning Mac tasks, not relearning Windows.

The Mac Way

Printing is what a Mac is made for! Okay, that and a lot of other stuff, but I digress. The Mac has always been the preference of publishers, artists, designers, and the like since the beginning of Mac time, and there's a reason for that: graphics and printing on the Mac is just better than graphics and printing on Windows. I could be more detailed, but it really is just that simple.

As with Windows, however, every app is just a bit different from the app next door when it comes to its own printing options, so I'll keep this very vanilla and cover the universals only. In order to do so I'll use TextEdit to print my job.

Here are the basics of getting a print job from your Mac to your printer.

1. From within the app you want to print from (in my case, TextEdit), press **⌘-P** or choose **Print** from the File menu to open the print dialog sheet (Figure 12.7).
2. Enter the number of copies you want to print.
3. Select which pages in the document to print.
4. Click **Print** to send the job to the print queue, where it is then kicked over to the printer.

Figure 12.7: *A typical standard print dialog sheet.*

You're probably thinking, "There has to be more to it than that," and you're right. Or at least there can be more to it, if the very bare-bones basics aren't enough.

Should you want more control over your print options, please follow along:

1. From within the app you want to print from (again, TextEdit for me), press **⌘-P** or choose **Print** from the File menu to open the print dialog sheet.
2. Click the **Show Details** button at the bottom of the sheet, and you will see a whole new world of printing bliss that's been lying in wait for you to discover it. Figure 12.8 shows you a typical expanded print dialog sheet.
3. Make changes to the print options available. Here's a brief description of each item in the main print dialog sheet:
   - Printer: Select a printer from the pop-up menu.
   - Presets: If you find yourself making the same settings selections for most of your print jobs, you can create a preset that sets them instantly when you print. To create a preset, make the changes to all the settings you wish, click the **Presets** pop-up and choose **Save Current Settings as Preset**. Give the preset a descriptive name and you're done.
   - Copies: Set the number of copies of the document you want to print.
   - Pages: Select which pages in the document you want to print.
   - Paper Size: Choose a paper size from the pop-up.
   - Orientation: Decide whether to print portrait or landscape.
4. Click **Print** to send the job.

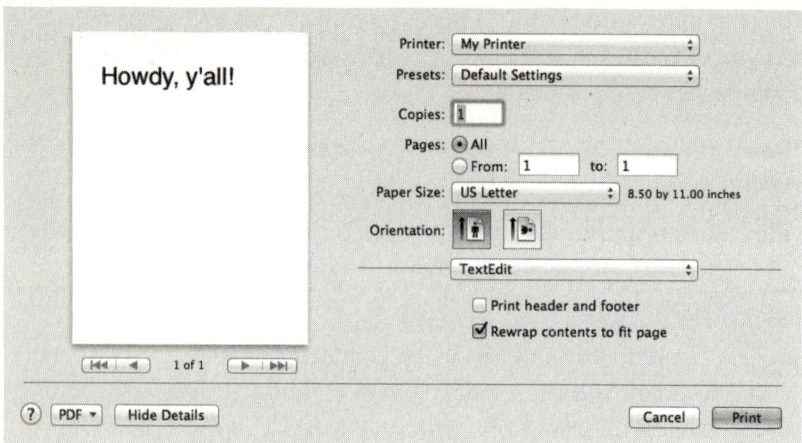

Figure 12.8: *An expanded print dialog sheet.*

Now, I'm sure you noticed that I skipped the pop-up menu under the Orientation option; I can explain. This pop-up offers access to other printing options within the expanded print dialog sheet. The first option in the pop-up is named according to the app you are printing from, and the items beneath the pop-up are application specific. The following tables offer brief descriptions for each of the typical Mac OS X printing options in this pop-up. Any items you may see in your pop-up that are not mentioned in these tables will be specific to the application you're printing from or to the printer you are using, so we won't be covering those.

Table 12.1 affords a brief description of Layout options.

Table 12.1 Layout Options

Option	Description
Pages per Sheet	Select the number of document pages you want to print on a single sheet of paper.
Layout Direction	If you choose anything other than 1 for Pages per Sheet, this option allows you to determine how the pages are placed on the sheet.
Border	Determine a border to place around the elements of your document.

Two-Sided	If you have a duplexer on your printer, you can choose to print on one side or both sides of a page.
Reverse Page Orientation	Causes the elements on your document pages to print upside down.
Flip Horizontally	Prints a mirror image of your document's elements.

Table 12.2 discusses Color Matching options.

Table 12.2 Color Matching Options

Option	Description
ColorSync/In Printer	Select **ColorSync** to allow the Mac to handle color matching, or select **In Printer** to allow the printer to handle it.
Profile	If you chose ColorSync in the previous selection, you can use this option to assign a color profile to the job.

Table 12.3 talks about Paper Handling options.

Table 12.3 Paper Handling Options

Option	Description
Collate pages	This option allows you to print all pages in a document in order before beginning the next set of copies.
Pages to Print	Print all, odd-, or even-numbered pages.
Page Order	This allows you to select Automatic, Normal, or Reverse page order.
Scale to fit paper size	Check this box to make the elements of your document fit the size you choose in the upcoming Destination Paper Size option.

Option	Description
Destination Paper Size	Only available if the Scale to fit paper size option is selected; this option allows you to print your document on a paper size other than the one specified in the main page of the expanded print dialog sheet.
Scale down only	Choosing this option keeps elements on the page from being scaled larger than they currently are.

Table 12.4 gives a description of Paper Feed options.

Table 12.4 Paper Feed Options

Option	Description
All pages from	If you have more than one paper tray on your printer, this option allows you to pick one to print all pages of the job from.
First page from	You can choose to print the first page of your document from a specific tray.
Remaining from	If you select the First page from option, you will get this option so that you can tell your Mac which tray to print the rest of your pages from.

Table 12.5 gives the lowdown on Cover Page options.

Table 12.5 Cover Page Options

Option	Description
Print Cover Page	If you want to print a cover page to help keep your printed documents separate from other users' documents, select this option and choose to print it before your actual document pages or after.

Cover Page Type	If you do decide to print a cover page, use this menu to select which kind to print.
Billing Info	If you're being billed for your print jobs, enter your identification here.

Managing Print Jobs

If you are a printing fanatic and send 10 print jobs a minute to your printer, managing those print jobs may become a necessity. Even if you only send one print job a month, if you send that job and nothing happens on the printer side, you might want to see what your computer is doing with the job. This is when it's handy to open a print queue and take a look at the jobs waiting to go to your printer.

The Windows Way

To see the print jobs you've got lined up on your Windows machine, go to Control Panel, open **Devices and Printers**, and double-click the icon for the printer in question. You will see a new window open and if there are print jobs waiting they will be displayed. From here you can view the progress of the print job, cancel it, pause it, or restart it.

The Mac Way

You might have noticed by now that when you print, a little icon of your printer shows up in the Dock, and then disappears as your job begins to print. This icon is your print queue, and if you click it you can see the progress of your print jobs. You can also open the print queue for a printer in this manner:

1. Open the Print & Scan preferences pane.
2. Click once to highlight the printer in the Printers list.
3. Click the **Open Print Queue** button.

When the print queue window (similar to the one in Figure 12.9) opens, you will be able to manage any pending print jobs.

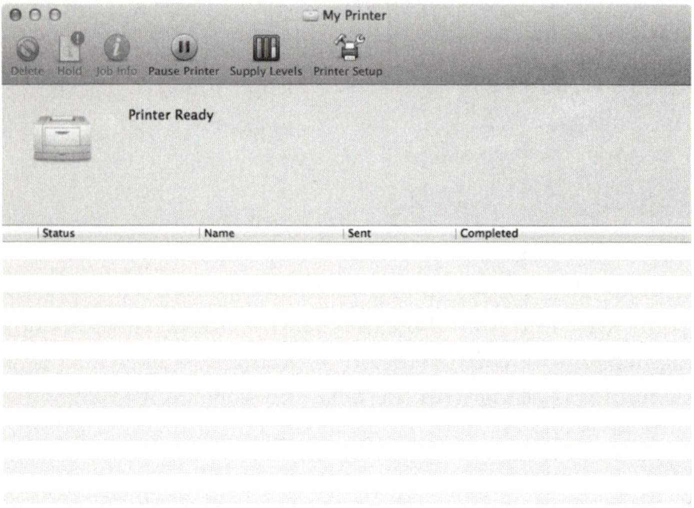

Figure 12.9: *Manage print jobs from within the print queue window.*

Here are a few of the basic tasks you can accomplish within the print queue:

- View a list of all the pending print jobs.
- Delete a job by selecting it in the job list and clicking the **Delete** icon in the toolbar.
- Hold a job (retain it for later printing) in the queue by selecting it and clicking **Hold**.
- View detailed information about a print job by highlighting it and clicking the **Job Info** button.
- Temporarily stop all print jobs in the queue by clicking the **Pause Printer** button. Start the job up again by clicking the **Resume Printer** button.
- If your printer supports the feature, click the **Supply Levels** button to check out the remaining life count of your printer supplies.
- Click the **Printer Setup** button to see information and make changes to the driver, and to configure options on the printer.

Sharing Your Printers

If you've got the only printer in the house or office and it's attached via USB to your computer only, it's only considered polite to share your printer with other computer users on the network.

When you share a printer, you aren't physically sharing the printer itself; you're actually sharing the print queue for it that resides on your computer.

The Windows Way

Back in the Devices and Printers control panel, right-click the icon for the printer you want to share, and choose **Printer Properties**. Click the **Sharing** tab and check the **Share this printer** option. Give the printer a share name and click **Apply** to make it stick. If the folks you are sharing with are running other versions of Windows, you begin to run into major headaches.

The Mac Way

Sharing your printer on a Mac is a snap:

1. Open the Sharing preferences pane found in the Internet & Wireless section of the System Preferences.
2. Check the box next to **Printer Sharing** to turn on printer sharing, as I've done in Figure 12.10.
3. In the Printers column, check the box next to the printers you want to share with other users.
4. Determine who can print to the printer using the Users column. To add users to the list, click the + button.

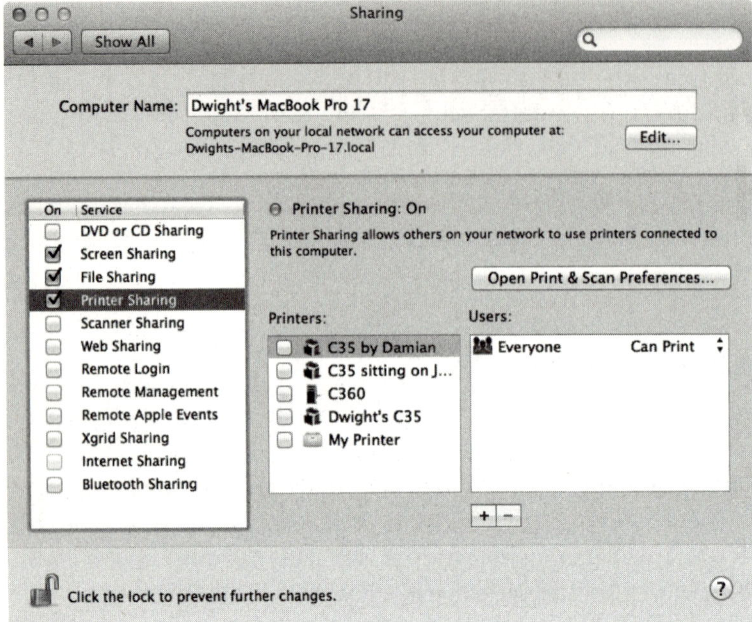

Figure 12.10: *Check the* ***Printer Sharing*** *box to begin sharing your printers over the network.*

Scanning Your Horizons

Although printing documents and pictures is great, digitally storing paper documents and photographs is pretty awesome, too.

By scanning your paper documents, you can archive them on your computer on a server as opposed to a big, bulky filing cabinet, not to mention easily send the document to others via email, thereby avoiding snail mail or some other parcel carrier.

Scanning printed photographs is a no-brainer. Thanks to this digital task, I'm able to scan deteriorating 50-year-old pictures and save them indefinitely, ensuring generations to come will be able to connect with their ancestors, if only through a smile captured decades earlier.

In this chapter, I'll show you basic installation and utilization of a scanner in Mac OS X.

It is always a good idea to have the documentation for your scanner handy, using it as we go along in case there is something special that the manufacturer recommends you do during installation or usage that I don't cover. There's nothing magic about all this, but this chapter is meant as a basic tutorial and translation of tasks for PC users who are using a scanner on a Mac, not the end-all, be-all tome for scanners of all makes and models.

Installing Scanner Drivers

Your scanner should come with a driver CD in its box, but if not you can always check out the manufacturer's website and download the newest drivers that correspond to your computer's operating system and version. To me, the second option of downloading the newest driver is the safest way to go in terms of ensuring proper functionality and connectivity.

Install Drivers Before Connecting Your Scanner

As with printers, it's best to install scanner drivers before you connect the scanner to your Mac. This way you can make sure that your computer has the software necessary for your scanner to operate properly as soon as you connect it.

The Windows Way

Insert the CD that came with your scanner into your PC's disc drive, and Windows should open its installer application. If not, double-click the CD in the Computer window, find the installer, and double-click to launch it. Simply follow the prompts to install the driver.

If you opt to download a scanner driver, you must extract the installer from the downloaded file, if your browser or some other utility doesn't handle that task automatically. Again, double-click to launch the scanner driver installer file and follow the prompts to complete installation.

The Mac Way

Installing drivers of any kind is a similar task on the Mac, so if these steps seem familiar after reading the previous chapter on printer installation, they should.

If you determine to install the scanner driver using the CD that was in the box:

1. Insert the CD into your Mac's optical drive.

2. The installer may begin automatically, if the scanner manufacturer created it to do so. If not, open the CD by double-clicking its icon on the desktop or by selecting it in a Finder window. You should see an installer file, which you must double-click to launch. If you can't find the installer file, contact the manufacturer's tech support or (first) check out the documentation that came with the scanner.
3. Go step-by-step through the installer to complete the scanner driver installation. You will be prompted to enter your user name and password at some point for security reasons; this is the same user name and password that you use to log in to your user account.

As I stated earlier, downloading the driver from the manufacturer's website is the safest thing to do.

1. Open a web browser and navigate to the website of the scanner manufacturer. Once there, you will need to find the driver files for your particular scanner model and download them. Typically, driver files are compressed disk images whose filenames end with a .dmg extension (see an example in Figure 13.1), but sometimes a manufacturer may opt to use the .zip format.
2. When the download finishes, the file should automatically decompress if you are using Safari. If you used a different web browser (like Firefox or Opera) or if Safari doesn't decompress the file on its own, find the file on your Mac and double-click its icon to decompress it. A window containing the installer package should open for you.
3. Double-click the installer package and follow the prompts (similar to those in Figure 13.2) to install the driver.

Figure 13.1: *Driver files you download from the web are typically disk images.*

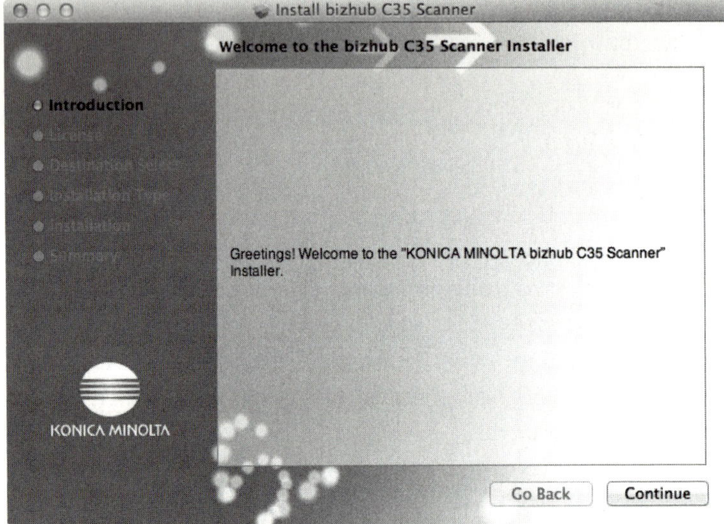

Figure 13.2: *Follow the installer's prompts to install your scanner driver.*

The scanner driver is now installed, so now you need to learn how to use your scanner.

Scanning Documents

A scanner isn't much good to you unless you actually use it to scan documents, pictures, and whatever else might strike your fancy. Scanning is usually pretty straightforward, but it can get a bit complicated if the job calls for it. For example, scanning a text document may require minimal settings changes, while scanning a photo may require extensive adjustments to color, contrast, resolution, and more settings. Most scanner manufacturers offer many settings that you can customize to fit your needs, but if you don't understand the driver software and its functionality, it can be quite daunting at times. You can never go wrong by reading the documentation that comes with your scanner!

The Windows Way

Windows Fax and Scan is a nifty tool for scanning documents and pictures to your PC, and it comes as part of the operating system.

Click the **Start** menu and select **Windows Fax and Scan** from the All Programs menu. Click the **New Scan** button in the toolbar (upper-left corner), choose a profile, and click **Preview** to get a snapshot of what your final scan will look like. Finally, click **Scan** to begin scanning the item to your PC.

There's more to it than just this little bit, such as cropping images and saving them to a folder, but you already know all that, right?

The Mac Way

Windows comes with Windows Fax and Scan as its default scanning app, and Mac OS X has a great little scanning gem of its own: Image Capture. Image Capture is a great tool for importing documents and images from scanners, and is also used for importing pictures from a digital camera or iPhone.

Let's make sure your scanner is able to get along with Image Capture before getting into scanning.

1. Before diving into Image Capture, go ahead and connect your scanner to one of your Mac's USB or FireWire ports.
2. Go to the Applications folder on your Mac to find Image Capture, and then double-click its icon to open it.
3. If you've correctly installed the scanner driver software, the scanner should automatically appear in Image Capture's window on the left-hand side under Devices, as shown in Figure 13.3.

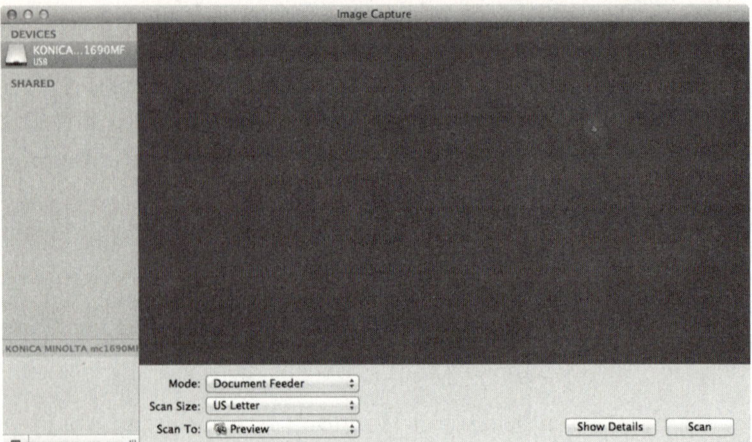

Figure 13.3: *If the driver is installed correctly, your scanner will appear in Image Capture.*

If the scanner doesn't show up in Image Capture, try the following:

- Check your connections for the USB cable at both the scanner and the Mac.
- Double-check that the scanner is turned on.
- Log out of your user account and log back in, and then reopen Image Capture.
- Try using a different USB cable.
- If you are connecting using a USB hub, disconnect from the hub and connect straight to your Mac.
- Try reinstalling the driver software.
- Restart your Mac.
- Should the other suggestions fail, it's time to call the scanner manufacturer's tech support. Call them before deciding to go to Apple tech support.

If all is right with the world and your scanner is showing up in Image Capture, it's time to get busy scanning.

To perform a basic scan with Image Capture:

1. Place the item you want to scan onto your scanner's flatbed or document feeder.
2. Select the mode of scanning: flatbed or document feeder.
3. Choose the size of your scan using the Scan Size menu.
4. Decide on a location or app to scan to using the Scan To pop-up.
5. Click **Scan** to begin the Scan.
6. The completed scan appears in the Image Capture window and in the Scan Results window, as shown in Figure 13.4. Click the document in the Scan Results window to view it in Preview, or click the magnifying glass to the right of the file name to open a Finder window to the file's location.

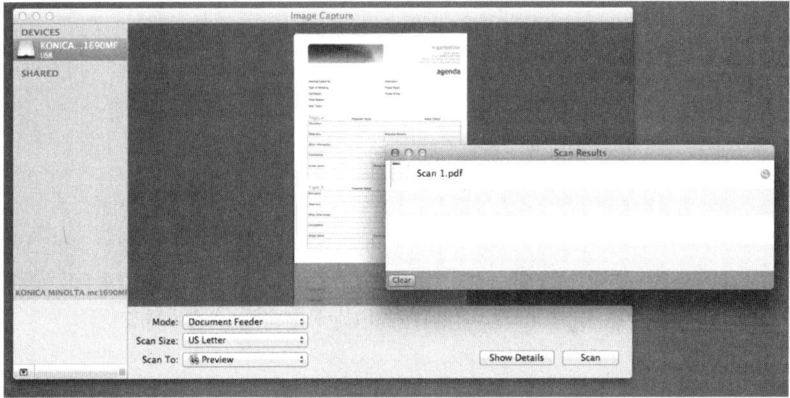

Figure 13.4: *The completed scan appears in the Scan Results window.*

That about sums up basic scanning, but you probably noticed the Show Details button at the bottom of the scan window. The Show Details button will provide you with more options for scanning your documents, assuming your scanner manufacturer has provided them with the driver software you installed.

Use the advanced scanning options supplied by your scanner manufacturer.

1. Place the item you want to scan onto your scanner's flatbed or document feeder.
2. Click the **Show Details** button and you will see more scanning options than you can throw a stick at (Figure 13.5).
3. Make whatever settings changes you need, depending on the type of scan job you want to perform. I can't be much help here, since I don't know what options you may have available for your scanner. Now would be a good time to consult your scanner's documentation or ask the scanner's tech support team.
4. Click the **Scan** button to begin the scan. Apple is kind enough to give you a progress bar so that you can see about how long your scan will take, as illustrated in Figure 13.6.
5. The completed scan appears in the window and can be found in the location you specified on your Mac.

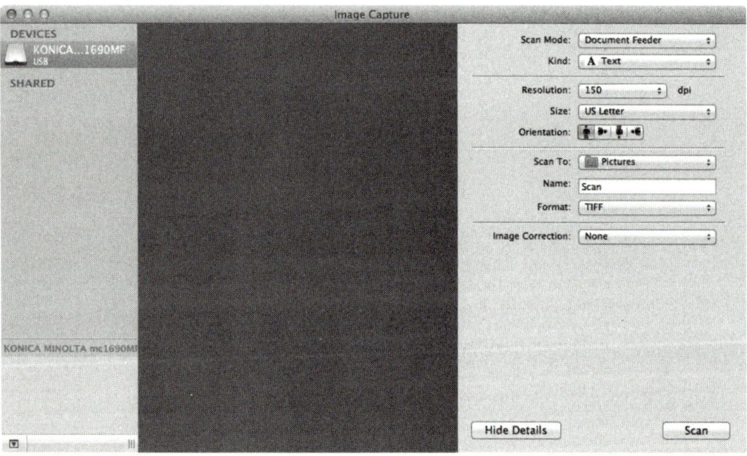

Figure 13.5: *Clicking the* ***Show Details*** *button reveals advanced scanning options, if provided by the scanner manufacturer.*

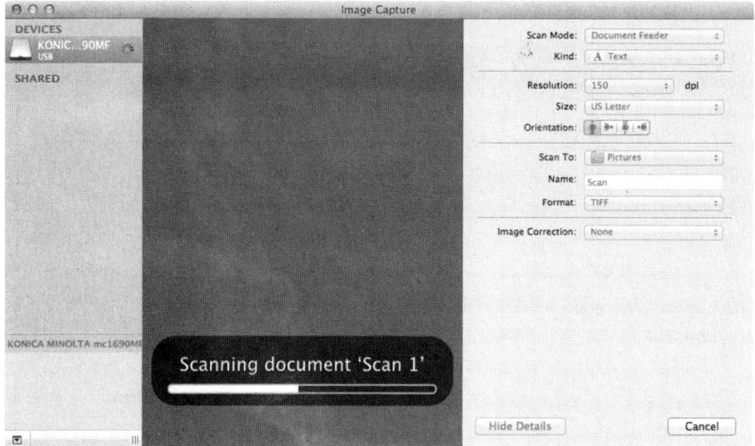

Figure 13.6: *A progress bar lets you know approximately how long your scan will take.*

You can also import items directly into Preview instead of Image Capture, if you prefer:

1. Open Preview.
2. Click the **File** menu, go to **Import from Scanner**, and select the name of your scanner.
3. You'll notice the scanning interface looks almost identical to Image Capture (Figure 13.7). Configure the scanning options to your liking and click **Scan**.
4. Select a destination on your Mac for the file you are about to scan and click the **Choose Destination** button.
5. The completed scan will open into Preview, where you can do with it what you like, as shown in Figure 13.8.

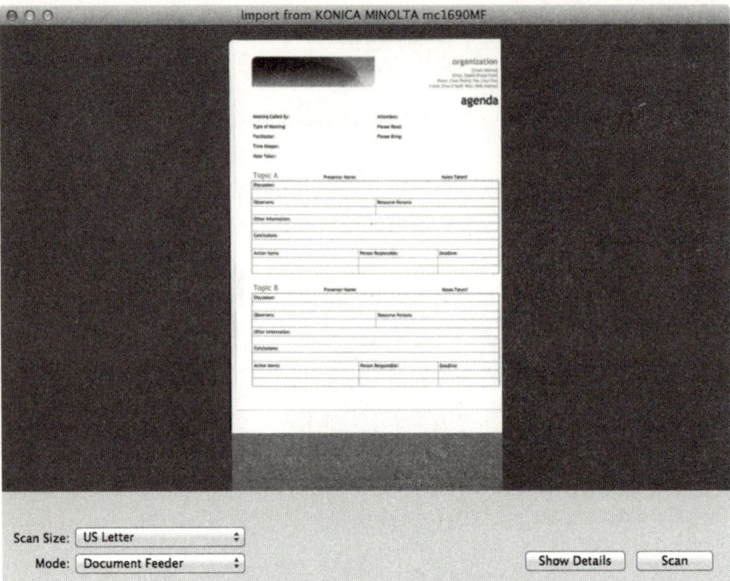

Figure 13.7: *You can scan from within the Preview app, too.*

Figure 13.8: *Your scan will open directly into Preview.*

Sharing Your Scanner

Who wants to buy a scanner for every computer in your home or office? Not me. One scanner is usually enough to do the trick, especially if you are a nice person and your parents taught you to share. Sharing is definitely the way to go since scanners aren't typically used nearly as often as other devices, such as printers.

The Windows Way

Short answer: You can't on Windows.

Slightly longer answer: Windows does not support sharing for locally attached (USB) scanners out of the box. There are some third-party applications that can accommodate this task for you, but Windows won't do so on its own.

The Mac Way

Mac OS X has scanner sharing built right in, my friend! Pull up a seat and see how it's done.

Sharing your USB-connected scanner on a Mac is simple:

1. Open the Sharing preferences pane found in the Internet & Wireless section of the System Preferences.
2. Check the box next to **Scanner Sharing** to turn scanner sharing on.
3. Check the box next to the scanner you want to share with other users, as shown in Figure 13.9.

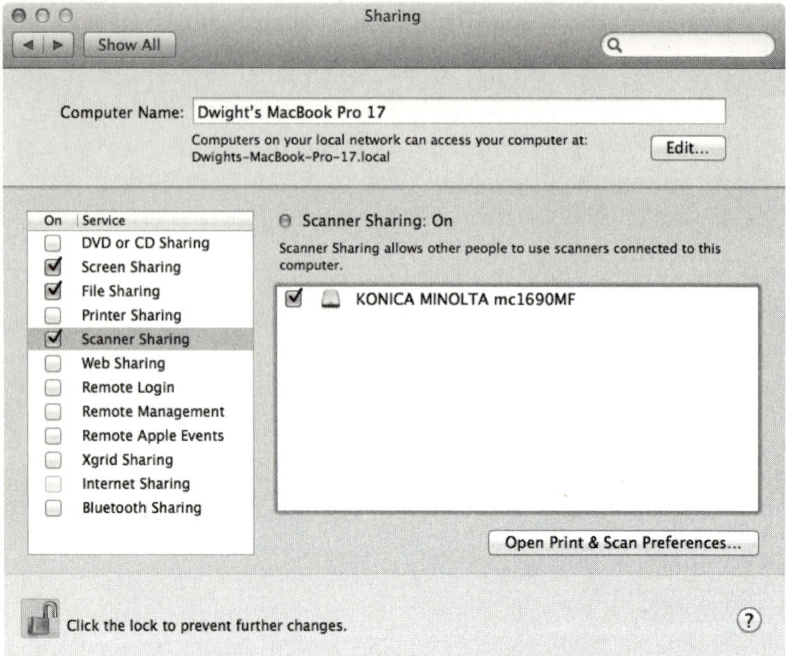

Figure 13.9: *Share your scanner with other folks on your network.*

Other Mac users can access your shared scanner by opening their Image Capture apps and selecting your scanner, which should appear under the Shared heading on the left side of the window.

Being Productive with Documents

We all know computers are great for fun and organizing, but we also know there's another use for computers: the four-letter "w" word. That's right—work.

Work is what computers were meant for in the first place, contrary to the rumor they were invented to play *Space Invaders.* Don't be fooled by the Mac's attractive interface; it's just as capable of spreadsheet heavy lifting as it is of creating vector graphics.

Basic Word Processing Tools

What most folks think of as "work" on their computer usually involves some level of word processing. In terms of importance, the ability to write letters and reports is right up there with the ability to get email for many users.

Neither Windows nor Mac OS X comes loaded with a full-bore, top-of-the-line word processor, but there are third-party alternatives galore for both platforms. However, both do come with adequate basic word processors.

The Windows Way

If you've used Windows for more than a total of three minutes, you are certainly familiar with the venerable Notepad. Notepad is about as basic a word processor as it gets. There are not a whole lot of bells and whistles—for example, you can change fonts, but you can't change the color of your text—but if all you need to do is enter or edit text, you're good to go.

WordPad also comes with most Windows installations, and it offers a bit more punch than Notepad. You can do basic tasks such as changing colors of text or adding pictures to your documents.

The Mac Way

TextEdit is the Mac OS X equivalent of WordPad, and has been a part of Mac OS X since the earliest days. TextEdit isn't the equivalent of Microsoft Word or Apple's Pages, but it is a great tool if your main objective is entering and editing text.

Open TextEdit by going to the Applications folder and double-clicking its icon. TextEdit will automatically open a blank document and patiently await your input, as shown in Figure 14.1.

Figure 14.1: *TextEdit will open a new blank document the first time you launch it.*

When it comes to working with TextEdit, it's always my recommendation for new users to set its preferences before beginning to work. There may be some default behaviors in TextEdit that you would prefer be changed. To see TextEdit's preferences (Figure 14.2), select **Preferences** from the TextEdit menu.

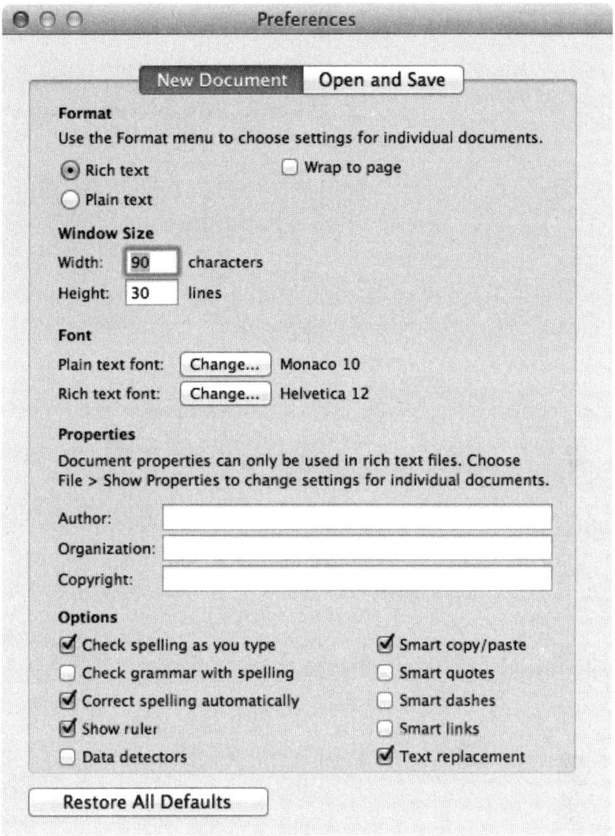

Figure 14.2: *Adjust TextEdit's preferences to suit your work style.*

Table 14.1 explains the options available under the New Document tab.

Table 14.1 New Document Preferences

Option	Description
Format	Use rich text (RTF) or plain text (txt) as your default format (the format can be changed for individual documents at any time).
Wrap to page	Wraps text to document margins instead of window margins.
Window Size	Sets the default window size.
Font	Selects the default font for plain text or rich text documents.
Properties (only pertains to RTF docs)	Enter author, organization, and copyright information if necessary.
Check spelling as you type and Check grammar with spelling	Enables automatic checking of spelling and grammar.
Correct spelling automatically	Enables automatic spelling correction.
Show ruler	Places a ruler at the top of the window, which helps with margins and text placement.
Data detectors	Recognizes dates, locations, contacts, and times, which can be used to create iCal events, Address Book contacts, and the like.
Smart copy/paste	Adds spaces when text is added or deleted, if necessary.
Smart quotes	Applies curly quote marks instead of straight quotes.

Smart dashes	Substitutes an em dash (—) when you type double hyphens (--).
Smart links	Converts internet addresses you type into web links.
Text replacement	Flags possibly misspelled words (such as "aniwhere") and automatically replaces them with the perceived correct spelling ("anywhere").
Restore All Defaults	Sets all preferences back to TextEdit's original defaults.

Table 14.2 details options in the Open and Save tab.

Table 14.2 Open and Save Preferences

Option	Description
Ignore rich text commands in HTML and RTF files	Opens HTML and RTF files as plain text.
Add ".txt" extension to plain text files	Adds the .txt extension to the end of plain text files automatically.
Plain Text File Encoding	Determines a text encoding to use by default when working with plain text files. Stay with Automatic unless you have reason to change this.
HTML Saving Options	Determines the default document type, styling, and encoding to use when saving documents as HTML files.
Preserve white space	Prevents blank areas in a document from being lost during formatting.
Restore All Defaults	Sets all preferences back to TextEdit's original defaults.

Now that we've gotten your preferences ironed out, you can begin typing in the new document TextEdit offered when you first opened it. You could also open an existing document by double-clicking it or by dragging its icon to the TextEdit icon in the Dock.

To save a new or edited document:

1. Press **⌘-S** to open the Save window.
2. If this is a new document or you want to save an edited document under a new name, enter a name in the Save As field.
3. Browse to the location you want to save the document.
4. Click **Save**.

Did you notice the File Format pop-up at the bottom of the Save As window (Figure 14.3)? TextEdit's default file format is rich text format, which most word processors can open, but you should be aware of the other options, which Table 14.3 explains.

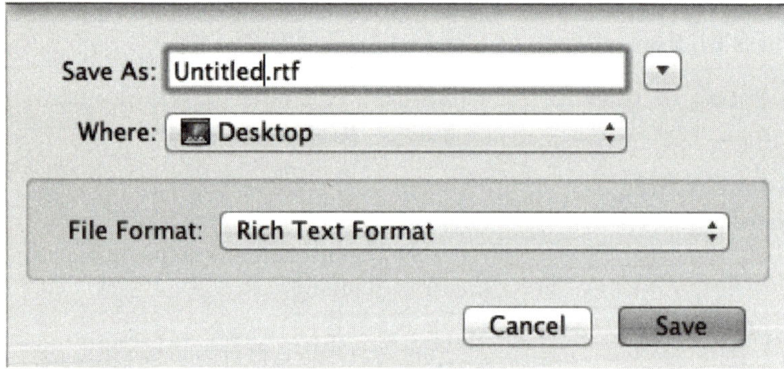

Figure 14.3: *The File Format pop-up menu affords many different format options.*

Table 14.3 File Formats Supported by TextEdit

Format	Description
Rich Text Format with Attachments (RTFD)	This is for RTF documents that include graphics.
Web Page (.html)	Allows you to create or edit web pages within TextEdit.
Web Archive	This is the format Safari uses to save web pages.
OpenDocument Text (.odt)	This format is native to the OpenOffice.org office suite.
Word 2007 Format (.docx)	Microsoft's default format for its newest versions of Word.
Word 2003 Format (.xml)	Save as an XML (Extensible Markup Language) file that's used for web pages.
Word 97 Format (.doc)	Microsoft's default format for Word documents prior to Word 2007.
Plain Text	Creates a plain text document with no graphic formatting.

Should you feel like gussying up a document, the first items to work on would be your text. Mac OS X is loaded with a wide variety of fonts, so you won't have much trouble finding a good one.

To change text settings within a document:

1. Select text you want to change by clicking-and-dragging the mouse over it, or select all the text in the document by pressing **⌘-A**.
2. Hold your mouse pointer over **Font** in the Format menu to perform actions such as changing the font size, underlining words, changing the text's color, and more.
3. Hold your mouse pointer over **Text** in the Format menu to perform actions such as aligning text, changing the spacing widths between lines, creating tables from text, and more.

The Font and Text items under the Format menu are good for quick changes, but you can get a little more detailed in your tinkering by using the Fonts window, seen in Figure 14.4, which you can open by pressing **⌘-T**.

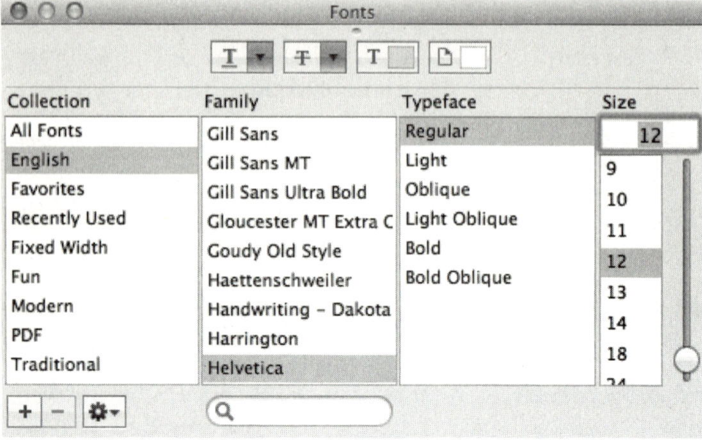

Figure 14.4: *You can make many adjustments to your fonts using the Fonts window.*

Browse the font selection in the Fonts window to find the perfect look and feel for your text. Use the **Action** button (looks like a gear) at the bottom of the window to really fine-tune your text by changing typography options and viewing character sets.

The effects items at the top of the Fonts window allow you to do the following:

- The Text Underline and Text Strikethrough buttons allow you to use a single or double line for the underline or strikethrough, as well as change line color.
- Text Color lets you change the color of the text.
- Document Color lets you change the background color of your document.

Working with Microsoft Office Documents

The Microsoft suite of production tools known as Office is perhaps the most popular set of software in the world. Comprised of Word for word processing, Excel for spreadsheets, PowerPoint for presentations, and Outlook for email and calendaring, Microsoft Office is pervasive in most offices (both large and small). Many homes own copies of Office, both for home businesses and students.

Needless to say, if you do any kind of work with your computer, you've probably used one of the Office suite products at some point. Having the ability to still work with documents of these types is imperative to some who are contemplating a change in OS platforms.

The Windows Way

It doesn't get much simpler than this: to work with Microsoft Office documents, get a copy of Microsoft Office.

Of course, that's not your only option, as there are a few quality third-party offerings on the market that are compatible with the file formats used by Microsoft Office apps. However, to guarantee compatibility, getting a copy of Office is the way to go.

The Mac Way

This does sometimes come as a surprise to many coming over to the Mac from Windows, but Microsoft offers a Mac version of the Office suite, complete with its four main products: Word, Excel, PowerPoint, and Outlook. I have to recommend this as your first approach to working with Office documents, as, once again, the best way to guarantee compatibility is to use the same product as the folks who are sending the documents to you.

Don't believe me that there's actually a version of Office for Mac? Well, just check out Figure 14.5 to see a screenshot of my Mac running all four apps (you can also see their icons in my Dock).

And if that doesn't convince you, please head on over to Microsoft's own website to check things out for yourself: www.microsoft.com/mac. You can even download a free 30-day trial to see how you like it.

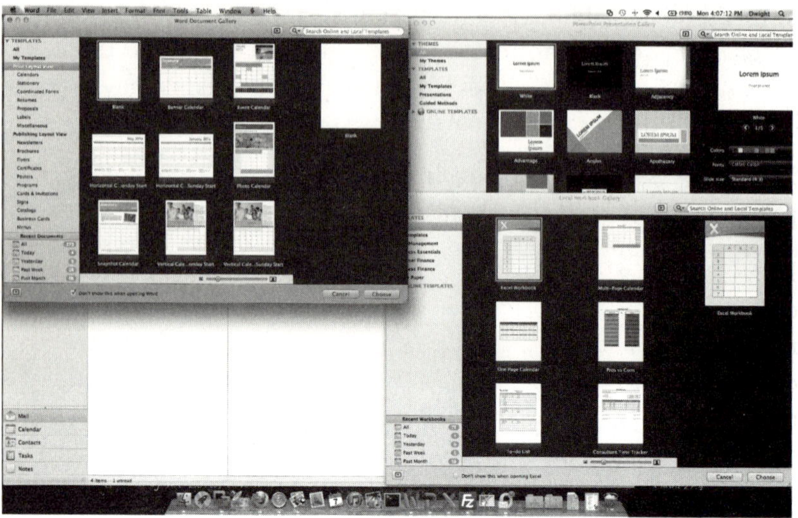

Figure 14.5: *Word, Excel, PowerPoint, and Outlook for Mac. That's right: I said Mac!*

Now, I'm certain there are quite a number of you who are pulling your hair out right now because one of the main reasons you went to the Mac in the first place was to escape the grasp of Microsoft, and here I am telling you to go back to them. As a die-hard Mac user, I can vouch for the fact that Microsoft Office for Mac is a darned good product. Having said that, you will be happy to know that there are alternatives.

The first alternative would be Apple's own suite of productivity software: iWork. iWork contains Pages (word processing), Numbers (spreadsheets), and Keynote (presentations); Mail and iCal are already parts of Mac OS X, so there is no bundled equivalent to Outlook.

If you simply want a word processing tool without the worries of Word compatibility, I would heartily recommend Pages over Word for its sheer simplicity. It is a fantastic word processing tool. Even if Word compatibility is a concern, I can attest to the fact that I've not run into a standard Word document yet that Pages doesn't open and edit. That's not to say that some such Word document doesn't exist—it's just that I personally have not run into it. However, I would issue a caution if you use macros in your Word documents; Pages won't be able to provide much help there, so Word might be your only option.

The same can be said of Numbers and Keynote. Both can work with Excel and PowerPoint documents respectively, and can export documents into those formats, but Excel macros will cause problems in Numbers, as will PowerPoint macros with Keynote.

Be aware that when Pages, Numbers, and Keynote open Office documents, said documents are converted to iWork formats. If you need an Office version of the edited document, you would need to export the document from the particular iWork format (depending on which iWork app you're working with) back to the appropriate Office document format.

Please check out iWork at www.apple.com/iwork. Despite the caveats regarding Office macros, the iWork suite is a really top-notch set of tools that make this kind of work seem easier than it should. As with Office, you can download a free 30-day trial, so go ahead and give both suites a go so that you can compare them yourself.

Is There a Free Office Alternative?

Yes! There are several, as a matter of fact, but your best bet is the suite of free productivity tools from OpenOffice.org. Writer, Calc, and Impress are the respective equivalents of Word, Excel, and PowerPoint, and they can open, edit, and save to the native formats of the latter. Check it out at www.openoffice.org.

Working with PDF Files

PDF (Portable Document Format) files are every bit as important these days as any other file format. PDFs can be exchanged with anyone using any operating system, and they are great ways of passing graphics-rich information along in small files (small in terms of bytes, that is). PDFs are used these days for anything from tax return documents to entire books, and everything in between.

The Windows Way

Windows does not natively support PDF files, which is a downer, but you can easily go to Adobe's website and download their free Adobe Reader software, which allows you to open and print PDFs. However, if you want to edit a PDF, you will need Adobe's Acrobat Pro software, which will set your bank account back a decent sum. There are alternative PDF readers and editors for Windows as well, but the Adobe products tend to do the best job, in my opinion.

The Mac Way

Mac OS X has PDF technology built right into it. As a matter of fact, much of what you see rendered on your Mac's screen is some form of PDF. This makes working with PDFs easy right out of the gate, and there's no need to download any third-party software to read, print, or create PDFs (you will still need third-party software if you need to edit them, however).

Preview is an application that comes with Mac OS X, and it is the default for opening and annotating PDF files. To open Preview, double-click its icon in the Applications folder or double-click a PDF file.

Figure 14.6 shows Preview with an open PDF file, and gives you the layout of its interface.

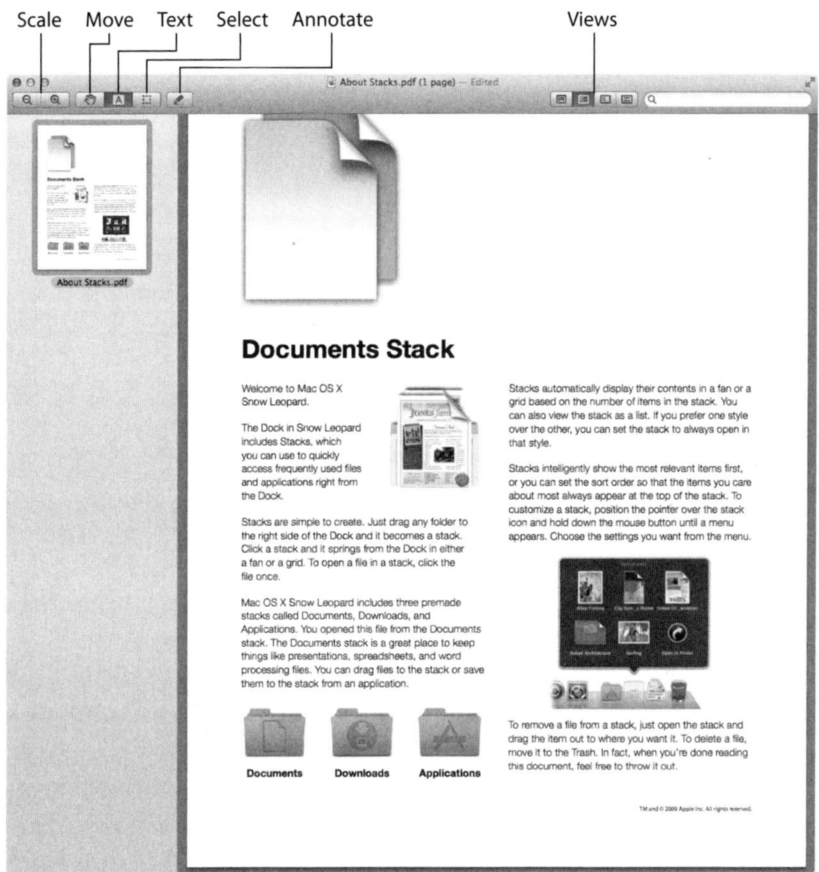

Figure 14.6: *Preview is a great tool for viewing, annotating, and printing PDFs.*

The scale buttons allow you to zoom in or out of the pages in your PDF, and the Views buttons help to show the pages of a PDF in the sidebar or as a contact sheet.

You can use the Move button to move the PDF around in the window, but its best use (in my opinion) is for rearranging the page order of a PDF, as shown in Figure 14.7. Simply click-and-drag a page to the order you want it to be in the document, and drop it in place. Save the document by pressing **⌘-S**.

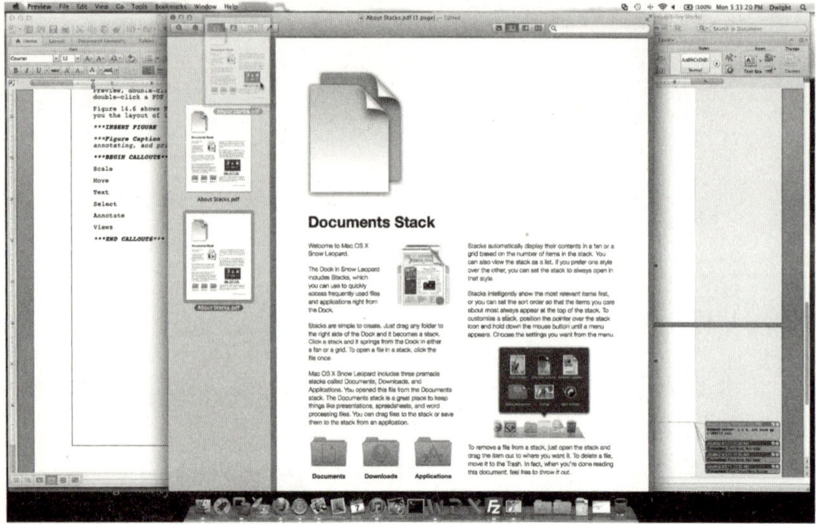

Figure 14.7: *Use the Move tool to rearrange pages within a PDF.*

Click the **Text** button so that you can select and copy text from a PDF, and use **Select** to click-and-drag over an area in a PDF; a selection box will appear in the PDF. Press **⌘-C** to copy the selected portion of the PDF, and then press **⌘-N** to create a new PDF using the selection from the original.

Click the **Annotate** button to make the Annotations bar visible under the toolbar (Figure 14.8).

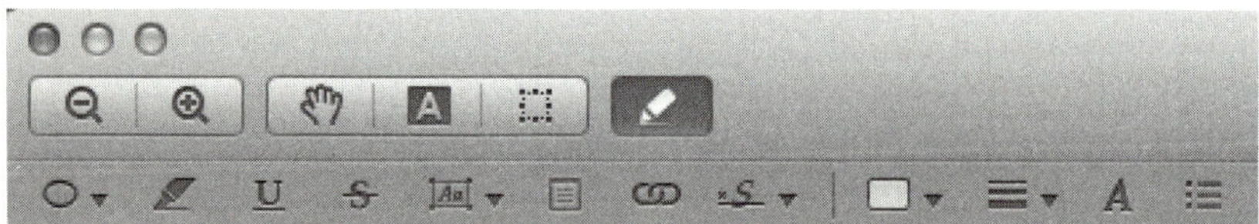

Figure 14.8: *Open the Annotations bar by clicking the* ***Annotate*** *button (looks like a pencil) in the toolbar.*

Use the tools in the Annotations bar to add elements to a PDF, such as comments, underline or strikethrough text, and your own text or notes, as well as a few more tricks. Figure 14.9 shows you some examples of annotations.

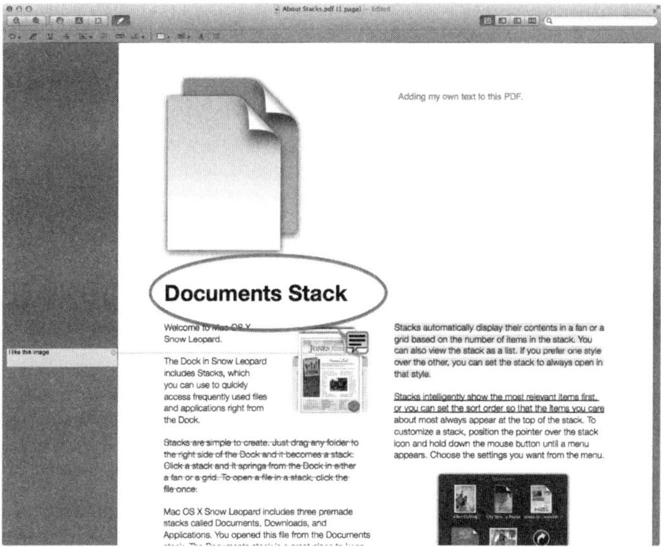

Figure 14.9: *The Annotations bar allows you to add comments and other items to a PDF.*

You can do all sorts of neat things with PDFs, but how about learning how to create your own? You don't need the third-party apps to do so, since Preview is built into Mac OS X. You can convert anything that you view on your screen into a PDF, including documents from any application. Do you have a Word document that you want to send out, but it's chock-full of graphics and its size is bloated? Convert it into a PDF and problem solved!

Here's how to convert documents into PDFs:

1. Open a document in any application you like.
2. Press **⌘-P**, or choose **Print** from the File menu, to open the Print dialog.
3. Click the **PDF** button in the lower-left corner of the Print dialog and select **Save As PDF** from the menu.
4. In the Save window (Figure 14.10), give the PDF a name, pick a place to save it on your hard drive, and enter any other information you deem pertinent in the fields provided.

5. Should you feel the need to lock down the PDF, click the **Security Options** button. The options given are to require passwords to open the PDF; to copy text, images, and other items from it; or to even print it. Click **OK** when done setting your options.
6. Click **Save**.

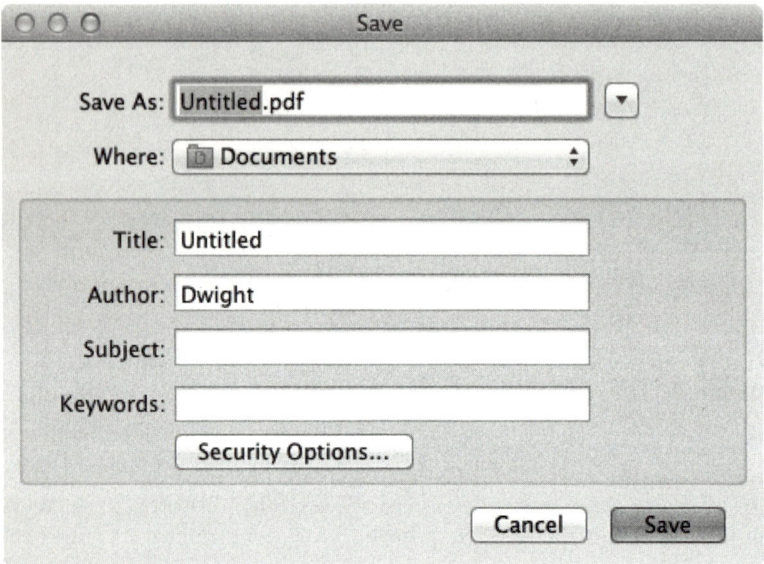

Figure 14.10: *Give your document a name and save it as a PDF.*

When it comes to PDFs, Preview is a great tool, but should you feel yourself missing Adobe's Reader app, don't fret; they offer it for the Mac, too.

Managing Your System

Managing your system (i.e., making proper configurations and maintaining functionality) is one of the most important and potentially time-consuming tasks a computer user experiences. Keeping up-to-date with the latest software, protecting your computer from computer-nerd hooligans who are up to no good, and backing up your important files are but a few of the tasks you must undertake to properly manage your computer's operating system and files. In this chapter, I will show you how to do those things, and more, on your Mac.

Viewing System Information

It's always a good idea to know the things you own, whether they be automobiles, homes, boats, and, yes, computers. Understanding the size of your car's engine is often helpful when buying parts for it; similarly, knowing the types of rewritable media your computer supports will be good information when you're out buying blank CDs and DVDs. Knowing basic information about your computer is good, but knowing how to acquire even more detailed information is better, and that's what I'll cover in this section of the chapter.

The Windows Way

Right-click on the **Computer** (or My Computer) icon that you see on your desktop or in the Start menu, and select **Properties**; you'll get a host of good information about what operating system version you're running, how much memory you have installed, and the like. But if you really want details, you'll want to pay a visit to the Device Manager.

The Mac Way

A quick and easy way to find basic information about your computer is to click the **Apple** menu in the upper-left corner of your Mac's screen and select **About This Mac**. The About This Mac window (shown in Figure 15.1) shows you the version of Mac OS X you are running, as well as the type of processor and amount of memory you have installed.

Figure 15.1: *The About This Mac window gives you the OS version you are running, as well as processor and memory information.*

While this is a nice start, it gets even better.

Click the **More Info** button in the About This Mac window to open System Information, which affords you even more insight into your Mac's underpinnings. Let's check out the various tabs in System Information:

- The Overview tab (Figure 15.2) gives you a bit more information than the standard About This Mac window. From here you can also see a System Report (more on that in just a bit) and whether there are any updates available.

Figure 15.2: *The Overview tab of System Information gives you a bit more info about your Mac.*

- Displays shows you detailed information about the displays you are currently using with your Mac. You can click the **Displays Preferences** button to make adjustments to your display's settings.
- Storage details the amount of free space on your hard drive, as well as how the rest of the space is being utilized (Figure 15.3). You can also see what disc formats your Mac can write to, as well as open the Disk Utility with the click of a button.

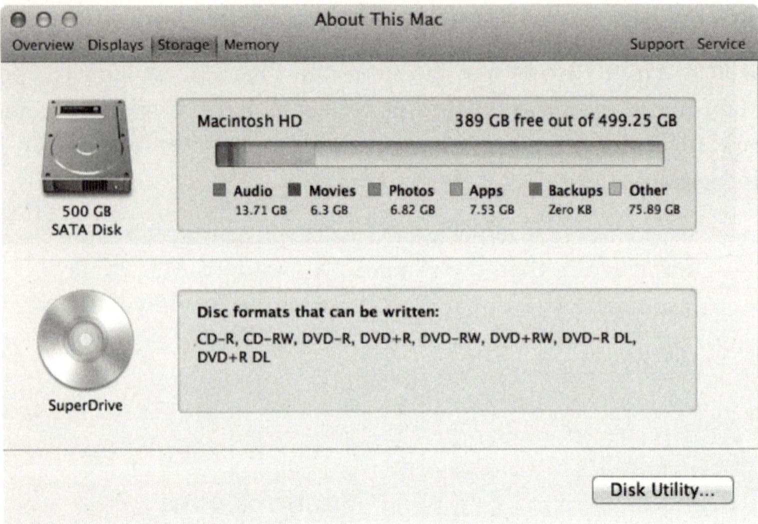

Figure 15.3: *The Storage tab lets you see how your hard drive space is allocated and what rewritable disc formats your Mac supports.*

- The Memory tab lets you quickly see how much RAM you have installed in your Mac, as well as how many memory slots your Mac supports.
- The Support tab offers you links to several support topics for your particular Mac model.
- The Service tab offers links that allow you to check the service and support coverage status, as well as any repair options that might be available. You can also learn more about the AppleCare Protection Plan.

Up to this point you've seen good information and even better information, and now it's time to see the best information. I say the best because it is so much more detailed than the good and better options, and for a supergeek like me … well, I digress.

To see the most detailed information possible about your Mac, go back to the Overview tab in the System Information utility and click the **System Report** button. The system report, an example of which can be seen in Figure 15.4, gives you a thorough breakdown of your

Mac's hardware components, your network vitals, and the software that you have installed.

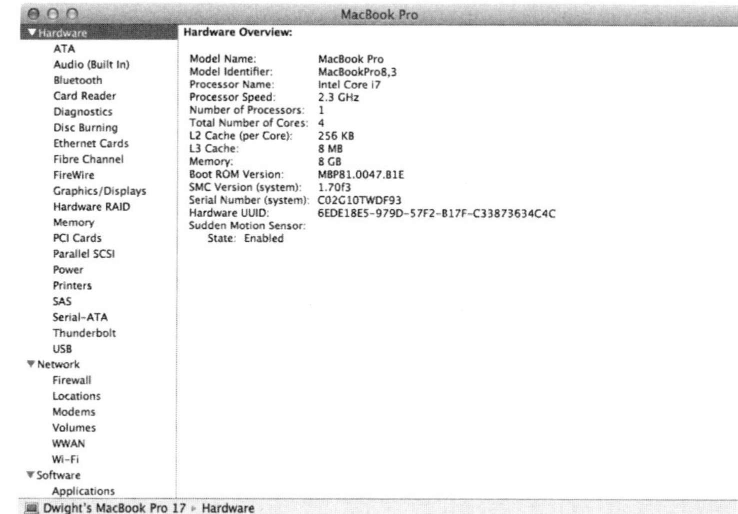

Figure 15.4: *The system report is the Holy Grail of information about your Mac.*

Click on one of the three main topics (Hardware, Network, or Software) in the left pane to see lots of detailed information about each, or click the subtopics to drill even deeper into your Mac's inner machinations.

Managing Color Profiles

Color management is a part of every operating system that strives to make sure that color is accurately represented across devices. Color profiles are basically descriptions of how a device, such as a computer display or a laser printer, renders color. Your computer uses these profiles to help most closely match the colors you see on your monitor to the output you might get from a device such as a printer. Color profiles are also important to devices such as cameras or printing presses. Some readers may never need to touch a profile, but for others (such as photographers or graphic designers) this is critical info.

 The Windows Way

Windows handles color profiles through the Color Management control panel. From there you can view the profiles that are installed, as well as install new profiles. Color profiles can be assigned to individual devices, and you can also change the systemwide color defaults from the Advanced tab.

 The Mac Way

Mac OS X comes with a nifty app called ColorSync Utility, which is your one-stop shop for color management on your Mac. ColorSync can do all that Windows' Color Management control panel can do, plus a little more, as you'll see.

ColorSync Utility can be found in the Applications/Utilities directory; double-click to launch it. Once you've got ColorSync Utility open, notice the five tabs (some may call them buttons) in the toolbar; here's a quick rundown:

- Profile First Aid allows you to scan your Mac's color profiles to see if any do not properly conform to the standards set by the International Color Consortium (ICC). If a profile does not meet these standards, ColorSync Utility attempts to repair the profile for you. Click **Verify** to run a check of your profiles (Figure 15.5), and click **Repair** if any errors are found.
- Profiles allows you to see each of the color profiles installed for systemwide use. Select a category, such as System or User, by clicking the gray triangle to its left and click a profile to see its information. ColorSync Utility even gives you a three-dimensional graph of the profile's color gamut, which you can rotate by clicking-and-dragging with your mouse or trackpad (Figure 15.6).
- The Devices tab allows you to assign a color profile to an individual device, such as a scanner or printer. Most manufacturers of these kinds of devices provide color profiles to help you accurately match color.

Figure 15.5: *Check your color profiles to make sure they meet correct ICC standards.*

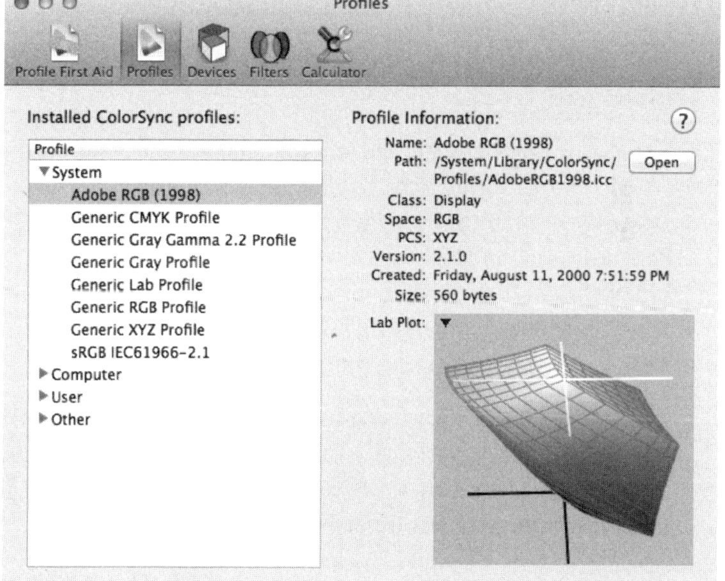

Figure 15.6: *Click-and-drag the 3D graph of a profile's color gamut.*

- The Filters tab lets you modify, create, or delete Quartz filters. A Quartz filter is a set of color rendering rules that perform several color management steps in one fell swoop when applied to a document or image.
- The Calculator helps you convert the values from one color space into a different color space.

Setting Parental Controls

For kids, the computer can have a mind-numbing effect, much like a television. Also like TV, the computer can be used for good, and also for bad. Giving parents the ability to control what their kids are viewing or which applications they are using is a huge deal, which any parent worth their salt will appreciate immensely (sorry, but I'm not pulling any punches when it comes to protecting kids from the dangers lurking on the internet).

The Windows Way

Windows has a very good set of tools for helping parents monitor and restrict their child's computer time and use. You can set up times for your children to use the computer, restrict game play, and even limit them to using only certain applications. However, there are some features that are sadly lacking, such as the ability to allow only certain websites to be accessed and for parents to be alerted when their child tries to do something he or she isn't supposed to do.

The Mac Way

Mac OS X comes with a surprisingly robust set of parental controls that can really ease the mind of a mom or dad. The Parental Controls preferences pane allows you to do quite a bit more than Windows' Parental Controls control panel, as you're about to see.

Mac OS X applies parental controls to standard user accounts; administrator accounts cannot be set with parental controls.

To set up a user account for parental control:

1. Open System Preferences by clicking its icon in the Dock or selecting **System Preferences** from the Apple menu.
2. Select **Users & Groups** from the System section of the System Preferences window.
3. Select the user account you want to apply parental controls to and check the box next to **Enable parental controls** (as shown in Figure 15.7).

Figure 15.7: *Select a user account to apply parental controls to.*

Now that you have an account set up to be under parental control, it's time to configure the settings for it.

If you are still in the Users & Groups preferences pane, select the user account under parental control and click the **Open Parental Controls** button. Otherwise, open System Preferences and select **Parental Controls** in the System section. Click on the user account in the pane to the left to see the parental control options, as shown in Figure 15.8.

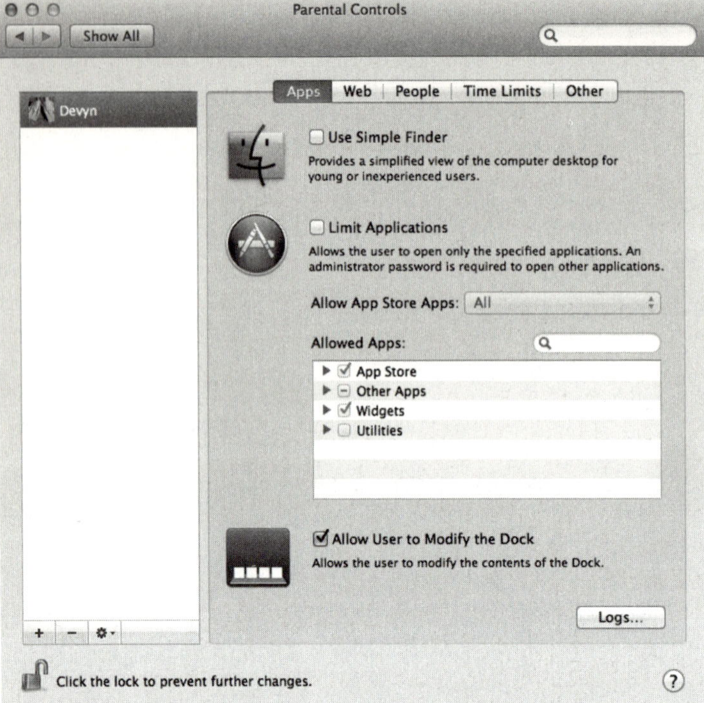

Figure 15.8: *Click an account to apply parental controls to.*

The Apps tab in Parental Controls helps you with the following:

- Check the **Use Simple Finder** box to give the user a (much) more simplified desktop. Basically, what they can't see they can't break, so Simple Finder hides much of the interface.
- Limit Applications lets you choose which apps your child can use.
- Check the **Allow User to Modify the Dock** option to let users make whatever changes they want (within the other defined rules) to their Dock.
- The Logs button is Mac OS X's version of a built-in tattletale. Click **Logs** to see what websites have been visited or blocked, what applications were used, and who the user of the account has been chatting (instant messaging) with (Figure 15.9). The Logs button can be accessed from the Apps tab, as well as the Web and People tabs.

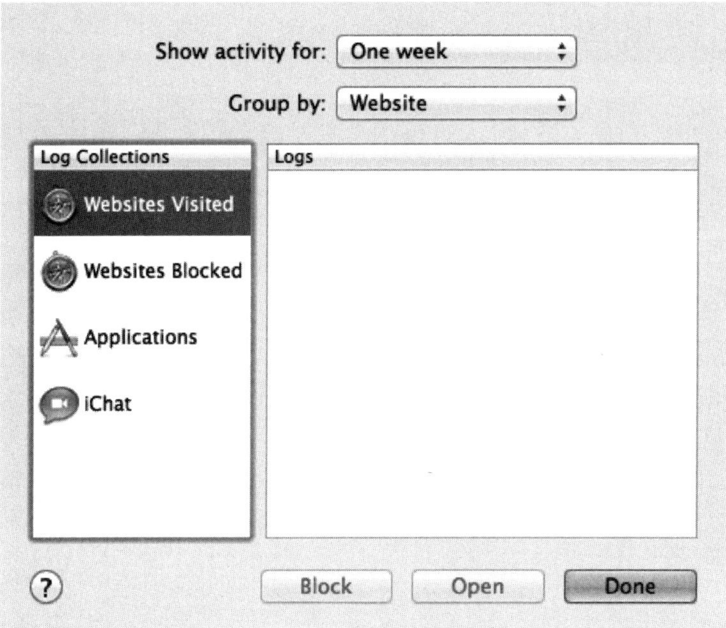

Figure 15.9: *Logs will show you what the user of the controlled account has been up to.*

The Web tab (Figure 15.10) is really good for limiting access to specific websites in the following ways:

- You can allow unrestricted access to websites (bad idea; if you select this option and you're trying to invoke parental controls, please call me so that I can hopefully change your mind).
- Have Parental Controls try to block access to adult websites automatically (good idea, assuming a site has identified itself as "adult").
- Click the **Customize** button to provide lists of approved and banned websites (better idea).
- Strictly allow access to only a certain list of websites *(ding, ding, ding!)*.

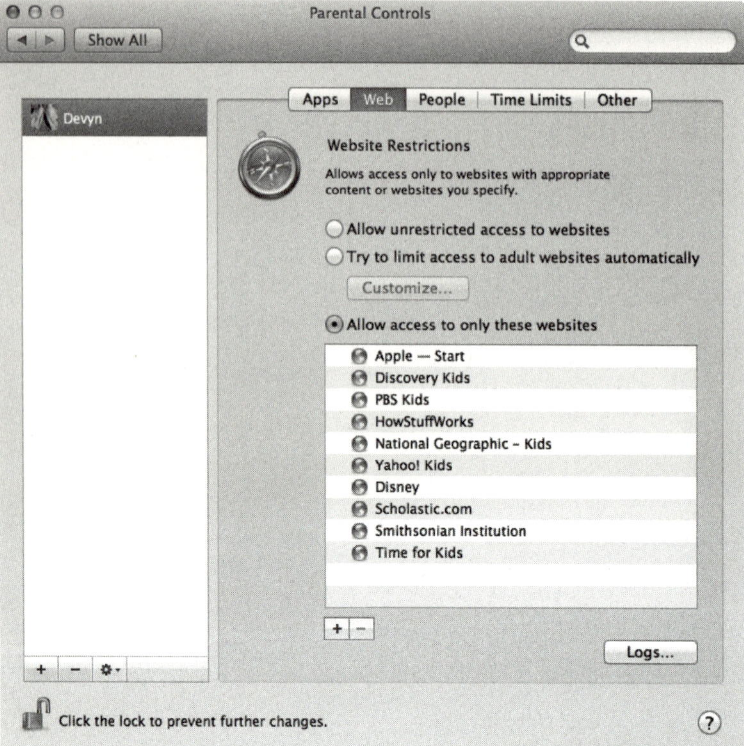

Figure 15.10: *Limit your kids' access to websites, I beseech you!*

The People tab (Figure 15.11) is great for restricting your children's email and instant messaging communications to only certain people. With the settings in this pane, you decide who they can and cannot talk to, and can let the user of the account send you email requests when he or she wants to add someone new to the approved list.

Figure 15.11: *Restrict email and instant messaging to only certain contacts.*

The Time Limits tab (Figure 15.12) is great for setting time limits for computer usage during weekdays and weekends, as well as restricting this usage between certain hours of the day.

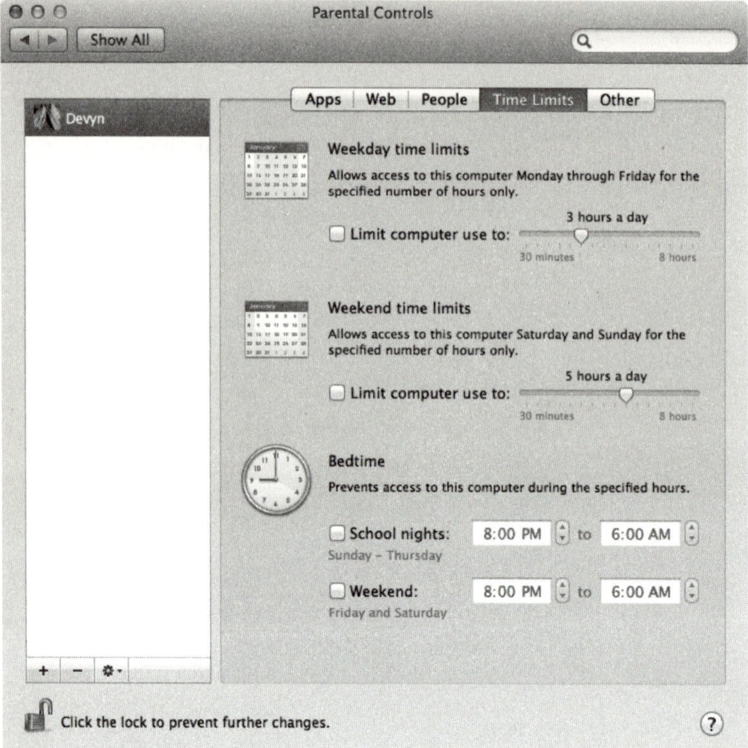

Figure 15.12: *Restrict computer usage to certain hours during the day and for particular time intervals.*

The Other tab keeps the kids' grubby paws off of various other sundry items:

- Hide Profanity in Dictionary does just what it says.
- Limit printer administration keeps the user from adding or removing printers, and from changing printer settings.
- Limit CD and DVD burning prevents the user from burning optical discs.
- To keep the user from changing his or her password to something you don't know (your kids wouldn't do that—would they?), check the option **Disable changing the password**.

Protecting Your Computer from Viruses

Computers may be machines, but that doesn't make them immune from getting the human equivalent of the common cold, or even worse. Unless you've been hiding under a rock for the last 30 years, you've heard of computers catching viruses from cyberbullies. These cyberbullies are basically folks who can't punch their way out of a wet paper bag, so to compensate they attack the computers of perfect strangers. Even some nerds have mean streaks, apparently.

The Windows Way

There's no doubt that if you've been a Windows user for any appreciable amount of time, your PC has most likely contracted a virus or been infiltrated by malware or spyware of some kind. That's just the law of the land when you own a Windows-based PC. Windows does provide Windows Defender to help protect against spyware, but I wouldn't exactly say it was the best way to go. You will definitely want to acquire a third-party antivirus/antimalware software, no question.

The Mac Way

Macs have a well-deserved reputation for being relatively virus-free. Some would debate as to the reasons for this, with one group claiming that the user base is smaller than Windows so the cyberbullies only attack the operating system with the most users (which is fair to say, up to a point). Another group, however, would also correctly point out that Mac OS X is built around a UNIX core, and it's just not as simple to write a virus for the Mac as it is for Windows. That doesn't mean it can't be done, mind you: it has been done before and will be done again.

Having said all that, you may be disappointed to know that Mac OS X doesn't provide any native protection against viruses. However, there are great third-party alternatives, such as those by Intego and Norton, should you feel the need for such protection.

Setting Up Speech Recognition

Don't you just love the sci-fi movies and television shows that depict a character talking to a computer, and the computer actually understanding what she is saying and carrying out her orders flawlessly? Now that's a day most computer users are ready for! That day is almost here, as speech recognition software is progressing by leaps and bounds all the time.

Speech recognition is a tool that some computer users simply must use, due to physical maladies such as deficient eyesight. To these folks, speech recognition is a godsend, no matter how clunky today's iterations may be.

The Windows Way

Windows comes with pretty decent speech recognition software built right in, which can be accessed within Control Panels. You need to "train" Windows Speech Recognition, which can be a bit trying at times, but considering it's free, Windows Speech Recognition does a fairly good job at understanding commands and taking dictation. Thumbs up.

The Mac Way

I must give Windows Speech Recognition the upper hand here, mainly due to the fact that its dictation feature works quite well, while dictation on the Mac is strangely nonexistent—that's a big omission, in my opinion. However, Mac OS X does handle the recognition of spoken commands quite well.

To enable and use speech recognition in Mac OS X:

1. Open System Preferences and select **Speech** in the System section.
2. Click the **Speech Recognition** tab at the top of the Speech window, shown in Figure 15.13.

3. Turn on Speakable Items, which allows you to speak commands to your Mac, by selecting the **On** radio button. The first time you enable Speakable Items, Mac OS X gives you some helpful tips that will enhance your success with speaking commands to your computer.

4. When you turn on Speakable Items, a microphone window, shown in Figure 15.14, will appear on your desktop. This microphone will hover above all windows while Speakable Items is on. The microphone window shows you when Mac OS X is listening (icon is active) and when it is not (icon is grayed out).

5. Choose the microphone you want to use to issue spoken commands to your Mac using the Microphone pop-up menu. You should click the **Calibrate** button and calibrate your microphone so the Mac will better understand your commands.

6. By default, your Mac is set to listen for your commands only when the Esc key is held. You can change this key, called the Listening Key, by clicking the **Change Key** button.

7. You can change the Mac's listening method from the Listening Key to a spoken keyword. The default keyword is "Computer," so you Trekkies can pretend you're Scottie barking orders to the Enterprise's computer in the heat of a fierce battle with the Klingons. Of course, feel free to change the keyword if you like. Your Mac will listen for the keyword, and once you utter it the Mac will begin listening for your spoken commands.

8. Mac OS X can acknowledge your commands by speaking an acknowledgement and by playing a distinct sound when the command is carried out.

9. To see a list of spoken commands you can use, click the **Commands** tab directly under the Speakable Items On/Off buttons. From there (Figure 15.15), you can enable or disable sets of commands for certain applications or settings, and even configure them by clicking the **Configure** button.

10. Click the **Open Speakable Items Folder** to see the commands that you can use with Speakable Items (Figure 15.16). Select the **Application Speakable Items** folder to see commands that are specific to applications you have running. You can also see a list of speech commands by clicking the triangle at the bottom of the microphone window and selecting the **Open Speech Commands** window.

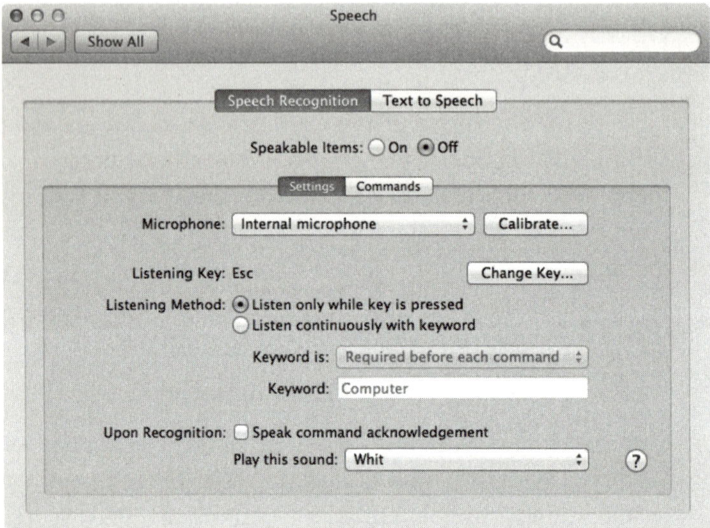

Figure 15.13: *Settings can be modified in the Speech Recognition tab of the Speech preferences pane.*

Figure 15.14: *Follow Mac OS X's tips for successful spoken commands.*

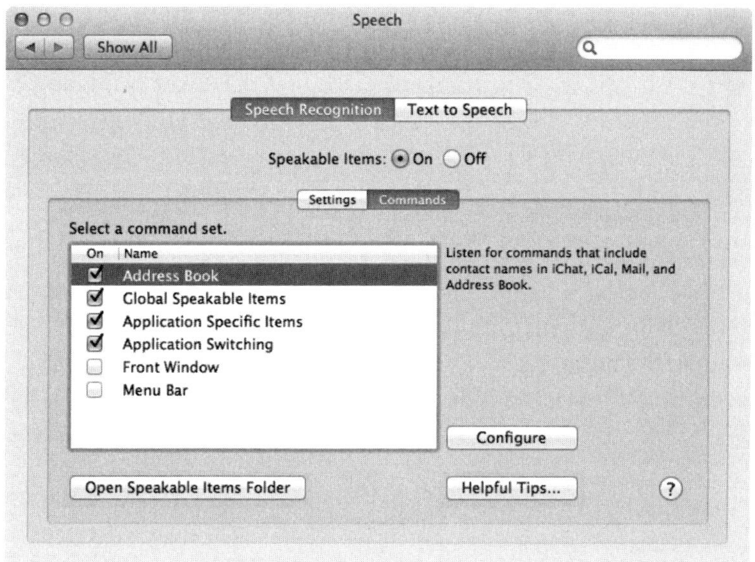

Figure 15.15: *Enable, disable, or configure command sets from the Commands tab.*

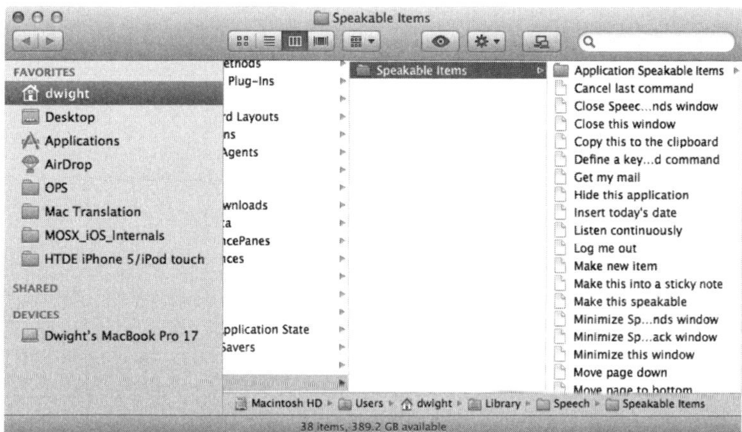

Figure 15.16: *The Speakable Items folder contains the built-in commands that you can speak to your Mac.*

A Good Microphone Is Key

When it comes to speech recognition, a good microphone can make or break the experience for you. The microphone that's built into your Mac is a good one, but if you're in an area with a modicum of ambient noise you'll want to get a good third-party microphone. Also, a headset microphone will enhance the experience more than a free-standing one.

Now that you have Speech Recognition set up, you can issue commands verbally to your Mac. But wouldn't it be cool if your Mac spoke back? You can enable this feature by clicking the **Text to Speech** tab in the Speech preferences pane, as I've done in Figure 15.17.

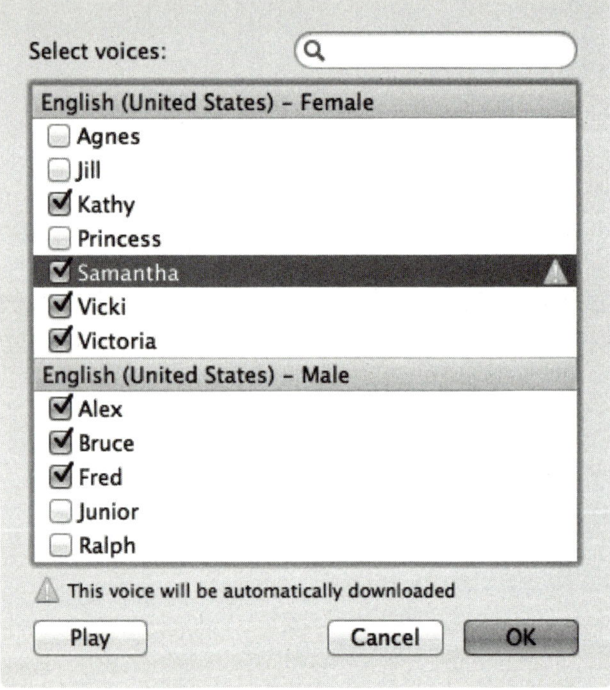

Figure 15.17: *Your Mac can talk back to you if you configure the settings in the Text to Speech preferences.*

Choose a voice for your Mac from the System Voice pop-up menu. The voices that are built in are okay, but if you click the pop-up menu and choose **Customize**, you can download alternative voices that are quite good and the annunciation is very clear. For example, click the check box next to Samantha under English (United States)—Female and then click the **Play** button at the bottom of the window; Samantha's voice is much clearer than those that come with Mac OS X. Note that when you click the check box next to a voice, a yellow triangle appears to the right of it (Figure 15.17); this indicates that when you click **OK** the voice will be downloaded and permanently stored on your computer. Beware, though: the file sizes can be quite large (Samantha is 469MB!).

Configure the settings in the Text to Speech tab to your liking, and your Mac will happily converse with you.

Keeping Your Software Up-to-Date

Some folks like to keep their software up to the very latest releases, while others tend to hold back from updates (especially major ones) until the rest of the masses have put them through their paces and discovered any pitfalls they may entail. I must say, though, I've been using computers since the early 1980s, and software updates have not generally been a problem. Based on my experience, I recommend you keep all your software updated to the newest releases.

The Windows Way

The Windows Update control panel is where Windows users go to check for the latest updates and install them on their computer. As long as you have Windows Update configured properly—and by that I mean changing its defaults—it is a fairly good utility. I say that because the default setting is to have Windows Update download and install updates automatically. This is a bad idea in my opinion, because I like to know what updates are being applied and what it is that they resolve. Another reason I don't care for the automatic updates is that you will put your computer to sleep one minute, and come back the next to find that it has been automatically rebooted in order to install the latest software updates. Not a fan of that, I must say.

The Mac Way

Mac OS X does updates the right way; there is no automatic update by default. Mac OS X prompts you when there are new updates available, and you have the option of simply updating or taking a gander at the updates so you can decide whether or not they should be performed at this time.

You can manually check whether updates are available:

1. Click the **Apple** menu and select **Software Update**, which opens the Software Update window. Software Update checks with Apple to see if there are any updates available for your operating system and other Apple software.
2. If updates are available, as they are in Figure 15.18, Software Update will ask if you want to see the details of the updates (recommended by me), not bother with them right now, or allow it to go ahead and install them (which, judging by the blue button, is what Apple wants you to do).
3. Should you follow my recommendations and click **Show Details**, you will see a list of the updates that are available to you. If there are more than one, you can check the boxes next to the updates you want to install now. Updates that require a restart of your computer will appear with a gray circle containing a small white arrow to the left of their check boxes. Click an update to see what it is for and how it will affect you (Figure 15.19).
4. Click the **Install** button at the bottom of the window to begin installing the update(s), or click **Not Now** to wait until another time.

Figure 15.18: *Software Update will alert you when updates are available.*

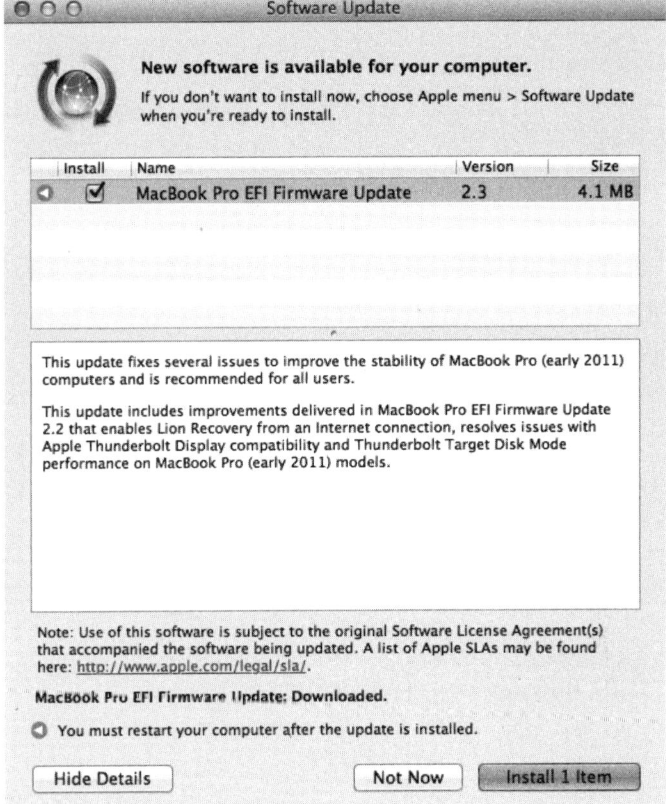

Figure 15.19: *Software Update affords details on what the update will affect.*

Setting Default Programs for Specific File Types

Computer operating systems have ways of associating file types with specific applications; this is the reason that when you double-click on a Word document, the Word application automatically opens. But what if you have multiple applications on your system that can open the same type of files? For example, every OS has native software that will allow you to view TIFF files, but let's say that you want to use Adobe Photoshop to open TIFF files automatically. What to do?

The Windows Way

Right-click on a file of a particular type and select **Open With** from the contextual menu. In the resulting Open With window, find the application you want to open the file with and select it. Next, check the box at the bottom of the list called **Always use the selected program to open this kind of file** and click **OK**. Super simple!

The Mac Way

Changing a file type association in Mac OS X is just as simple:

1. Right-click (Control-click) the file you want to open and select **Get Info** from the contextual menu.
2. When the Info window opens (Figure 15.20), click the pop-up menu in the Open with section to see a list of apps that can open this type of file, and select one.
3. Click the **Change All** button to associate this application with all files of this type.

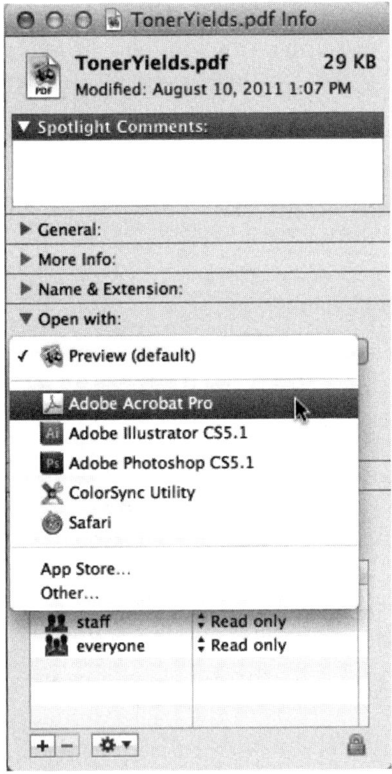

Figure 15.20: *Select an application to associate with the type of file you are getting info about.*

Backing Up Your Important Stuff

You're happily editing the photos from last week's family reunion and all is right with the world, when all of a sudden—blip—the power goes out. You shrug your shoulders, wait for the power to come back on, and then start your computer back up. Lo and behold, your operating system has been fried, and the only way to resolve the problem is to format the drive and reload everything from scratch.

At this point you are in one of two states of frustration: extremely irritated or completely devastated. The extremely irritated state would indicate that you are really ticked that you have to take so much time restoring the operating system and all of the files you have backed up. The completely devastated state tells the world that you have just lost every last thing you had stored on your computer, because you never made any backups of your files.

Backing up the files stored on your computer is the best way to ensure that you don't lose everything in the event of a catastrophic hardware or software failure.

The Windows Way

Backup and Restore is a control panel within Windows that helps you back up the information on your PC. Backup and Restore is a good utility and can restore anything from individual files to an entire system. It is relatively easy to use and is a breeze to set up.

The Mac Way

Mac OS X uses a really neat utility called Time Machine to back up your system. Time Machine makes a full backup initially, and from then on backs up only the items you change or add. All of this backing-up business happens in the background, too, keeping you blissfully unaware of the flurry of activity occurring out of sight.

Time Machine can back up your information in one of the following ways:

- To an external hard drive (recommended)
- To a USB flash drive
- To a partition on your Mac's hard drive
- To a network volume

Next, you need to set up a drive to back up to. The first thing you'll need to do is format the drive using Disk Utility, like so:

1. Open Disk Utility.
2. Connect the drive to your Mac.
3. Select the drive in the Disk Utility window.
4. Click the **Erase** tab near the top of the window.

5. Set the Format option to Mac OS Extended (Journaled).
6. Click the **Erase** button once, and then click the **Erase** button a second time in the verification window.
7. When Disk Utility is finished formatting the disk, it is now ready for use with Time Machine.

The next step is to tell Time Machine which drive you want to use for backing up your files:

1. Go to System Preferences and open the Time Machine preferences.
2. Click the **Select Disk** button (Figure 15.21).
3. Select a disk and click the **Use Backup Disk** button.
4. Time Machine will start counting down to when it will begin its first backup. If you want Time Machine to automatically start backing up everything on the system, you don't need to do a thing; if you only want to back up certain files, click the **On/Off** switch on the left side of the Time Machine preferences pane to set the switch to Off.

Figure 15.21: *Click the* ***Select Disk*** *button to choose a disk for your Time Machine backups.*

At this point, if you turned off Time Machine, you will want to set up Time Machine to back up only certain files. Here's how to tell Time Machine which files to back up:

1. Click the **Options** button in the Time Machine preferences pane.
2. Click the **+** button under the left corner of the Exclude these items from backups window.
3. Browse your Mac for items that you do not want to include in your backups, select them, and then click the **Exclude** button.
4. Click **Save** when finished excluding items from the backup procedures (Figure 15.22).

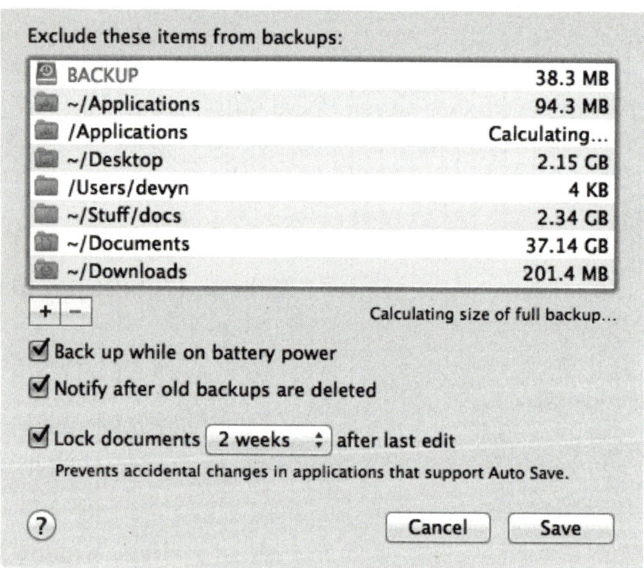

Figure 15.22: *Exclude items that you do not want Time Machine to back up.*

Now that you've set up Time Machine for manual backups, it's time to perform one:

1. Within the Time Machine preferences, check the **Show Time Machine status in menu bar** box.

2. Toggle the On/Off switch to **On**.
3. Click the **Time Machine** icon in the menu bar and select **Back Up Now**. Time Machine will back up the files you have selected (Figure 15.23).

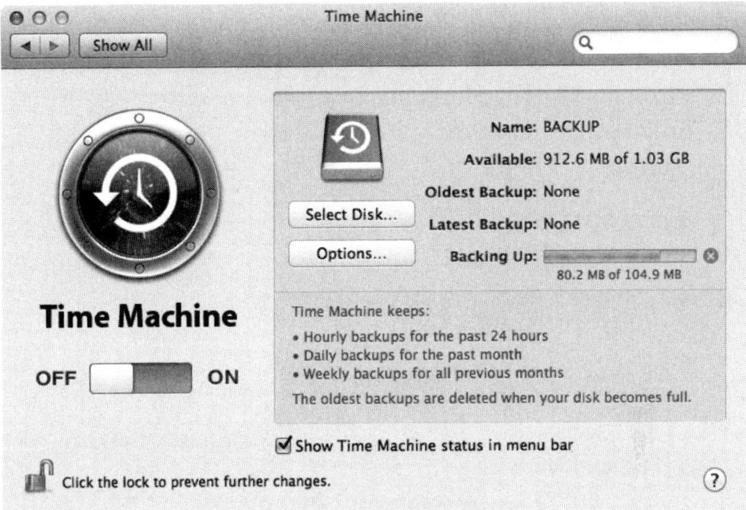

Figure 15.23: *A backup in progress.*

Now that you know how to perform backups, I'll be happy to show you how to use them to retrieve information.

To restore individual files and folders:

1. With the backup drive connected to your Mac, click the **Time Machine** icon in the Dock, or double-click its icon in the Applications folder.
2. Time Machine will open and reveal a Finder window (Figure 15.24).
3. To find the date at which time the item you want to restore was backed up, navigate using the timeline on the right side of the screen, or the arrow buttons next to it.
4. Find the item you want to restore within the Finder window.

5. Once you've found the item you need, select it and click the **Restore** button in the lower-right corner of the Time Machine window. The item flies forward in time to today, and Time Machine closes.

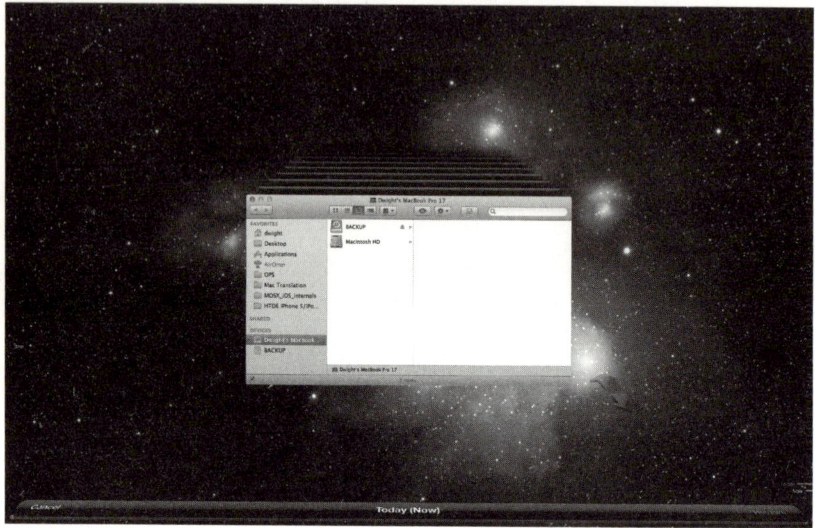

Figure 15.24: *Flying through space with Time Machine.*

How about if you need to restore your entire system? Here we go:

1. Connect your backup drive to your Mac.
2. Select **Restart** from the Apple menu, and then press and hold **⌘-R** while the computer restarts.
3. When the Mac OS X Utilities window appears, click **Restore From Time Machine Backup** and click **Continue**.
4. Do one of the following, depending on the type of backup disk you are using to restore from:
   - If using an external hard drive or USB flash, select it and click **Continue**.
   - If using a network disk, select it and click **Connect to Remote Disk**.

- If using one of Apple's Time Capsules, select your Airport (wireless) network using the Airport menu on the menu bar, select your Time Capsule, and then click **Connect to Remote Disk**.

5. If needed, enter your user name and password to connect to your backup drive, and then click **Connect**.
6. Determine the date of the backup you want to restore your system from and follow the onscreen instructions to complete the process, which could potentially take quite a bit of time.

Taming the Unruly

Sometimes things can get a bit funky with a computer. Computers start freezing, applications start crashing, everything in general begins slowing down, bean sprouts start growing up through the keyboard ... you name it.

When things get a little weird, it may be time to do some work under the hood. Maybe your computer needs a little housecleaning or a good swift kick in the rear, but either way it needs help to right the ship. The following tasks can help rectify odd behavior and restore balance to your computing universe.

Monitoring Your Computer's Usage and Performance

When things start to get a little slow, or even feel like they are crawling to a dead halt, it's good to take a look at your system to see how well it's performing.

The Windows Way

Resource Monitor is a mighty nice utility that comes with Windows. Resource Monitor gives you the skinny on all the processes and activities that might be taxing your PC. You can view all the goings-on for the CPU, hard drive, network, and memory. Good stuff.

The Mac Way

Mac OS X has quite the venerable tool itself for monitoring the happenings on your Mac: Activity Monitor.

Activity Monitor lets you get a bird's-eye view of the following:

- The percentage of your Mac's CPU power that is currently being utilized.
- The amount of memory that is currently being used on your Mac, as well as how it is being used.
- The activity that is currently affecting your Mac's hard drive.
- How much hard drive space you have available.
- The amount of network activity that's occurring over your Mac's wired or wireless network connections.

To see what's going on in Activity Monitor:

1. Find Activity Monitor in the /Applications/Utilities folder and double-click its icon to open it.
2. Click the **CPU** tab at the bottom of the window to view CPU usage.
3. Select the **System Memory** tab to see how RAM is being used (Figure 16.1).
4. Choose the **Disk Activity** tab to check out what's going on with your Mac's hard drive.
5. Click the **Disk Usage** tab to see a graphical representation of the used and free space on your Mac's hard drive.
6. Select the **Network** tab (Figure 16.2) to peek at the activity between you and your network.

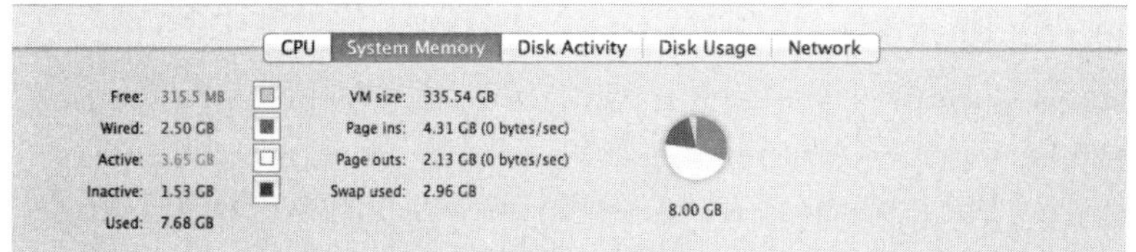

Figure 16.1: *System Memory shows in real time how your RAM is being utilized on your Mac.*

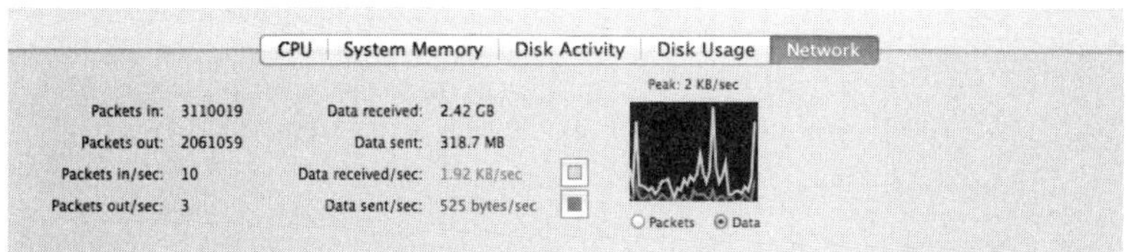

Figure 16.2: *Monitor the network traffic flowing to and from your Mac.*

If you want to keep near-constant tabs on your system, you can actually change Activity Monitor's icon in the Dock to have it give you a visual representation of current activity on your Mac. Simply right-click (Control-click) the **Activity Monitor** icon in the Dock, hover your mouse pointer over the Dock Icon option, and select one of the six options. Figure 16.3 shows the standard Activity Monitor icon on the left, and a graphical representation of the disk activity on the right.

Once you change the icon from the standard to an activity, you can close the Activity Monitor window but still view the activity running in the Dock. Click the icon in the Dock to reopen the Activity Monitor, should the need arise.

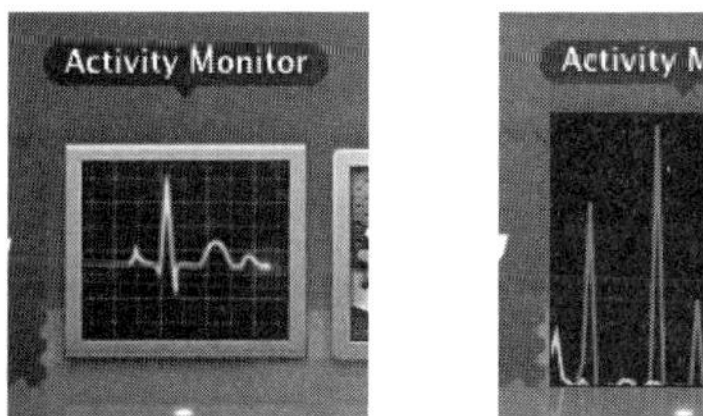

Figure 16.3: *You can change Activity Monitor's icon in the Dock to let you watch your system at all times.*

Starting and Stopping System Services

There are many tasks that are running in the background of any computer operating system, and these background tasks are called services. These services are meant to run without you even being aware of them, so that you can perform tasks on the fly. Examples of services would be printing services and network clients.

Sometimes these services may give you a hiccup and prevent you from performing a task. For example, let's pick on the printing services—your print queue may freeze and you are unable to clear a print job. Stopping and restarting the print services may clear up the issue.

The Windows Way

Any PC user worth his or her salt knows how to access the Task Manager, right? Well, if you're one of the unsalted, access the Task Manager by pressing **Control-Alt-Delete** on the keyboard and clicking **Task Manager**. When the Task Manager opens, you should go to the Services tab and find the service that may be causing an issue. Click the **Services** button, find the problematic service, and click it to start, stop, or restart it.

The Mac Way

Activity Monitor can be used for more than just seeing what's going on. You can also start, stop, and restart key system services from within its environs. Oops, I said "system services," but technically Apple refers to them as "processes."

Activity Monitor can show a particular set of processes, or it can show you all of them at once. By default, the processes pop-up (found in the upper middle of the Activity Monitor window) is set to My Processes (as seen in Figure 16.4), but you can choose to see processes in several configurations:

- All Processes
- All Processes, Hierarchically
- System Processes

- Other User Processes
- Active Processes
- Inactive Processes
- Windowed Processes
- Selected Processes

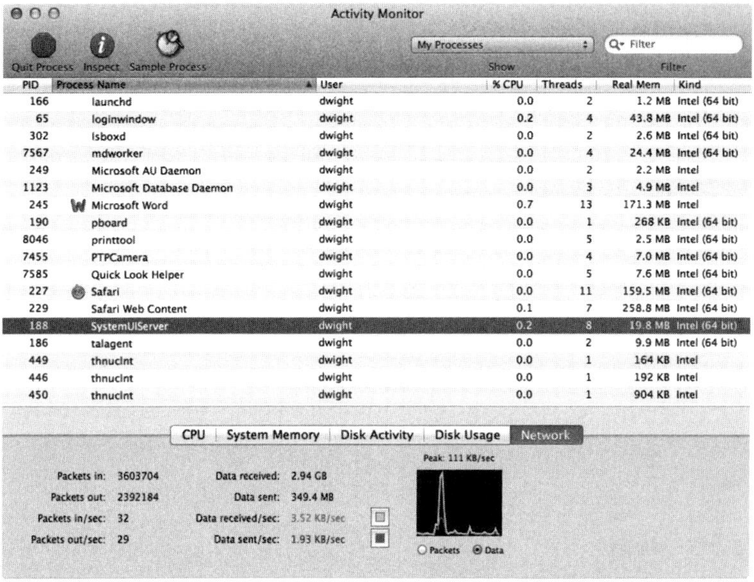

Figure 16.4: *My Processes is the default configuration for viewing processes in Activity Monitor.*

Should a process be slowing down your Mac (or worse), you can quit the process from here. To see which processes could be the culprit, click the **% CPU** column header to arrange the list of processes according to which ones are using the most CPU power.

1. Select the process you want to quit from the list.
2. Click the **Quit Process** button in the toolbar.
3. Select **Quit**, **Cancel**, or **Force Quit**, as seen in Figure 16.5.

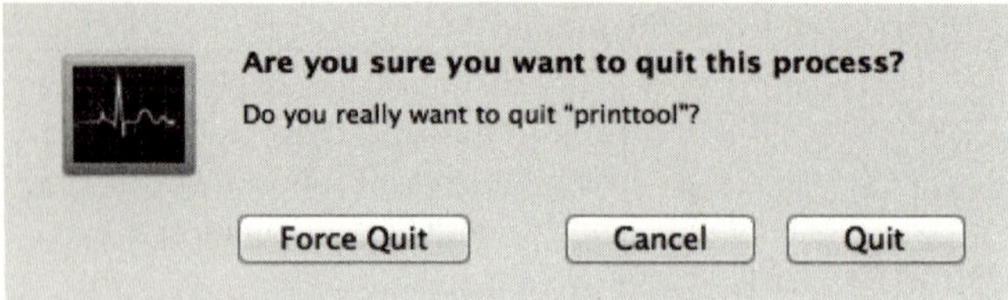

Figure 16.5: *Quit or Force Quit?*

Quit or Force Quit a Process

Your Mac is on top of what's going on, so if you tell it to quit a process that it knows may cause you to lose data or create problems with open applications, it won't quit the process. However, if you know you have no other alternative, you can override the Mac by clicking **Force Quit**.

Performing Disk Maintenance

After many moons of much toil, any hard drive will eventually need a bit of a helping hand. We've all heard of "defragging" a disk, and there's also the need to sometimes repair permissions of files. A computer may need several different types of upkeep, and even some preventive maintenance from time to time.

The Windows Way

Gotta say that Windows does a nice job here, due to Disk Defragmenter and Disk Cleanup. Disk Defragmenter basically tidies up your hard drive, making it easier for your hard drive to find items it's looking for. Disk Cleanup looks for and removes files that you really don't need, potentially freeing up huge chunks of wasted hard drive space. These two are nice tools to have if you're a PC.

The Mac Way

Disk Utility is used for many disk-related tasks, but when it comes to maintenance it excels at two tasks: verifying and repairing disk permissions, and verifying and repairing problems with the disk itself.

What Are Disk Permissions?

Mac OS X assigns specific access privileges, or permissions, to all of your files, folders, and apps. If these permissions become corrupt, it can cause massive problems, such as significantly slowing down your computer or causing apps to crash (if they launch at all).

To repair disk permissions:

1. Open Disk Utility, which can be found in /Applications/Utilities.
2. Select the hard drive whose permissions you want to check and repair (if necessary) from the list on the left.
3. Click the **Verify Disk Permissions** button to see if there are any problems with permissions on the hard drive, as in Figure 16.6.
4. If Disk Utility finds permissions issues, click the **Repair Disk Permissions** button to restore order.

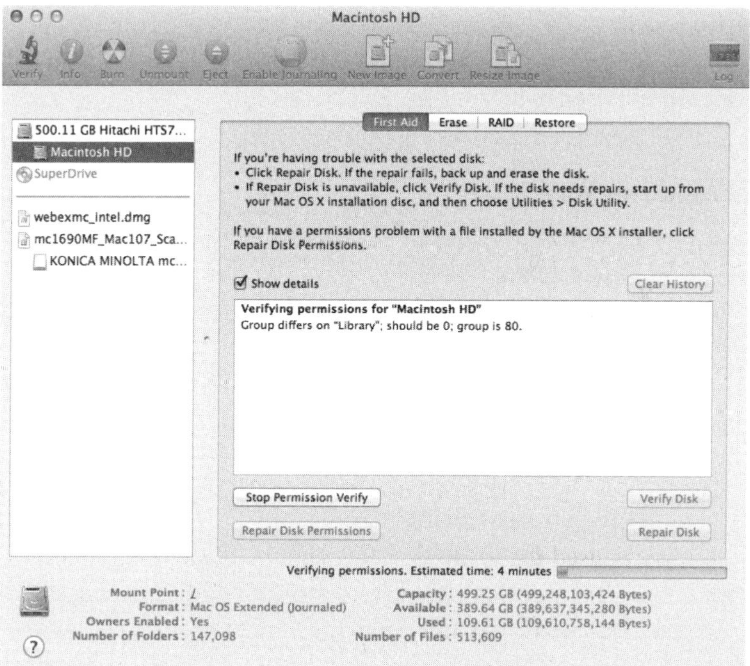

Figure 16.6: *Click* ***Verify Disk Permissions*** *to see if there are any permissions-related problems.*

To repair the directory structure of a disk:

1. Open Disk Utility, which is found in /Applications/Utilities.
2. Select the hard drive you want to check and repair (if necessary) from the list on the left.
3. Click the **Verify Disk** button to check if the directory structure is corrupt, as shown in Figure 16.7.
4. If there are problems with the directory structure, click the **Repair Disk** button to set things right.

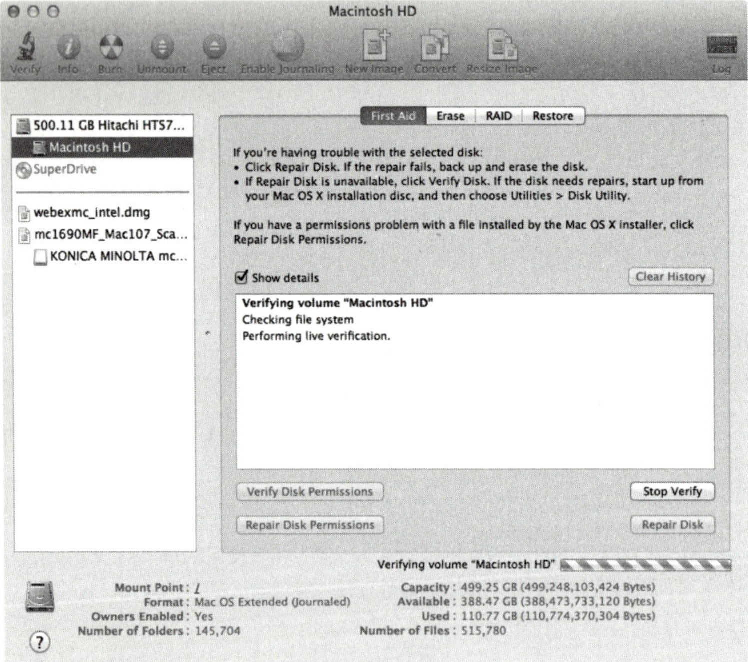

Figure 16.7: *Verify a disk to find out if there are any major issues with the directory structure.*

Killing Problem Apps Dead

You're working along, enjoying the feel of the keyboard and guiding your mouse effortlessly under the breeze of your ceiling fan, when all of a sudden the app you're working in can't seem to do a darned thing. You move the mouse some more, you all but pound on the keyboard, you throw paper at your cat, but the app still seems to be frozen in a time warp.

What to do when the unthinkable happens?

The Windows Way

Task Manager to the rescue, again! Press **Control-Alt-Delete**, click the **Task Manager** button, and go to the Applications tab. Find the application that's causing you grief in the list, select it, and click the **End Task** button. Get a cup of coffee, take an ibuprofen, and get back to work.

The Mac Way

With Mac OS X, you can get forceful with those problematic apps. By that, I mean you can force quit them. This task can't get much more simple:

1. Press **⌘-Option-Esc** to open the Force Quit window, seen in Figure 16.8.
2. Select the cantankerous application from the list.
3. Click the **Force Quit** button.
4. Mac OS X wants to be nice and ask if you're sure about taking this drastic action. If you are, click **Force Quit** again.

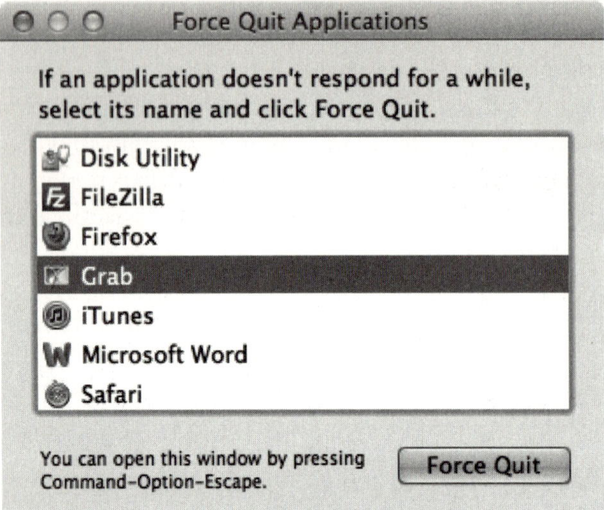

Figure 16.8: *Force those problematic applications to quit!*

At this point, you can try to reopen the problematic application and see if the issue is corrected. If not, a reboot might be in order.

Command Line Maintenance

The command line is so 1970s, but it can still be relevant today, at least in a small part for most computer users. Some of you may even be wondering what I could mean by "command line." Remember the good old days of computers where you had to type everything? Back when there was no mouse? If you do, you know what I mean by command line. If you don't, you're making me feel pretty old.

There are a number of housekeeping tasks that can easily be performed by using the command line, as well as other uses, such as finding items on the network.

The Windows Way

If you've used Windows for an appreciable length of time, you know what the DOS command prompt looks like. From there you can run a Check Disk, which can be executed with the chkdsk command. You can also defragment the hard drive by executing a defrag.exe command. There are lots more, but I can sense the boredom creeping into your very heart and soul as I type this, so I'll have mercy.

 The Mac Way

If you were bored to tears with the DOS prompt, the Terminal app in Mac OS X probably won't make you jump up and down with joy. Terminal is the Mac's portal to its underlying UNIX core, and it's all command line, my friend.

"Why on earth would anyone want to run this insidious Terminal app anyway?" you may be asking. Mac OS X uses a set of maintenance scripts that can help keep your Mac running smoothly, but Apple has determined that those scripts should automatically run at 3:15 A.M. and 5:30 A.M. local time on a daily, weekly, and monthly basis (depending on the specific function of the script). However, if your Mac is turned off or in sleep mode at those times, the scripts won't run. So unless you keep very early morning hours, the chances of these scripts ever being run are fairly low. You can use Terminal to make those scripts run on command:

1. Find Terminal in the /Applications/Utilities folder, and double-click its icon to open it. The resulting window will be quite nondescript, like the one in Figure 16.9.
2. Type "sudo periodic daily weekly monthly" and enter your user account's password when prompted, and then press **Return**.
3. Terminal looks like it's not doing a thing in the world until the scripts complete, at which time the blinking cursor reappears. The length of time it takes to complete a script depends on the script and the amount of information on your Mac's hard drive.

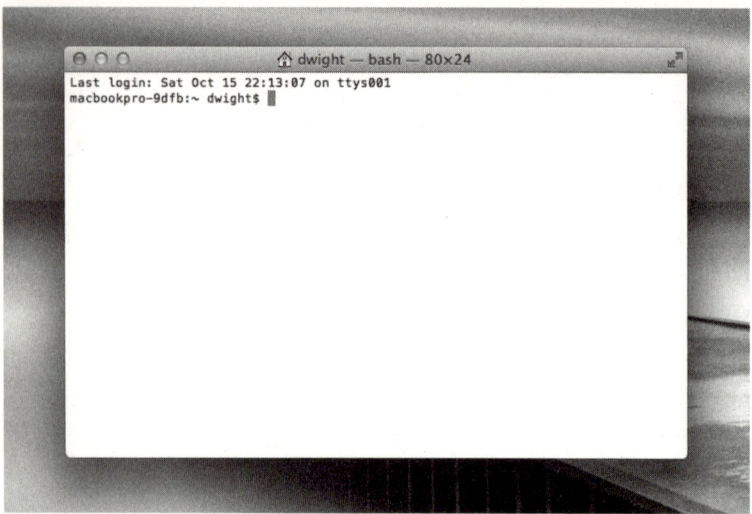

Figure 16.9: *Terminal may look boring, but it's one very powerful place to be, if you know the right commands.*

Recovering a Wayward System

You just installed a new driver in your computer, and all of a sudden it's acting totally wonky. Nothing seems to help, and it's beginning to drive you crazier than someone dragging nails on a chalkboard. This is just one scenario in which you may need to simply start over with your computer, or at least return it to a time when all was right with it. Let's see how Windows and Mac OS X handles this major dilemma.

The Windows Way

Windows has a very nice tool to recover your temperamental system, and it's called the System Recovery Options menu. From there you can fix startup problems, restore your files to an earlier time when all worked properly, completely recover your entire system using a personalized system image, check your computer's memory for errors, and access the command line so you can use diagnostic and troubleshooting tools.

The System Recovery Options menu can run from your computer, the Windows installation disc, a USB flash drive, or a system repair disc.

The Mac Way

Mac OS X uses Lion Recovery in much the same fashion as Windows' System Recovery Options menu. Lion Recovery can repair your hard drive, reinstall Mac OS X, or restore a Time Machine backup of your system (see Chapter 15 for more information on backing up with Time Machine).

Mac OS X Lion creates an invisible partition on your Mac's hard drive that is called Recovery HD, and it contains several tools that can help get your Mac back up to speed.

Note: To reinstall Mac OS X using Lion Recovery, you must have an internet connection. No ifs, ands, or buts. No internet, no reinstall.

To utilize Lion Recovery:

1. Restart your Mac and immediately press **⌘-R**. Keep pressing the keys until you see the Apple logo. In a few seconds the Mac OS X Utilities window will appear.
2. From the Mac OS X Utilities window you can do the following:
   - Restore your files, folder, and even your entire system, from a Time Machine backup.
   - Reinstall Mac OS X from scratch.
   - Open Safari to get support help from Apple online.
   - Open Disk Utility so that you can repair or even erase your hard drive, if necessary.

Glossary

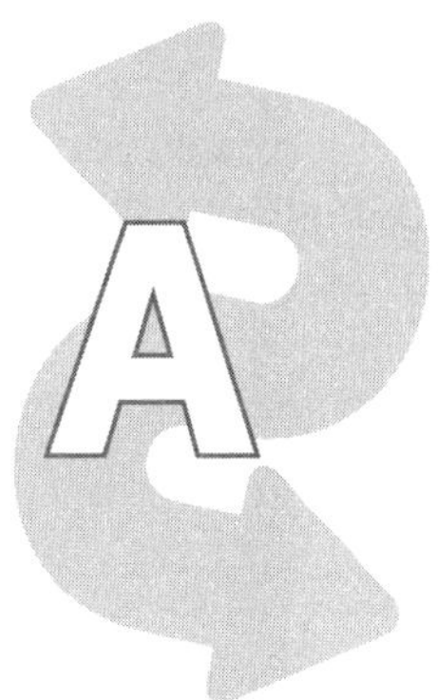

access point A network device that allows two or more computers to connect over a wireless network.

Address Book An application for maintaining lists of personal contacts and their pertinent information, such as their phone number, email address, street address, and relevant web pages.

administrator A powerful user account that has the ability to make permanent changes to your Mac's operating system. An administrator can perform many functions, including deleting other users (even other administrators), installing software, installing device drivers, and so on.

AFP Apple Filing Protocol. A network protocol used to share files and network services among Macs.

AirDrop A feature that allows simple drag-and-drop file sharing with other Macs running AirDrop. You simply click the AirDrop icon in a Finder window's sidebar, locate the computer you want to share files with, and then drag-and-drop your file onto that computer's icon. The file is automatically copied to the recipient's Downloads folder.

AirPort Apple's range of wireless networking products.

Apple menu Home to a few key commands, such as Software Update, System Preferences, Sleep, Restart, Shut Down, and Log Out.

application or app Software that you can install on your Mac. Applications are created for specific purposes, such as word processors, web browsers, email clients, page layout, and so on.

application menu The area of the menu bar between the Apple menu icon and the menu extras. The application menu displays menus associated with the application that's currently active.

application preferences The options and settings that you can set for a particular application via the Preferences option in the application menu.

backup The process of creating copies of the information you have stored on your computer. Making frequent backups prevents losing all of your information should your Mac experience serious hardware problems.

Bluetooth A wireless networking technology standard based on radio transmission that allows two devices to communicate when they are within range of one another.

Bonjour Bonjour allows for the automatic discovery of other devices running the Bonjour protocol. There is no setup needed; devices running Bonjour simply discover one another and can then share services. For example, a Mac running Bonjour can discover and print to a printer that's also running Bonjour without having to know anything else about it.

BSD Berkeley Software Distribution. BSD is a UNIX-based operating system that was developed by the University of California, Berkeley. Mac OS X runs on a derivative of BSD called Darwin.

CD Compact disc. CDs are one of the most common media formats today, and are great for storing information portably. We most commonly associate CDs with music, but you can also store computer data on them.

ColorSync Mac OS X's color management technology that uses other industry-standard technologies, such as ICC profiles, to keep color consistent among applications, your Mac, and input (scanners and cameras) and output (displays and printers) devices.

Command key The Command key (⌘) is located next to the Spacebar (on both sides) on the keyboard. This key can be used in conjunction with other keys to perform tasks. For example, pressing ⌘-P causes an application to open its print dialog box and pressing ⌘-A selects all of the items in the active window.

command line interface A text-only interface used to display information for the user and to send commands to the computer.

compression The process of making a file, or a folder containing many files, smaller in data size.

Cover Flow A Finder view that shows a split screen with a List view of the contents on the bottom and a preview of the current item on the top.

CPU Central Processing Unit. Every computer contains a CPU, which is the microprocessor that executes the commands given to it by the user or the operating system. Today's Macs use Intel processors for their CPUs.

CUPS Common UNIX Printing System. The printing system used by most UNIX-based operating systems, including Mac OS X. Apple purchased CUPS in 2007.

cursor The arrow that moves when you reposition your mouse. The cursor is essential for knowing where you are on the screen and what objects you will interact with if you click your mouse button.

Darwin The name of the open source BSD UNIX that Mac OS X is based on. Darwin is developed by Apple and is the core of your Mac's operating system services, such as networking and file systems.

Dashboard An application that runs other mini-applications, called widgets.

Device Driver Software written by a hardware device's manufacturer that allows the operating system to interact with that hardware.

DHCP Dynamic Host Configuration Protocol. A protocol used to automatically assign IP addresses to computers and other devices in a network environment.

directory Another name for a folder.

disk image A data file that acts exactly like a physical disc would on your Mac. Disk images are created by Disk Utility, and you can copy or place items into it just as you would any other directory. Many application installers that you download from the internet use disk images to transport their data. Disk Utility will mount disk images just as it would an actual CD, DVD, or hard drive.

Dock Located at the bottom of your screen, the Dock is a convenient place to store links to items or applications you use frequently.

Drop Box A directory in your home folder that can be used by others on your network to share files with you. They can drag-and-drop files into your Drop Box to share them with you, but they cannot view its contents.

Eject key Press this key, usually located in the upper-right corner of the keyboard, to eject a previously inserted CD or DVD.

email Electronic mail is used for sending messages and data to other computer users in lieu of traditional mail.

Ethernet The most common network standard in use today, Ethernet links computers together via a system of cables and hubs, or routers. Data transmission speed can range from 10 to as fast as 1,000 megabits per second, depending on the cabling and hardware used.

event An appointment or meeting scheduled in iCal.

Exposé Allows the user to press the F9 key to see all open windows at once, the F10 to see only the windows associated with the currently active application, or the F11 to hide all open windows.

fast user switching A Mac feature that allows more than one user to be logged in at once. Leaves programs running when a user logs out and reinstates them just as they were when the same user logs back in.

file Simply a container for information. Think of it as a modern digital equivalent to a paper document.

file system Method of storing and organizing files on a storage device, such as a hard disk or CD. Mac OS X supports many different file systems, but its default is HFS+.

Finder The one application that you can interact with that is running all the time on your Mac. The Finder is what you use to navigate your Mac's disks for files, folders, applications, other volumes, and so on.

firewall Software that protects your computer or network from outside intrusion.

FireWire A high-speed serial bus standard developed by Apple for the speedy transmission of large amounts of data. Also known as IEEE 1394, FireWire is cross-platform and can transmit between 400 and 800 megabits per second, depending on which version your Mac's hardware supports.

font A complete set of characters for a particular typeface that defines how the typeface appears on the Mac's display and on printed documents.

FTP File Transfer Protocol. An IP protocol used for transferring, creating, and deleting files and folders located on an FTP server.

group A collection of Address Book contacts.

guest operating system An operating system that runs inside a virtual machine using virtualization software.

HFS+ Hierarchical File System Plus. The default file system for Mac OS X, which uses a hierarchical system for storing and organizing files and folders.

home directory This is the directory that contains all of a user's personal documents and files. Every user account created on your Mac is assigned a home directory. These directories are located in the Users folder at the root of your hard drive.

HTML HyperText Markup Language. The main programming language used to render the graphics and text of a simple web page.

HTTP HyperText Transfer Protocol. A protocol responsible for linking and exchanging files on the internet.

iCal Mac OS X's default scheduling application.

iChat A Mac application used to converse with other people in real time by sending each other online text messages.

iLife A suite of applications that can be installed on a Mac. Includes programs such as iDVD, iPhoto, and iWeb.

Image Capture The Mac application that you use to connect to a device (such as a digital camera, scanner, or digital camcorder) and download that device's photos or videos to your Mac.

IP Internet Protocol. A protocol that delivers packets of information from one host computer to another based on each host's unique address. Internet Protocol Version 4 (IPv4) is the most common in use today.

IP address Internet Protocol address. A unique number that identifies each device on a network so that it can exchange information with other devices on that network. For example, many home routers use a default IP address, such as 192.168.0.1.

iTunes Mac OS X's default media player application. iTunes is also used to sync iPhones, iPads, and iPods of all varieties.

iWork A productivity suite that consists of three programs: Pages, a word processor; Numbers, a spreadsheet program; and Keynote, a presentation program.

JPEG Joint Photographic Experts Group. Perhaps the most common format for pictures on computers and the internet, JPEG can compress the data size of the image while still retaining reasonable image quality.

kernel The central component of Mac OS X's UNIX underpinnings. The main responsibility of the kernel is the management of the system's resources. The kernel makes sure that each running process is allocated the amount of computing resources, such as memory, it needs to complete its task.

LAN Local Area Network. A network that is confined to one particular area, such as in a small office or home.

Launchpad Provides instant access to applications through an iOS-like interface.

login items The applications, files, folders, network shares, and other items that start or connect automatically when a user logs in to their account.

LPD Line Printer Daemon. An industry-standard protocol for printing via TCP/IP over a network.

Mac OS X Pronounced *Mac Oh-Ess Ten*, this is the default operating system developed by Apple for use on their Mac computers. Mac OS X 10.7, also known as Lion, is the latest version of the operating system as of this writing.

Mail Mac OS X's default email application. Mail can handle multiple email accounts using different protocols, such as IMAP, POP, and even Exchange.

menu bar The semi-transparent strip that runs across the top of the Mac screen.

menu extras These icons appear on the right side of the menu bar and show the status of certain Mac features, such as the wireless network connection or progress of a Time Machine backup. They also allow the configuration of other features, such as the volume and Bluetooth functionality.

Mission Control Displays an organized overview of every open item in Mac OS X, such as all the windows associated with an application, Dashboard, and full-screen applications.

modifier key These are keys pressed in conjunction with one or more other keys to launch some action. Most Mac keyboard shortcuts involve the Command key.

mouse An input device for your computer. The mouse controls movement of the cursor on the screen, and also facilitates the launch of applications, the opening of documents, and the placement of files using its buttons.

network A collection of computers and other devices (such as printers) that communicate with one another through a central location, such as a wired or wireless hub (router).

open source The software development methodology that allows for free access to source code, and the modification and redistribution of the code (under certain conditions).

pair To connect one Bluetooth device with another by entering a passkey.

partition A portion of a hard drive's space that has been set apart from the rest of the drive. Your Mac views each partition as a separate hard disk, and you can use the partition for anything you want, such as installing Windows or storing particular types of files.

PDF Portable Document Format. PDF is a cross-platform file format mainly used for the distribution of documents.

permissions Every file and folder (both visible and invisible) on your Mac is owned by a user account. Permissions are access rights given to the owner and other users of the Mac. Without the correct permissions, a user may not view or access the file or folder owned by another user, even if they are an administrator (however, the root user can see anything and everything).

Photo Booth A Mac OS X application for taking pictures with the built-in Mac camera and adding special effects.

preference files Documents that store options and other data entered using an application's Preferences command.

Preview A native Mac OS X application that is used for viewing and annotating PDF files and images. Preview is capable of opening more than 25+ file formats, including almost all of the popular image formats.

printer queue Repository for print jobs you send to your printers. Whenever you print a document, the print data goes to the printer queue that was created when you originally installed the printer on your Mac. The printer queue passes the data from Mac OS X to your printer. If there is a problem, the print data will be stored in the printer queue and wait until such time that it can resume printing.

protocol A set of standards or rules that govern the communication of information between computers and other network devices.

QuickTime Apple's default multimedia framework designed for the creation and handling of various digital media formats in the areas of video, sound, and animation.

QuickTime Player The Mac's default digital video player.

Safari Mac OS X's default web browser.

server A computer whose function is to provide a variety of services to other computers, such as file and printer sharing. There are many types of servers providing their own unique services. Two examples: mail servers provide storage and retrieval of email for clients, and print servers manage print jobs for multiple users.

sidebar The pane on the left side of any Finder window that offers a number of shortcuts to objects such as connected devices, network shares, and local folders.

sleep mode A low-power state in which a Mac uses only marginally more electricity than if it were powered off altogether, while still preserving all running applications, windows, and documents.

Smart Folder A kind of virtual folder where the contents depend on the criteria specified by the user. Mac adjusts the contents automatically as the files change.

Smart Group A collection of Address Book contacts in which each member has one or more things in common. Address Book automatically updates a Smart Group as contacts are added, edited, or deleted.

Smart Mailbox A Mail folder that consolidates all messages that meet one or more conditions.

SMB Server Message Block. A protocol used primarily by Windows computers for accessing shared files, printers, and other network services. Mac OS X has the built-in ability to communicate with Windows-based PCs through SMB.

SMTP Simple Mail Transfer Protocol. An internet standard protocol that is used mainly for sending email, but rarely for receiving email.

Spaces An application that allows you to work with multiple desktops on which you can run applications and view documents. You can use each space for a different task, which is a good way to keep yourself organized.

Spotlight A Mac feature used to search for files, folders, applications, Mail messages, images, and other data.

System folder Located at the root of the hard drive, this folder contains the core components needed to boot your Mac system and run it efficiently after the boot process occurs. Your Mac will not be able to boot correctly if this folder is tampered with (such as by changing its name), so it's best to steer totally clear of this folder.

TCP/IP Transfer Control Protocol/Internet Protocol. A set of industry-standard protocols used for communications via the internet. Under this protocol suite, information is transferred in packets consisting of the user's data (payload) and control information. TCP's job is to keep up with the packets of data being sent, while IP is the actual vehicle for delivering the packets.

Terminal A program used for accessing the command-line interface of Mac OS X.

TextEdit Your Mac's default word processor.

Time Machine A Mac application that you use to create and access backups of your files.

URL Uniform Resource Locator. Used to point to a specific file on a computer that either resides on a network or on the internet. URLs are the addresses you type into the address field of your favorite web browser. The beginning of the URL states the protocol needed to access the file (such as HTTP or FTP); the next part is the IP address, computer name, or website name where the file is located (such as www.apple.com, 127.0.0.1, or dwightsmac); and the last part is a hierarchical location for the file (such as /support.html or /hard_drive/users/Dwight).

user accounts Every person who uses your Mac needs an account to access personal files and folders, and these are called user accounts. Each user account contains folders dedicated to that user alone, and no other users—even administrators—can access them without permission.

utility Utilities are software applications dedicated to managing and tuning your Mac's software and, to some degree, hardware. Each utility has its own specialty; for example, the Grab utility's function is to capture screenshots, and that's all it does. Some utilities may perform a variety of tasks, but the tasks are designed around a specific theme, such as Disk Utility, whose functions pertain to disks (formatting, mounting, and so on).

virtual machines Software files that virtualize applications, like Parallels Desktop for Mac or VMware Fusion, recognize and utilize as if they were separate computers. You can install almost any Intel-based operating system on your Mac using virtual machines. The virtual machine runs within Mac OS X, allowing you to use Mac OS X and the OS on the virtual machine at the same time.

virtualization Running a guest operating system (such as Windows on a Mac) in a virtual machine.

VPN Virtual Private Network. A private network that utilizes software and IP protocols to remotely communicate via the internet. A good example of how a VPN can be useful is when it allows a user to access his or her company's network while traveling.

WAN Wide Area Network. WANs are networks that span facilities in separate geographic locations.

widgets Mini-applications that are launched with Dashboard. Widgets typically concentrate on one particular task, such as local weather, movie show times, sports scores, recent news, and the like.

XML Extensible Markup Language. An open standard specification for creating documents that contain structured information. XML is used quite extensively on the web and is becoming increasingly used for electronic publishing.

Additional Resources

While it's my intention to make this book your go-to source for PC-to-Mac translation, there are many other fine resources available on the internet that can be of assistance, not only in the context of helping longtime PC users make a smooth transition to the Mac, but regarding all aspects of the Mac universe. This appendix is a compilation of those resources that I have found to be most helpful and useful over my many years with both computing platforms.

Apple Websites

www.apple.com

Apple's website simply must be the first stop for anyone new to their products. From here you can get a bird's-eye view of the world of Apple, and delve as deeply as you like.

www.apple.com/mac

The Mac portion of Apple's website gives you the scoop on the latest Mac-related hardware.

www.apple.com/macosx

This site keeps you informed on the latest version of Mac OS X.

www.apple.com/itunes

You can download the latest version of iTunes for Mac or PC from here, as well as check out the hottest items on the iTunes Charts, learn how to use iTunes more efficiently, and more.

www.apple.com/support

Apple's Support site is where you can go to get help with your Mac, Mac OS X, or other Apple software and devices. From video tutorials and product manuals to technical specifications and the latest software and firmware downloads, you'll find them here.

This site also affords access to Apple's Communities forums, where you can discuss issues and concerns with other Apple users from all around the world.

www.apple.com/usergroups

If you find yourself so enamored with your Mac that you simply must get in touch with others in your local area to discuss the merits of all things Mac face-to-face, go here to find your local group of Mac users.

http://store.apple.com

Apple has a great online store for all your Apple-related needs.

www.apple.com/why-mac/compare

Still having a difficult time deciding between a Mac and a PC for your full-time computing attention? Try visiting this site to find out more regarding how Macs stack up to their Windows-wielding brethren.

http://training.apple.com/#certification

There are some of you who are going to fall so head-over-heels in love with your Mac that you simply must know all there is to know. Some folks may think you're certifiable, but you can do them one better and become officially certified—by Apple! Go here to find out how to obtain your Apple certifications for hardware and software.

Mac Instruction

www.apple.com/findouthow/mac/
Apple's own tutorial site to help you learn many of the basics of operating your Mac.

www.macforbeginners.com
This site has several articles on how to do many Mac-related tasks but is definitely slanted toward the complete novice.

www.myfirstmac.com
A wealth of information for new Mac users can be found here, and there's even a special section for those making the switch from Windows.

www.macinstruct.com
Find lots of tutorials and articles here for getting more familiar with your Mac.

www.macosxhints.com
This is one of my favorite sites for Mac tips and tricks.

www.macfixit.com
MacFixIt has been a great site for all your Mac hardware needs for many a year.

http://macscripter.net/
This site is a big help for users of AppleScript and Automator, both of which are necessary to carry out tasks automatically on your Mac, should that be your bent. This is definitely up the alleys of more experienced computer users, though.

http://smokingapples.com/software/tutorials/mac-terminal-tips/
Learn about how to use the Terminal, which is Mac OS X's command line interface (similar to Command Prompt in Windows operating systems) into its UNIX-like underpinnings.

Mac News and Rumors

www.macworld.com
This is the premiere Mac news site, but does offer much more, such as in-depth software and hardware reviews.

www.macintouch.com
Plenty of Mac news and reviews.

www.macnn.com
Get the latest Mac news, podcasts, reviews, and more!

www.appleinsider.com
There is a certain segment of the Mac community that simply cannot go a day without their latest fix of Mac rumors, and this is one of their favorite sites to assuage these gossipy appetites.

http://macosrumors.com
I have personally visited these folks for my Mac rumors fix for almost two decades.

http://db.tidbits.com
Rumor has it that this site was started by some guy named Methuselah. Regardless of how long it's been around, it is an outstanding site for Mac news.

www.macrumors.com
This site is a nice mix of both news and rumors.

www.macdailynews.com
Yet another of my favorites, you can also track the headlines with their app for iPhones and iPads.

A

B

C

D

E

F

G–H

I–J

K–L

M

Q–R

S

T

U–V

W–X–Y–Z